MEMOIRS OF A MEDIOCRE TEACHER

MEMOIRS OF A MEDIOCRE TEACHER

A Book for Teachers Stumbling, Struggling, and Somehow Still Loving Their Job

Blair Clinton

ISBN 13: 978-1-63489-580-4
Library of Congress Catalog Number has been applied for.
Printed in the United States of America
First Printing: 2023

27   26   25   24   23   5   4   3   2   1

Cover design by Luke Bird
Interior design by Vivian Steckline

Wise Ink Creative Publishing
807 Broadway St. NE
Suite 46
Minneapolis, MN 55413

PREFACE

....

It's easier for us to write about what we know. That's what my colleagues and I always tell our students to do. So in writing about teaching, I didn't want to create a memoir about inspiration.

In movies like *Dangerous Minds, Stand and Deliver,* and *Dead Poets Society,* we see teachers saving a group of students from the wrong path, transforming them into the next poet laureates, or turning struggling readers or math students around so that they score the highest grades on standardized tests. Not that these movies are bad; it's just that sometimes you feel like those heights of teaching greatness are unattainable. I also despise these storylines, because they make me feel like I'm doing something wrong with my students. How can I get all my struggling readers on the path toward college scholarships, dammit? What did they do in those movies to create successful students that I can do with mine?

I wanted this memoir to be about how an average boy grew up to become an average teacher. Most of us teachers are not like those teachers from those movies. Most of us are not going to have a movie made about us, and that's okay.

One of my favorite authors, Frank McCourt, has probably the most famous passage on what it's like to be a teacher. In his book, *Teacher Man,* he states:

> In the high school classroom you are a drill sergeant, a rabbi, a shoulder to cry on, a disciplinarian, a singer, a low-level scholar, a clerk, a referee, a clown, a counselor, a dress-code enforcer, a conductor, an apologist, a philosopher, a collaborator, a tap dancer, a politician, a therapist, a fool, a traffic cop, a priest, a mother-father-brother-sister-uncle-aunt, a bookkeeper, a critic, a psychologist, the last straw.

Had I read this before I pursued a career in teaching, chances are I would have enlisted in a different profession!

Chapter 1

AN UNSPECTACULAR, EDUCATIONAL CHILDHOOD

If you had told my childhood friends that I was going to be a teacher, they would have laughed both you and me off the block. But here I am today, a middle school reading interventions teacher. A *reading* teacher, of all possible teaching positions! I've lasted twenty years in this trade; and even with the dizzying array of hats a teacher must wear, I consider myself one of the luckiest beings on Earth to be involved in it—even if I'm rather average at it.

Growing up, I wasn't particularly fond of education. I guess you could say I was indifferent to it. Part of that was due to my family background. I didn't grow up in a family that was stellar in academics. If you look back at the chain of family connections, you'll probably see this was quite obvious.

MEDIOCRACY: IT'S IN OUR BLOOD

My parents had to raise five of us kids, and they had to work with the education they had obtained growing up in the 1940s and '50s. My dad's dad was a farmer; and as far as I know, that was what most of his kin were involved in, besides one of them being a Catholic priest. He even told me about how much he hated school. He would go home crying because he didn't know how to learn what they were teaching him, particularly in math.

After high school (which he barely graduated from), my dad got a job at a lumber mill, then in simple architecture, and finally in carpet sales, which was his profession for the rest of his life. He did some work for carpet companies, then started his own floor covering business.

My dad was a simple man—in terms of his interests, not his smarts.

He didn't want to get caught up in anything complicated or emotional that required deep thought. He wanted to have his beer at the end of the night, and not to be bothered by any of us kids—and that was that! When I was a child, I wanted my dad to read to me and my brother. But most of the time, that didn't happen. We would come up with a comic book for him to read, and his response was usually, "Nope, not tonight." There were a few occasions where we convinced him to do it, but not many.

Asking my dad for help with schoolwork was out of the question. I could see the pained expression on his face whenever I did. It was almost like he was going back to the school he'd hated. This was the case with almost every subject. So my siblings and I learned fairly early that our dad was not to be bothered with homework help.

It wasn't as if he didn't care about our education. It was just that he had a lot going on with five kids and figuring out if he would sell enough carpet to get groceries and have enough for himself at the bar, which often seemed like his second office. Despite our dad's lack of formal education, he did a phenomenal job in getting us through school.

If it hadn't been for our mom, I know for a fact that my siblings and I wouldn't be where we are today. Like in many families, our mom was the rock. Just like our dad, she didn't grow up in a family that valued education. Her family consisted of six boys who were constantly getting into trouble, two girls (including herself), and a rocky marriage between her parents. So while my mom was growing up, her home was in no way supportive of advancing beyond high school. Most of her brothers enlisted in the military, then did quite well on the entrepreneurial front with restaurants and lodging, all without a formal college education.

With no support for higher education, my mom was accepted into a two-year college and became a radiology technologist, taking X-rays. She ended up working in this trade for over forty years.

Despite not growing up with much educational support, our mom valued my and my siblings' education and made sure we were on track for college. I think that was partly because my parents had some extremely lean years, and my mom didn't want us to scrape by as she and our dad did. Our dad often complained about his lack of business, and I wasn't setting kid fashion on fire with hand-me-downs from my brothers. Also, the older I got, the more I think my parents didn't want me and my sibling to be burdens on them! But my mom disagrees with this; she calls it "striving for independence."

My mom was a tireless worker. As an X-ray tech, she often worked late into the night and was on call other days during my formative years. Again, this made it difficult not only for me but also for my siblings to get the help we needed if we were stuck on schoolwork or needed that boost of motivation. When her overnight on-call shifts ended, our mom would come home tired, and we knew she needed to catch up on her sleep. And with us five kids engaged in sports or working part-time jobs, it was especially hard to get attention. It's not that we were upset about this; we just thought it was normal.

Whenever our mom had time to herself, she would be in her bed, reading. Her favorite authors were Agatha Christie and Stephen King. I was also really interested in King's work, because I loved horror movies; and his writing inspired some of my favorite movies growing up, like *Children of the Corn* and *Cujo*. I often wondered what reading his books would be like if those were his movies. This became my first serious foray into reading for enjoyment, and my mom noticed and encouraged it—no matter how inappropriate the writing was for my age.

The only time my siblings and I *did* get attention for our academics was when somebody from school called to tell our mom that we were underperforming, either by failing a class or some behavioral issue. Then holy hell would break loose. We would do anything in our power to hide, lie, or cover up potential bad news from school. If we were caught, it was game over.

It would start with the stare once we got home. Our mom had this low, glowering stare, as if she was deciding how to skin us alive. The second tell was her breathing. If she was breathing like a lion about to square off with its nemesis, then we knew there was no hope. The third tell was her hair. If it was springing up in different places, we knew we were entering the death cage we couldn't escape.

This would be followed by about an hour and a half of yelling. As I grew older, I understood that the more I tried to defend myself from our mom's anger, the worse it would get. So by the time high school rolled around, I had learned to just sit there and take it.

The second round of interrogation was questions from our mom about how we were going to get ourselves out of this mess. It always seemed as if there were no right answers.

"How are you going to get out of this mess?" my mom would ask.

"Well," the child in question would answer, "I don't . . . study harder?"

"That's not good enough!"

"I don't know! Get better grades?"

"How are you going to do that?"

And around and around we would go.

The third round was typically a staring match—more like a one-way staring match. We would just stare at the ground, and our mom would stare at us in disgust. The shaming was palpable.

The worst part was the longest part. While we would eventually be ungrounded, our mom's silent treatment went on even longer. That would go on for days, weeks, or even months. Even if you had one glimmer of a chance to redeem yourself and showed her the good deed you'd accomplished, all you'd get would be a grunt and maybe a week off the silent treatment.

I was lucky to not face the wrath of our mom as much as my two older brothers and my sister did. They *loved* to party, and school was secondary. My mom saw them sliding the way she and my dad had in terms of academic achievement, and she would not have it. So when my younger brother, Brandon, and I were boys, we had front row seats to some of the family's greatest firework fights. There was a lot more of the shouting back and forth and a door or two slamming. But in the end, our mom wouldn't fall back. The looks, interrogation, and silent treatment would start all over for our other siblings. So by observing how they each went through their middle and high school years, I learned how to avoid verbal spats with my mother.

MONKEY SEE, MONKEY DON'T DO

I closely observed my sister, Carrie, but she was twelve years older than me. So everything she was going through in high school was too complicated for me to comprehend. I did know, though, that she and our mom were constantly squabbling about her doing well in school and focusing on her future. Her friends were over at our house often, and she was going out to party quite a bit. This wasn't unusual for a high school teenager, however, and she did end up graduating and going to a pretty good college. Interestingly, she graduated from that college and got a teaching job at the school where I would be teaching with her years later.

The most entertaining part of this time in our lives was Carrie's relationship with my older brother Ren. They were the prototypical brother and sister from *Ferris Bueller's Day Off*, with Ren seemingly getting away with everything under the sun, while Carrie was constantly getting caught with her extracurricular activities. One time, she ratted him out for going to a party where drinking had been going on. But Ren had an ace up his sleeve: Earlier, he had found a pot pipe in one of Carrie's tampon boxes. (He claimed he'd heard rattling while moving it in the bathroom cupboard.) When our mom found out about Ren and the party, he just held up his hand to stop her railing and led her to the bathroom. To Carrie's horror, Ren handed the tampon box to Mom, and he was off the hook again.

But for whatever Ren would get away with, it would come back to bite him in the end. He had zero interest in school. But he was popular, athletic, and the smartest D student to ever graduate from Lakeville High School, in my opinion.

Ren was ten years older than me, but my memories of him growing up with his friends are still vivid. This group would come over and harass me and Brandon by pitting us against each other in wrestling matches and pulling practical jokes and other torturous disturbances on us. Once they were bored with us, they would go off and find their own lunacy.

My parents had a hard time reining Ren in to get him serious about school. Being a D student wasn't helping him, and he graduated without a diploma. He had to go to summer school to get it. Our mom was on a warpath to get Ren into a college. He was a pretty good pitcher in high school, and colleges were legitimately interested in him. But his grades kept them away. Our mom dragged him from one school's administration office to the next, but he wasn't getting in. Even a local college we used to make fun of for their low standards wouldn't accept him. For some reason, though, a college in Minneapolis took him in on strict education probation. To stay, Ren needed to maintain a 3.0 GPA during his first year, which we thought would be impossible.

Thankfully, Brandon and I didn't need that much pushing to get into college. Both of us were relatively close in age, so we were practically twins. We shared the same friends and did almost the same activities all the time; and together, we watched our older siblings succeed and fail at being adolescents. Studying how they grew up helped us understand what we could get away with—and what we definitely couldn't get away with.

Since I knew most of my parents' tics and what would set them off, I knew I was going to have an easier time in high school than my older siblings. However, the bar wasn't exactly set high for me. So I knew that if I could just keep my grades in the B to B- range, I'd be living on easy street. And that's exactly what I did. I kept my nose clean enough (Brandon and I were like angels compared to our other siblings), and I did just well enough in the grades department. Nothing more, nothing less.

Chapter 2

COLLEGE? WHAT AM I DOING HERE?

By the time I arrived at the University of Minnesota (U of M), I felt like I had a pretty good grasp of what college would be like. I had two older brothers and a sister who had all gone and graduated. And when they had been in college, they had sometimes invited me and Brandon to stay with them on campus, which made us feel mature and cool. So I felt like college was going to be fairly easy—and it was, in a way. But I didn't know what I was going to study.

Not knowing what career I wanted to get into bothered me. I had friends who were starting to create a vision for themselves, and I felt like I wasn't. I knew I had at least two years of taking general classes to figure it out, but that window was starting to close.

It wasn't until I finally took a hard look at what my sister was doing—which was teaching—that I thought it might be a fun career to get into. I guess that was the sole element I had in my head when deciding on my career: Was it going to be fun? Even now, I wish somebody had slapped me upside the head and yelled at me about overlooking the second element: income!

But to hell with income! If you're a teacher, you're not constantly sitting behind a desk (if you like to stand and talk). And best of all, you have three months off! Also, let's be honest: It seemed like 70 percent of the students in the College of Education and Human Development (CEHD) were female, which was fine by me! I saw my good friend and roommate, Dan, go to his engineering classes, which he told me were roughly 90 percent male. How boring!

Now, I have to admit: I did catch some grief from my friends when they found out I was heading into the CEHD. They called it "teachers' school," and oftentimes they didn't consider it real college. Why go to school to go back to school to teach school? In a strange way, it seemed that they viewed me as not having moved on from school and that they were doing something real, like getting an office job, rather than heading back to the classroom. It was almost as if they saw me as somebody with no skill. As the old saying goes, "Those who can't do, teach."

THE BUG

The majority of my classes were situated in old Peik Hall, which, I believe, used to be a high school before the U of M took it in. It stood on the east bank of the Mississippi River. By the time I arrived thirty years later, it still looked like an old high school. The halls still had lockers. The fluorescent lighting had that asylum yellow tint to it. The floors had checkered tiles, and the halls were cacophonous when students were moving between classes. The classrooms had those rudimentary wooden desktops and straight-back chairs attached to them. There were no whiteboards to speak of, but rather the good old-fashioned blackboards. It was up there for the blandest building interior on the whole campus.

And, most importantly, it is also where I was introduced to Professor Buggey.

Professor JoAnne Buggey was an educator who was both revered and feared. She had the students' attention from the moment she stepped into the classroom. She seemed to glide across the room without moving her legs. Her wardrobe reminded me of what my kindergarten teacher had worn, which was always a ladybug-themed shirt or overalls. (Yes, overalls. All the time, it seemed.) Professor Buggey appeared to be in her early seventies at the time. Her dark, graying hair was pulled back in a bun that resembled something straight out of the Laura Ingalls Wilder era. And she had those beady eyes that, when she looked right at you, knew everything you were going to say even before you knew what you'd say. When she talked, her voice was high-pitched, formal, and righteous. Sometimes it would get downright acerbic. Her tone brought to mind a grandmother who disapproved of anything you did, no matter how hard you tried. I didn't quite know what to make of her. I felt like if she was a professor here, then she must know what she's talking about, right?

Professor Buggey started me and my classmates with an introduction to elementary teaching. Like most of my classes, I felt that it was pretty easy; and once again, I could fade into the background and do just enough. Since I wasn't exactly positive that I wanted to be a teacher, I didn't feel the need to participate and become fully invested with the class quite yet. My mindset was in wait-and-see mode.

That first part of Foundations of Education involved a lot of work that I felt was unnecessary at the time. One time after class, I came back to the house I was sharing with my roommates and started coloring in letters for an alphabet wall, while my civil engineering friend was solving problems for Calculus 6. My roommates often looked at me in disdain over how easy my classes seemed. Sure, I was taking classes that involved child development. But looking back, I wished the education program had better prepared me and my peers for what we were going to face. Some of the aspects of teaching I felt we could have used more help with—and would have loved to have seen parts of our classes devoted to—were classroom management, parental interaction (i.e., communicating with parents through conferences or phone calls), and awareness of different curricula.

INTO THE CLASSROOM—YIKES!

Part of being in Foundations of Education at the U of M was that after my peers and I graduated with our bachelor's in education, we still had to go into the master's program so we could student teach. Going into the master's program right away proved to be beneficial for us. For one, it was only for a year, and none of us had a full-time job yet, so we could focus solely on our schoolwork. And during this time, we had classes that focused on all of the major core disciplines of math, science, social studies, and language arts.

As my peers and I were going through these "core" classes, we were dispatched throughout the metropolitan area for our practicum of teaching. One school I distinctly remember doing some of my student teaching at was in southern Minneapolis. This was the first time I was involved in a class of equally mixed races. I had grown up in a pretty much all-white, outer-ring suburb that was as sheltered as it could have been. The teacher I was observing was a middle-aged man who had probably twenty to twenty-five years of experience. He had his classroom management down pat, with an air of authority. Since I had come in the middle of the school year, I didn't get to see how he had established this management at the beginning of the year. He would have been great to learn from. His students didn't blurt out answers, and they kept their hands to themselves and worked in an engaging way. If there was any hint of nonsense, the teacher would stare at the student. The class would start with a morning meeting routine, and what I found fascinating was that all the students called their teacher by his first name. These students were from all parts of the socioeconomic scale, and it was great to see them working as a cooperating classroom.

At one point, the teacher and I were doing a math/geography lesson on the Alaskan sled dog race, the Iditarod. We discussed distance in miles and the terrain the teams would travel throughout the race. The students were pretty focused on what we were teaching, and I don't think we damaged their learning too badly with our lesson. I tried as best I could to emulate the actual teacher. Plus, it helped that he was there to keep tabs on the students' behavior.

Some environments were culturally foreign to me—and I was not prepared for them. One of these was a practicum where my peers and I had to do a special education observation for two weeks. For this, we were sent to an upper elementary school in a poverty-stricken area of Saint Paul, which was probably about 60 percent Black and 40 percent Hmong. I had never dealt directly with a school that was this diversified, and I was woefully ill-equipped to understand the cultural differences and the needs of these students compared to where I had come from. So I had to observe the staff to see how they worked with this.

My and my peers' objective was to observe what it was like in special education classes. At one point, I observed a student who had severe attention deficit hyperactivity disorder (ADHD) and had to wear a lead vest to control his hyperactivity. This was the first time I'd ever witnessed such a thing, and I honestly don't know if they even practice this anymore.

The other part of this observation was to watch a regular classroom. When I walked into the classroom, the teacher—a man who was probably in his early forties—looked like he hadn't slept for a week and had just walked out of a tumbling dryer. This was the look of a teacher who was worn down to the bone, and I could see why. When his sixth-grade class came in, it was evident from the start that he had no control over them—and I made that assessment without having had any proper teaching on classroom management yet! These students were climbing all over the walls. The teacher tried to get a math lesson going, but his students were not having it. At one point, an argument flared up between two girls who were yelling at each other from across the room. This sparked hoots and hollers from the other students and provided them cover to ignore what was going on and carry on with their loud conversations, totally disregarding the teacher. The look on the teacher's face said it all: *Here we go again.* He did have an out, but it took about fifteen minutes of bribing the students into a math game with a promise of candy. The students half-complied with this, which made it doable for him.

When the class left, the teacher had a prep hour for the next class. It looked like he had just gotten through twelve rounds against Muhammad Ali. I asked if this was what it was like every day. He sighed and said yes. Later, he told me that this was his second year of teaching. He had quit his job at a business institution to do something more meaningful. I wondered if he now regretted making that decision. And truthfully, in my early years of teaching, I would end up going through the same struggles he went through.

Chapter 3

RACIAL INEQUALITY
EYE-OPENER

While going through Foundations of Education, my peers and I had to have a certain number of volunteer hours in the education field. The best option, I felt, was volunteering through the U of M's YMCA, in a program called Fresh Force. It dispatched volunteers all over the metro area to schools and held after-school activities for students. At this point, I was still naive about what I was getting into and wasn't taking this volunteering stuff seriously. I thought that volunteering in teaching wasn't going to be that useful for me, whereas I wanted to work and make a little money rather than donating time to volunteer. So I thought I could sleepwalk through this as well. Just tell me what to do, and I'd do it. I didn't want to put any creative juice into it.

Most of the other students signed up to volunteer with Fresh Force, which partnered us up with other schools in the area. Then they would get us in contact with a liaison at the school to help us get acquainted with the students and figure out what plans and activities we would do with them. It turned out that my partner, Lisa, and I were going to one of the most economically deprived schools in northern Minneapolis.

Lisa made a connection with the students much more easily than I did since, unlike me, she had grown up in the area. The students ranged from fourth to eighth grade, and they were full of energy. One way I connected with them was through playing basketball with them, but that wasn't what we had been sent there to do. We were there to plan and execute activities for the students.

Our first activity was fairly simple. Lisa and I asked the students to make a collage about themselves using pictures from magazines we had compiled. This led to the first of many signs of ignorance I would display in this job. Once Lisa and I explained the topic to the students, we started handing out magazines. To my horror, I realized that the magazines we were giving them included almost exclusively white people. One student laughed and said, "Man, what am I going to cut out with all of these white people in this magazine?" Lisa and I shot embarrassed looks at each other.

Luckily, I had some *Sports Illustrated* magazines, and the boys were by and large content with cutting out the sports players they dreamed of being. But *Seventeen, Cosmopolitan,* and *Girls' Life* weren't the most integrated magazines yet. This was a big learning experience for me to wake the hell up, be more conscious of the students I could be teaching in the future, and learn how to cater to their cultural needs in the classroom.

Sometimes Lisa and I would plan an after-school field trip with the students. Our first field trip—which Lisa had planned, since I hadn't fully grasped the concept of organizing at all—was to the bowling alley at Coffman Memorial Union, located right on campus. We piled into the van right after school and headed over to throw the rock. It was a great time! The students enjoyed being out of the stuffy school and in a different environment. As for me and Lisa, we enjoyed bowling and developing a rapport with the students. Even though this interaction was small, I grew a ton from it. I had lived in a racially homogenized bubble my whole life, and this experience helped me break down the racial stereotypes I may have had when growing up. These kids were just kids, looking for an escape and to have fun, as we all do.

Afterward, Lisa and I had to drive them home and drop them off. Again, my naivety about the conditions in northern Minneapolis came into play. The homes where we dropped students off were in the most crime-ridden areas of the city. This was another education for me on the economic and social disadvantages inner-city students had to deal with. At one point, I dropped off one particular student who was excited to see her uncle. As she got out of the van, she commented, "What is Uncle Jimmy doing here? He's not supposed to get out for another six months!" Again, Lisa and I shared a look of sorrow for these students. This was a learning point for me. Whereas I'd be devastated over incarcerated loved ones, these students seemed to take it as just a normal day. So I developed an extreme respect for them and how they dealt with constant hardships. I felt like they were much stronger than I was.

For our grand finale, Lisa and I were going to be involved in a community festival, and it turned into a flop. We thought we had enough students going with us and set up some games we would play there. This was unique, because it was taking place on a weekend day. We had a list of about ten students who were coming. But when we showed up at the school, only two students were there. We made it work at the festival, though; our students interacted with the crowd and played the bean bag game we'd brought with anyone who visited our setup. But it didn't go over well with the school counselor when he found out about it. He gave me and Lisa this look that implied we were a complete waste of his time. I felt like a failure big-time and wondered if this was going to happen often. I couldn't blame the administrator, as we hadn't had the same number of students we'd said we'd have. This was my first brush with disappointment from a superior—and it wouldn't be my last.

Lisa and I had one final after-school activity day with our students before our time with Fresh Force wrapped up. As I was playing basketball with the students, it struck me how they had taught and influenced my future teaching way more than I could ever reciprocate. They opened my eyes to something I'd been blinded to my entire life: the reality of enduring social and economic inequality. Now, being a teacher, it was important for me to understand where my students were coming from and the situations they were facing. I felt ashamed for being so ignorant. Here I was, going back to my safe space on campus, where I wouldn't have to worry about being rejected for job offers because of my background or race, and where I knew I would be relatively safe economically and didn't have to worry about my family members getting caught up with the law.

There was an emptiness and helplessness as the final minutes of the day ticked away and all the students said their goodbyes and gave me and Lisa hugs. One student was left as I was walking to my car. He was one of the brightest, funniest, and most outgoing students in the group. He came up to me and said, "Mr. Clinton, when I grow up, I want to

be just like you. Thanks!" To this day, this is one of the greatest compliments I've ever received. I still don't know what I did to deserve that,
and I hope he has been much more prosperous in life than I have been.

THE SUMMER JUNGLE

In the end, Fresh Force and the YMCA were valuable in helping me get
acclimated to students, especially those from different socioeconomic
areas. It was also valuable for student teachers like myself who hadn't
experienced much outside of their home territory by getting them involved in a different community.

After Fresh Force, I was lucky enough to get a job for the after-school
program Kids' Safari in the Bloomington school district. This was sort
of like a daycare but with structured activities and classes. During the
school year, Safari would open right after the school day ended and
give students options like an art class, a homework area, a phys ed activities area, and so on. And during the summer, Safari was an all-day
program, starting at six in the morning and going all the way to six in
the afternoon.

I was kind of an outsider when I started. Most of the leads, who
were about my age or a little older, were from the Bloomington-area
schools. Since I was starting out in the program, I was an assistant to
the leads. Each week, I would get together with whichever lead I was
working with and help them draw up plans for that week. But in my
first year, I just observed what the leads were doing, since it was a whole
new experience.

This was the first time that I looked at daily planning and what went
into it. It also prepared me for figuring out how to manage classroom
supplies. This would be incredibly important for when I became a full-
time teacher.

Eventually, as I gained more experience with Kids' Safari, and after
some of the leads moved on to their own careers, I became a lead. Each
hour of the day had to be planned with some sort of activity, like art,
outdoors, or group activities like a game club. Being responsible for
creating my own lessons and managing student behavior was a big step

for me. The planning was easy, but I struggled with classroom management.

How hard do you go after a student who repeatedly doesn't follow class expectations? What's their background like? And if you don't enforce discipline with that student, are you being fair to the other students? All of this comes into play, and it's incredibly difficult for a young adult to sort it out—especially when the students view you as their older brother and not necessarily as an adult!

What I considered student misbehavior was way more lax than it should have been, and it showed when I had the responsibility of a lead in Safari. If we had a student who was acting out, the general rule was to put that student in a "two-minute" time-out. But with me, if a student was roughhousing or making fun of another student, I would just give a verbal warning and not put them in time-out. Students would get wise about this and push me further and further to see if I would ever do it.

I was hardly behaving myself in my personal life, also. So why be so hard on these kids? I admired the leads who had their students in order whenever we were doing classroom activities. They maintained discipline and kept the environment safe and fun. They weren't like me, letting bad behaviors fester. Instead, they set parameters right away and were consistent. There was the flip side of this, too. The lead of the class pretty much let the students do whatever they wanted; and sometimes as an assistant, this bothered me. I found I was becoming that kind of lead.

When I became a lead, the biggest thing I was nervous about wasn't coming up with ideas for activities. It was how well I was going to manage the students on any given day. Observing Safari's administrators and my coworkers really helped me out. Although I clearly wasn't perfect, no student died on my watch. So there's that!

Another aspect of Safari was that most of our students came from a single-parent family or a mixed family background. It didn't matter if a student came from a traditional family background. There was always something we didn't know that could have been inflicting trauma on that student, no matter how happy their home looked from the outside.

But students with single parents typically had more difficulties adjusting, and for a couple of reasons. First, they were often at school from six in the morning until we closed at six at night. Second, the parents sometimes had other children or responsibilities, and so the student in question might not have received the same support compared to students who had both parents. So I learned that I had to start taking the environment students came from into account while teaching. This was exactly what I'd needed to do with the students at Fresh Force. If there were behavior issues, it could very well correlate to their home life. If a student was sleepy or always hungry, I (along with the rest of the staff) found it important to give that student more food or time to rest. Despite any disadvantages, many students showed resilience. They were incredibly inspiring to me through what they accomplished educationally and socially.

Chapter 4

STUDENT TEACHER LUCK

A fter finishing our undergraduate work, my peers and I entered the master's part of Foundations of Education. In this cohort, you could pick the grade levels you wanted to teach. I wanted grades four through eight. I was nowhere near nurturing enough to be teaching the primary grades and nowhere near mature enough to be teaching high school. In fact, one of our professors told us that high school teachers should be no younger than thirty-five years old. (I totally agree with this! Most young teachers are easy prey for seasoned high school students to take advantage of, and I remember these shenanigans being performed when I was in high school.)

When we finally found out which schools we were going to, it was kind of like looking to see which team picked you for your town's local sports team. I was going to be teaching at a southern suburban school called Echo Park, right on the border of Apple Valley and Burnsville—right next door to where I had grown up.

I was picked for fourth grade. This was the grade level I had some familiarity with, thanks to my volunteer work with Kids' Safari and Fresh Force; and the kids were at that age where they weren't hopelessly independent yet weren't going to run you over with severe behavior issues—or so I hoped! This grade is also great because, most of the time, the students look up to you, and it's easier to convince them that you know what you're talking about even when you clearly don't.

When I got to the school, I was surprised to see that it had an "open" format. The classrooms weren't quite enclosed. The walls that surrounded each one were only about four feet high. For example, the classroom where I was going to teach had two walls that stretched up to the ceiling. The wall along the main hallway was the half wall, if you could call it that. On that half, students would hang up their jackets, hats, or whatever they would need to store. In the back of the room was another half wall, so I could just turn around and see what the math teacher was teaching in her classroom.

HERE COMES THE ROOKIE

I immediately became apprehensive. I was new, and I knew I was lacking expertise in classroom management. What would each of those teachers think if I couldn't keep the class in order? I was afraid I was going to have to raise my voice and yell at the students if they weren't behaving—and I didn't want the other teachers to hear me yell! Also, our education program was pushing cooperative learning in an inquiry-based setting. This meant that I needed the students to do quite a bit of group work. What if my groups were too loud but were doing what they needed to do? I was also afraid that the other teachers would think I had no control over my class. I had no idea whether they would give me time to figure things out or whether it was normal to have a class that was a bit distracting in this open classroom setting, especially with a new teacher.

As it turned out, the teacher next to my classroom was a yeller! I was quite uncomfortable with this. Whenever he yelled, it seemed to disrupt my students' learning, since they would stop what they were working on and snicker over his outburst. The man was quite the paradox. He had posters of peace, Jimi Hendrix, and John Lennon all over his classroom and was a year away from retirement. You would think that if you walked into that classroom, you'd have the most laid-back teacher. But no way. This guy would go on a tirade for minutes. Sometimes it was so bad that I had to stop teaching because I couldn't hear myself over his booming voice. All of the students in my class had a look that said, *I hope I'm not getting that teacher next year!*

Also, the room I was going to teach in didn't have regular desks. The students would be sitting at tables. This was a first for me; my students wouldn't have their own place to store books, pencils, and the like. Instead, they would either have their supplies underneath the spot where they were sitting or put those items in their cubby alongside the back wall. Having tables would work, since we were focusing on cooperative learning anyway.

Aside from the open classroom layout, Echo Park was your typical one-level elementary school. At that time, there was nothing that stood out. Today, looking back after twenty years of teaching, I wonder how we got through the day with so little technology. My cooperating teacher, Tom Trefethen, was ahead of his time in programming for grades using an Excel spreadsheet. That blew my mind. I thought he was a technological genius! There was also nothing much in the way of media then. We just had two TVs on a cart. The Internet was just coming into play, but teachers (including student teachers like myself) didn't have any way of knowing how to use it to benefit the classroom. I kind of miss those days when we had to be creative and come up with our own lessons and not default to the Internet to look up (and steal!) ideas.

I Hope I Don't Suck in Front of You All

It's nerve-racking to guess what type of cooperating teacher (aka classroom teacher) you'll end up getting when you enter the world of student teaching. You might think to yourself, *Is my teacher going to be strict and criticize everything I do?* Or, *Are they going to report to my professors that I'm a bad teacher?* Or, *Is my teacher just going to hand over the keys entirely to me and not give me any guidance whatsoever, and I'm going to get swallowed up by the class because I have no clue what I'm doing?*

Another question that student teachers might ask themselves is, *Am I going to get the teacher that will help me plan and give me some constructive criticism to help me grow as a teacher?* This is normal for anybody heading into any profession. Are you going to have a boss who's going to help you out or push you out of the boat to let you sink? Having someone who's going to observe what could potentially be your life's work for the first time can be unnerving!

The first time I met Tom was rather uncomfortable. He looked like a short army general. He couldn't have been taller than five foot seven, and he had a stocky build. He also had a silver crew cut (he was pretty close to retirement at the time) and eyes that looked like they had seen a lot. Tom was a man of many interests. Outwardly, he looked regimental and would sometimes act like it, but he also had an artistic, eclectic side. He also had a reassuring sound to his voice.

That first meeting on day one was somewhat uncomfortable because I felt like Tom was sizing me up. He was warm and welcoming when I came into the classroom, but I felt like he was closely paying attention to what I was saying and even considering my movements. He would stand off to the side with his arms crossed and his head tilted, staring as if he was analyzing a painting. I got the feeling he thought that he might be dealing with some clueless college student and that he was going to be in major trouble!

Tom's room was a little different in that it wasn't decorated much for a fourth-grade classroom. Most of the time, if you go into an intermediate-grade classroom, you'll find posters with formulas, motivational quotes, general information, or cartoons or movie characters on them. Not with Tom. His classroom was bare-bones. Then again, since it was an open classroom, there wasn't a lot of wall space to hang posters.

Tom also showed me where I was going to be sitting, which was a small table in the back of the classroom. This is normal for a student teacher, but I wasn't planning on sitting much unless he had me grading tests or doing some other task. I wanted to move around the classroom when he was teaching and help him out that way. I felt like it would be something he would appreciate as well, and he wouldn't think of me as some lazy student teacher.

After a quick tour of the classroom, Tom took me around to visit the teachers in our hallway. The first teacher we met was Mr. Nelson, who was across the hallway from us. He was in his early sixties, a straight-up Norwegian with a Minnesotan accent. He was a kind and knowledgeable science teacher. The students loved him. He made a point of remembering their names before an open house. He also took great care in getting to know his students personally and making sure they knew they mattered. He took the time to get to their level and make connections to their personal lives. Any time we had outside recess, Mr. Nelson would rally the students and start a huge soccer game. The students all looked forward to that. To this day, I try to know the names of my students within the first two days of the school year. (Okay, so I don't remember them by open house, but I try!)

Mr. Nelson also had a quiet discipline that worked in his classroom. He probably had the best-managed class in the school. (All of the teachers were really good at this school, except for the yeller next to us.) It was due in part to the relationships and rapport he built with his students. Also, students were always excited to get him as a teacher. When you build relationships for nearly forty years, word spreads from brother to sister, parent to parent, and neighbor to neighbor about how good of a teacher you are—and that puts you in high demand.

I also met Mrs. Carrol, the math teacher who taught in the classroom connected to Tom's. She was organized and extremely friendly. I noticed that she was completely the opposite of Tom in terms of organization. It was the first time I saw somebody work with a planner and have it so detailed.

Mrs. Carrol helped me become that organized when I did my own planning, simply because I was terrible at winging it. Tom, on the other hand, wasn't necessarily disorganized. He was more of a framework kind of guy. He showed me how to make a framework for the year, meaning that he outlined the topics he would teach and how many days, weeks, or months they would take. But he didn't do the day-to-day planning. He had it all in his head. Today, I think it's harder to do that. But at that point, the No Child Left Behind Act hadn't come into effect yet, and we didn't have to follow state standards as we do now. And back then, the curriculum also helped you put together the framework.

Another thing that blew me away about Tom was that he had the curriculum—he just never used it! This is where his eclectic manner came in to teaching. He felt he had more important themes and topics to teach rather than what the curriculum held. Sure, he would delve into the commercial product once in a while, but he ultimately produced his own quasi curriculum. It's hard to make something out of nothing, but that was what Tom (and also the U of M) was expecting me and my fellow student teachers to do. Damn the curriculum—come up with your own inquiry lesson! This was something I needed to do.

However, Tom was more off the cuff, while I had to plan out what I was going to teach.

The last teacher I met and got to know fairly well was Marie, who was in her last year before retirement. She, just like everyone else, was extremely gracious and welcoming. It was interesting. Here I was, a kid trying to get into teaching, and there she was, a teacher who had been teaching for forty years and was now on her way out. When a holiday, lyceum, or school party was going on, Marie always reminded us that this was her last time participating in it. She always had a tear in her eye when she declared this. It got me thinking about whether teaching would make me that emotional if I made it as far as she did, and what it would be like to do activities for the last time in the profession I enjoyed.

Finally, I met the principal of the school. Since it would be my first time working under a principal, it was hard to judge just how good of a principal she was. Whenever she saw me in the hallway, she always stopped and asked how things were coming along. She was also effective during staff meetings. She would speak directly and to the point. She didn't supply any fluff or silly icebreaker activities, especially as the year went along. Instead, she would just go over what was going on at the school and address any issues that were on the horizon. She seemed like a straight shooter who didn't want to waste the staff's time. The staff also seemed to admire her.

The schedule that was set up for me and the other student teachers was all-encompassing. Our student teaching was going to be a full-year experience, whereas student teachers from most other colleges only teach for a semester. For the first month or so, I would only be in the classroom two or three times a week, and for a couple of hours each day. As the year moved on, we settled into more of a full-time routine at the school, and that was when we started teaching the bulk of our lessons. Then when spring rolled around in March, we would start relinquishing control back to the classroom teacher.

I loved this because I could be with the students for the whole year and watch them grow. I wasn't just dive-bombing in by the middle of the year or vanishing during the year without seeing them graduate from their grade. The yearlong experience also gave me and other student teachers a chance to witness and work on the extra pieces that go along with being a teacher, like student conferences, open houses, and getting students ready for the next grade. And it was valuable in that we could see what it was like to get a classroom ready before the school year started.

There was also something Tom identified about me that I hadn't been aware of previously: my difficulty with maintaining attention. During the week before school started, as we were getting the classroom set up for the students, Tom had noticed some of the behaviors I exhibited. He would often be talking to me, and I would just tune him out. I was either on information overload or thinking ahead to what I needed to get done, rather than listening to him talk about what he needed. Other times, Tom would tell me that I would need to have this or that ready to introduce myself to the students or to put up something on the walls of the classroom, and I would go off and do something else like work on my portfolio or plan for future lessons. Later, I would come back and realize I hadn't done the one thing he wanted me to do, or I would have to ask him again what he had wanted me to do.

About three days into that week, Tom asked me if I had attention deficit disorder (ADD). I was shocked! Nobody had ever asked me that before. Truth be known, I had only started learning about it in my child psychology classes at the U of M—and I was pissed that I was getting a diagnosis from my cooperating teacher! I asked him why he would even ask me about it, and what he said made me think about whether I did have ADD. This diagnosis was something I felt only occurred in students, not adults!

Tom admitted that he had ADD and was taking medicine for it. This was news to me, since I didn't think you needed to go through that in your fifties. He let me know that he saw a lot of himself in me, always kind of doing my own thing and not paying attention to what others wanted. I honestly didn't know what to say to him. I didn't want to get into an argument with him over it. I didn't want to say, "No way! Nobody ever told me I was ADD! I don't have a problem!" I came close to it, but he was too important to disagree with at that time, and having him relate to me made me feel like maybe I needed to step back and analyze myself.

Growing up, I had always been told twice what I had to do. I would often be deep in my thoughts and not realize what was going on around me. Now, as a student teacher, I started to think of all the instances that may have affected my life: my parents constantly repeating commands for me to do something (often to the point of anger), me not listening to my bosses during my menial middle and high school jobs, me not taking commands from my coaches in sports, and my less-than-perfect assignment completion rate in school. I had always done well on tests, but I had been horrible at following directions and timelines. It hadn't been to the point of concern, but now it was all rushing back to me, since my cooperating teacher was the first one to unofficially diagnose me.

After Tom hack-diagnosed me, I never seriously thought of getting tested—frankly, because I knew some people were worse off than I was. I also concluded that everybody has some degree of ADD. If I had gotten by all those years without anyone quite noticing, then maybe I'd just shape up a little for Tom. I did take what he said to heart, though; and whenever somebody admonished me for not paying attention or not doing what was clearly asked of me, Tom always came to mind—and I wanted to kick myself!

Here Come the Kids

We had an open house a few days before the students came. This was a nice way to see how the teachers conducted themselves in front of parents and students for the first time. The parents came in and listened to Tom give his spiel about what his class would be like in terms of what he was teaching and his expectations for behavior. Thankfully, because I was nervous as all get-out, I didn't have to say much. Tom just pointed me out in the back and introduced me. I got a few nods from the parents, and I feebly waved my hand and gave a nervous smile. I was wondering if the parents were thinking, *Oh, great. Look at that student teacher standing over there! He's going to get eaten up by these kids, and my child is going to get behind in learning compared to all the other kids in this school!* As you can tell, I was brimming with confidence.

When Tom's speech was over, the parents lingered in the classroom, looking at the setup and grabbing a word with Tom whenever they had the chance. He seemed to put the parents and their kids at ease. Some of the parents had other children who had had Tom in the past, and they were pleased to have him as a teacher for their second or third child. Seeing this made me hope that one day parents would be happy to have me teach their second or third child.

At the end of the night, Tom talked to me about some of the kids we were going to have in our class. He was pretty good at profiling (hey, most teachers do this!) and pointed out possible behaviors some of the students might exhibit. He had seen which ones were going to be the troublemakers, which ones were going to be the pleasers, which ones were going to be quiet, and which ones were going to be the wild cards.

Tom also went to the third-grade teachers who had taught these students the previous year to get the lowdown on them. There were files where he could look up their cumulative scores on standardized tests or behavior notices, but he wanted to hear it straight from the teachers, too. This made him strategize where each student was going to sit—and teachers all knew about the strategy we put into seating arrangements!

The students in Tom's class were extremely attentive on the first day of school, as any class usually is that day. Tom had a way of using humor by mispronouncing their names to make the students relax and laugh, but he also exuded an authority that wasn't going to let the class have too much of a leash when it came to silliness. Tom was also a great cartoonist, and he showed off his skill while telling stories to the students that day. He would use this talent on grading, too. He would doodle little characters on worksheets he'd hand back to the students, who would get a kick out of it.

After that first day, I felt good about possibly going into the profession. It was enjoyable to see the students come in all bright-eyed and cheery. They were all willing to get off on the right foot, and it made me think that this was what every first day of school would be like.

Even throughout that first week, Tom made that classroom feel welcoming by having fun with the students through slight jokes, but never to the point where he lost the boundary of being the teacher. The students knew what the expectations were, too. Tom did a great job showing a firm hand when he needed to. He didn't have the students come up with the expectations for the year; rather, he gave the expectations to them.

As the young year went on, Tom slowly gave me responsibilities to take over the classroom. I had certain areas I had to cover in teaching, but my main areas of focus were language arts and social studies. I didn't have to do any math or science—for which I was thankful!

If you had a Houghton Mifflin Harcourt language arts or math curriculum, then you'd go on what they had installed and just teach off that for the most part. The situation I had with Tom was that he hardly used any curriculum. At one point, he gave all our students mini Constitution packets and taught that for about a week. I was somewhat taken aback, since it was a complex subject. But Tom felt it was important for the students to know about it—and so he was going to teach it! During this lesson, I felt like the students were struggling to grasp the language of the Constitution, along with all the amendments. Since it was the beginning of the year, the students were still in that phase where they were too shy to ask questions or even complain about the complexity of it. This was the first time I noticed the possible negatives of coming up with your own curriculum.

Teaching off the cuff and coming up with your own material was what our program, I felt, was pushing anyway. Other teachers were strictly by the book, going by the prescribed materials that would be taught on such and such a date and in order. Nothing was wrong with that at all. I actually would have preferred doing that, since I was new; and I didn't know if what I was making up for my lessons was having any impact. Having Tom as my cooperating teacher made me feel comfortable with coming up with my own material. At one point, when we were going over our plans, he saw that one of my lessons was too grandiose and would take a considerable amount of time. He told me not to hit home runs every lesson or I'd strike out more often than not.

"Just go for the singles," he said. "They're quick, simple, and to the point, and the students will get more out of them."

There was one area where Tom and I differed quite drastically, and that was in how students were to learn in the classroom. Tom was extremely teacher-centered. There was hardly any group or partner work when he was teaching. He had an amazing capability to get down to the fourth graders' level and hold their attention throughout a lesson. He was a storyteller, in a sense, and would often use his art skills to get the lesson through to the students.

Part of his capability to hold the students' attention was his classroom management style. Some aspects of his management made me feel uncomfortable, because he would use subtle threats with his students. For example, if a student was having a difficult time paying attention or was side talking, Tom would stop teaching and ask that student what they were doing. The tone of Tom's voice would change ever so slightly so that the class knew this wasn't a question in which he was interested in the answer. Oftentimes the student would give a weak answer or an excuse, and Tom would have none of it. Then Tom would threaten the student by asking them if they would like to call their parents in front of the class and tell them why they were being disruptive. Now, Tom never raised his voice, which was great because I'm not one to do that myself. But there was something about Tom's tone and glare that was unsettling. The fact that he used public humiliation with a student was enough for the others to decide that they didn't want this to happen to them.

Using the threat of having a student call their parents because of the way they behaved was nothing new. But as a student teacher, there was something in my gut that told me I didn't like this use of authority. It put the rest of the students at unease—and maybe that was the point for some teachers, and to each their own. Still, upholding the students' dignity, no matter how much they misbehaved at the time, overruled my desire to publicly shame them. To each their own, though.

Tom's teacher-centered classroom flew in the face of the U of M's insistence on developing inquiry-based learning. Inquiry-based learning gave students more of a voice in learning by having them get involved with discussions, ask questions, and explore material within groups. In today's learning environment, students have the Internet and can learn through guidance from the teacher. But at the time, the Internet wasn't readily available for whole-class inquiry, so teachers had to come up with printed copies of materials or other means of literature for them to read and collect information. Since I had to use inquiry-based learning, it was difficult for Tom to give useful feedback, since he wasn't used to teaching through that method. Oftentimes he would leave the classroom and go down to the teachers' lounge and let me do my teaching solo. When this happened (and it's normal for cooperating teachers to do this), I would half expect the students' eyes to open wide and half of them to start drooling at the prospect of causing trouble. Sometimes this would be difficult, because I could have used the feedback on how certain lessons went—especially if they had flopped!

Chapter 5

BEGINNING TO TEACH DURING A NATIONAL TRAGEDY

During my first week of student teaching, the national tragedy we now call 9/11 struck. Tom and I were getting ready for the students to come in when he received a phone call from his wife. This was before anybody had a cell phone, so he took it on the classroom's landline phone. I wasn't paying attention to his conversation, but when he hung up he told me that a plane had crashed into the World Trade Center. We didn't think about it being anything big. Instead, we both thought it must have been a small propeller plane or something of that size.

Minutes later, the school principal spoke over the intercom to tell us that an actual passenger jet had crashed into the tower. Tom and I just stared at each other in disbelief. The next thing we knew, we and the rest of the staff were being summoned to one of the first-grade classrooms.

When we arrived, the staff had just rolled in one of the school's two TVs. As soon as Tom and I walked into the classroom, the second plane slammed into the other tower. There were audible gasps from the staff members; and I just stood there, dumbfounded. Nobody could comprehend what was happening. Just as we were coming to grips with what we had seen, the bell rang and the students came in—whether we were mentally ready or not.

Tom told me not to worry about any of the lessons I had planned on doing that day and that he would take it from there. Both of us were probably frazzled at that point.

As the fourth graders walked into the classroom, they were abuzz with what they had seen at home, which was the first tower on fire. They thought they were watching a movie, not an actual terrorist

attack. Of course, at that age, there was no way they could have com-
prehended it. Even we adults were having a difficult time understanding what we were witnessing.

There were no Epson projectors wired to the computers. Nor was
there Google to show images or even stream the news to try to explain
it all to our students, who had a never-ending stream of questions for
us. But Tom was an excellent illustrator, so he did his best to describe
what was going on by drawing on the whiteboard. He sketched two
large towers and two planes that looked like they were going to fly into
them. I stood back in disbelief. This was something we were actually
teaching the students. This was actually happening. The students sat
silently and listened to Tom patiently explain what was going down.
They sat there, mystified; and in the end, they didn't know what to
ask for. Instead, most of their questions were about whether it was a
movie and when they were going to put the fire out. Tom and I realized just by looking at each other that he had done the best he could
to explain what was going on, and we had better make it as normal a
day as possible.

The rest of the day was frantic horror. Tom taught while I was running back and forth to the staff workroom to find out the latest news.
There was a TV in that room, so I could get updates on what was happening and then relay the news to Tom throughout the day. Whenever
I made my way to the workroom, I would feel the school's intensity and
the solemnity of everything. It was as if life was sucked out of the place.
Whenever any teacher had a chance, they would find their way to the
workroom or wherever the second TV was.

Toward the end of the day, many parents were understandably coming to pick up their children rather than have them take the bus home.
Nobody knew if we were even going to have school the next day, because we didn't know when this carnage was going to end. I left the
school with two of my student teacher cohorts as we discussed if the U
of M was going to do something.

On my drive home, I wanted to drive into downtown Minneapolis,
even though I lived in Saint Paul with my brother, Ren. As I drove
northbound on Interstate 35W, I wanted to look at the IDS Center,

since that was the tallest building in Minneapolis. I needed to wrap my head around what had happened that day. I looked at the IDS tower and told myself that two buildings—each four times taller and four times wider than this building—had just collapsed. I still couldn't grasp it. It was a beautiful fall day, just like it had been in New York City.

When I arrived home in Saint Paul, I watched the news at Ren's house with my friend Grant. All three of us were awestruck, and the news was coming in fast about who might have been responsible for it. It was then that I found out we were going to have school the next day. For the rest of the night, the three of us sat there with our eyes glued to the TV, watching CNN. Ren's house was near the Minneapolis-Saint Paul International Airport; and on any normal night, there would be planes flying over his house all the time. But on this night, and for the rest of the week, the planes were grounded. We would go outside at night and look up into the dark sky and see just one fighter jet, circling the metro area over and over again. It was chilling.

The rest of the week, my student teacher cohorts and I, along with the regular teaching staff and the students, were still trying to figure out what was going on. My peers and I found it hard to focus during our lessons and at school. So many things were going on throughout the academic community. Everybody was trying to see if everyone else was okay and if there was another attack coming.

The teachers at the school in Echo Park did an excellent job of keeping things together. This was the moment when I learned that teaching was a job where you needed to compartmentalize quickly—because you were leading a group of young students who were looking up to you, so you needed to have your shit together. This was an important lesson, as I would have to teach through tragedy a few more times in my career.

Along with student teaching, I also had practicums sprinkled throughout Minneapolis that I had to be at on the days when I wasn't at Echo Park. One practicum I had was a first-grade classroom in a school just outside the U of M campus, and one of the students I was working with was a young boy named Saeed. He was quite possibly the cutest kid I've ever worked with. Each time I came into the classroom, he had the brightest smile and eyes that were full of wonder and excitement. He and I would go to a quiet part of the classroom and work on letters and sounds. Even though he was behind in this area compared to his classmates, he didn't care—or, quite frankly, he didn't know. He was so determined and positive, even when he was struggling; and he was so excited when he knew he was progressing and could read out of his rhyme book without stumbling. He was the epitome of what makes teachers want to teach.

It wasn't until our daily morning meeting that we started to see the effects that 9/11 would have on some of our students, including Saeed. During the meeting, students would sit in a circle and there would be a lesson about the calendar, weather, or happenings at school. Toward the end of the meeting, the students would have a share session. One student would share something, then call on two other students to politely comment or ask a question on their share. The cooperating teacher (who was fantastic) led the group in the share. As you can imagine, first graders *love* to share, and all of them had their little arms waving madly to be picked on. On this particular day, she picked Saeed, and he was *excited*!

When Saeed stood up to talk, he stated that his dad had been driving his taxi home while Saeed had been waiting for him. He went on to explain that two men had come out of the bushes and thrown eggs at his dad's taxi. The cooperating teacher and I looked at each other as it dawned on us exactly what this was about.

Saeed continued, saying that the two men had yelled something at his father. Oddly enough, he was recounting all of this as if it was amusing. As a first grader, Saeed had no idea of the nature of this act, even though the nation was aflame with Islamic hatred at the time. The cooperating teacher did a masterful job of moving the sharing along. The other first graders didn't know how to respond to Saeed's story anyway.

I often wondered how this event shaped Saeed's life as well as the lives of countless other students like him. It wasn't fair that this had to happen to him, and I hope everything turned out well for him as the years have passed by.

Chapter 6

ESCAPE THE REAPER

There was one matter I was nervous about during student teaching, and that was being observed by the infamous Professor Buggey. If my cohorts—who were much better at student teaching than I was—were getting negative feedback, then I couldn't imagine what Professor Buggey was going to say to me!

One way to see if my peers and I were progressing was to ask a cohort in our school to observe us. I was completely insecure about being observed. I wasn't yet ready for constructive criticism on my teaching, especially in the areas of lesson presentation or management, partly because I felt like I was nowhere near as competent as my two cohorts, Sarah and Sophia.

One day, Sophia asked if I would observe a lesson she was doing. I thought this was great, because it would give me a chance to measure how I was doing. Sophia was teaching first graders, which wasn't much help in terms of classroom management since I was dealing with older students. But I could see how long her lessons were, how well-organized they were, and if the students seemed to grab the concepts she was teaching and were engaged.

The lesson Sophia was teaching was how to tell time. She had the Big Time™ demonstration clocks, which were these large yellow clocks that had a blue minute hand and a red hour hand. She had the students in groups, and they would mimic what she was doing for each time on the clock she wanted them to show. As I was watching, I noticed that the students were engaged in what Sophia was doing and that she knew how to move about the room, making sure the students were up to the task. Sophia would move among the students gracefully, giving equal time to all of them and more precise one-on-one time with students who were struggling. When she was finished with the lesson, she asked me how I thought it had gone. I told her that it had been a really thought-out lesson and that she had done great. I was happy for her—but now it seemed that I had to make sure my lessons were as good as hers.

As for Sarah, I didn't get to observe her, but Sophia did. Both of them asked if I wanted some feedback on my teaching, but I sheepishly found a way out of being observed by them. This is something that all teachers need to get over, though—and most do! Most teachers have no problems with putting themselves out there, but I still get nervous whenever I'm being observed by my peers.

Aside from Professor Buggey coming to observe us, a few of our instructors and advisers came in to observe us teaching. This was usually unannounced—and it was nerve-racking for all of us. We would have our lessons all ready to go when it was our time to teach, but some of us had our inconsistencies. So whenever the advisers came to observe, I'd wonder if they were going to notice an area I was glaringly struggling in.

One area I was having trouble with was, of course, classroom management. I was having a hard time finding my voice of authority and learning when to get the students to calm down and pay attention. By and large, the students were really good, but this class knew that Tom—Mr. Trefethen to them—ran the show; and if they were going to give me trouble, then they were going to disappoint their teacher, which they didn't want happening. Still, the students liked to push my buttons, as all will do whenever the main teacher is away or not teaching. During my teaching, there would always be some form of side talking. At times, it seemed I was doing a whack-a-mole in shushing students. And during small group work, I would notice that the same students weren't participating, and I struggled to get them to put in their fair share.

After observing my teaching, an adviser pointed out my struggle with classroom management. She warned me that Professor Buggey was looking for class discipline, and I needed to tamp down the side talking and blurting out. I wasn't used to criticism, and this stung. It also made my anxiety ramp up, as I knew that Professor Buggey was going to be in for observations.

One time, I was finishing up for the day when Sophia came into my and Tom's classroom. Tom usually left right around the time his students left, and I usually stayed behind to make sure I knew what the heck I was going to do the next day. When Sophia arrived, I was surprised; we usually didn't come to each other's classrooms at the end of the day. So something was up—I could tell right away from the look on her face. She was pissed and on the verge of crying. Right then, I knew that Professor Buggey had come in to observe Sophia.

Sophia started by saying some unsavory comments about Professor Buggey that I won't repeat on this page. She then described her lesson and explained how everything had gone. What she told me seemed like a perfectly normal lesson. By Tom's account, it would have been a safe "single" rather than a "home run" type of lesson, which was what I was planning on doing when I was to be observed by Professor Buggey. Sophia felt her lesson had gone well, though, and even commented that her cooperating teacher had told her the lesson was strong.

However, when Sophia had the post-observation meeting with Professor Buggey, the professor had a very different take. Sophia relayed what was said to her; and as she was telling me this, she became more enraged at how the professor had denigrated her lesson. There wasn't one good thing Professor Buggey had said about it. In fact, she had recommended that Sophia take the rest of the semester off and come back the following semester, when she would be ready. She also suggested that teaching might not be the profession Sophia should sign up for. I could hardly believe what I was hearing!

In addition, Professor Buggey had torn into Sophia about the condition of her portfolio, which was a binder full of lessons we had to keep up and maintain. After this, I was shaken, because Sophia's portfolio was way more organized and fancier than mine. So as Sophia was venting, I was tuning her out because of the images of what would more than likely come my way. I was starting to sweat!

Sophia was so mad that she was ready to go to our program's administration to make a complaint and ask for all of her money back if she was going to be forced to drop out and then come back next year. I didn't blame her. Not once did Sophia say that Professor Buggey had offered suggestions about how she could improve her teaching. It was almost as if the professor had been expecting perfection the whole way through.

I didn't know what to tell Sophia. She was in a bad way, and I wanted her to do well. But I wasn't in a position to tell her exactly what was going to happen and what she should do. I was now in survival mode. Then, in the parking lot, we ran into Sarah, who was distressed. She told us that Professor Buggey had told her to quit for the year and come back next semester, because she felt that Sarah had missed too many days of student teaching due to a medical condition. Right away, Sophia became irate. I didn't blame her at all, after what she had just gone through with the professor. Sarah's medical condition was out of her control; and from what she was saying, she had only missed two weeks of student teaching. In fact, she wasn't even supposed to have come back that soon. She was putting her health at risk, and the stress wasn't making it any better.

So now my two student teacher cohorts had been shredded by Professor Buggey, and I was next. I was thankful that I was the last one, because now I could spend time trying to revise my portfolio.

Portfolios were all-encompassing in our program. They were graded by the professors who taught our core subject areas. Within these classes is where we taught our microlessons at the schools where we had practicums. The portfolios also had to be divided into educational standards that the professors were looking for us to teach. We were graded on these portfolios through quality, quantity, organization, neatness, and creativity. The rest of the graded materials and the standards that had the lessons in them were complimented well enough. I always scored a B or a B+. Nothing lower, nothing higher. To me, this was good enough to get by.

The main portfolio I was sweating over, though, was the one that was going to be graded by Professor Buggey. It was our Introduction to Elementary School Teaching binder, which was split into ten standards that included subject matter, student learning, diverse learners, instruction strategies, learning environments, communication, planning instruction, assessments, reflection and professional development, and collaboration. Everything associated with our student teaching had to be included in this massive portfolio. It also had to have a theme, and my theme was sports because I wasn't very creative. It was the easiest one I could think of.

I also realized I had no stickers to make my portfolio "theme-y" enough. This was something Professor Buggey had a strange obsession about, going back to her ladybug theme. So I ran all over to try to find sports stickers. I had never asked the newer teachers at Echo Park what examples they had kept from their student teaching days and how they had shown their portfolios to their professors. For better or for worse, my portfolio was just about complete. I had already received mediocre grades for my other core classes, and I felt I could do no worse with the portfolio I had prepared for Professor Buggey.

The next day and a half slogged by. Again, I had to make sure my lessons were airtight for the afternoon. I really wanted to tell the students that a special visitor was coming to the room to watch them—and that if anybody acted up, the visitor was going to drink all their blood and bury their corpses in the swamp out back. (That would have been inappropriate for the fourth graders, though.) Anyway, Tom and I had prep the third hour of the day, and we usually headed down to the teachers' lounge. Sometimes I wanted to stay back and double-check my lessons, but I needed to clear my head.

When we came back, I discovered a note on my portfolio. It was from Professor Buggey! She admitted in the note that she had mixed up the observation times, but not to worry about mine, because she was sure everything was going well! And while I had gone on our prep, the professor had gone through my portfolio and graded it right there. I got, of course, a B+.

I couldn't believe it. I felt like I had cheated death! My most feared part of the school year was over! I sat at my table in bewilderment for several minutes. How could Professor Buggey just totally blow off my observation?

The next day, Sophia asked me how the observation had gone. Suddenly I was worried about what she would think about me not being observed and getting a passing grade while she was on the verge of failing. For a split second, I felt like lying to her and saying that it was okay, that

Professor Buggey had nothing good to say about my lesson but hadn't told me to quit student teaching. I wanted to say this just to join Sophia in her misery so that she wouldn't be alone. Instead, I told her that Professor Buggey had never shown up and had given me a B. Needless to say, Sophia was livid. She started raging about how I had gotten a B and how she was possibly going to fail and have to repeat next year. I was afraid that she was going to take this up with the administration and rat me out for not being observed, which would make Professor Buggey come in again to do an observation. In the end, though, Sophia calmed down and just chalked it up to me being lucky. I was thankful that she wasn't going to make this bigger than it needed to be.

The more Sophia and I thought about it, though, the more we wondered if gender had a role in this. There were hardly any male teachers in our program. Sometimes our female cohorts thought that the male students were given higher grades because the profession needed more men and our program didn't want them to walk away. This always drove me nuts to hear it, and it still does even today. But there are instances where sexism can creep in.

Chapter 7

AM I EVEN WORTHY?

Once student teaching was over, my peers and I had to start looking for actual teaching jobs. It was kind of a complicated scenario, because most of us were looking and filling out applications. Plus, we had to take the Praxis exam, the test that would provide our certificate of teaching if we passed it.

I didn't know what to do. I was kind of paralyzed by indecision and self-doubt. It was taking a huge leap. Was this the profession I wanted to do for the rest of my life? And would I be any good at it? I still didn't know the answers. Plus, I didn't want to start looking for jobs and filling out applications because I hadn't taken the Praxis exam—and I was extremely pessimistic about it, since I didn't think I was going to pass. Today, I have no idea why I was thinking that way. My grades were fine, and I had done okay in my student teaching. But there was something about that test that made me uncomfortable.

During mid-May, a job fair for teaching positions was held at the Minneapolis Convention Center. I knew I was going to have an elementary license that would cover me in grades K-6, along with a social studies license in grades five through eight. So I decided to check out this fair, not knowing what the market was like for new teachers. And boy, did I find out how dire it was.

When I walked into the convention center, there were hundreds of tables representing every corner of Minnesota, all states, and even teaching abroad contingencies. I quickly noticed that the state of Minnesota wasn't in a hurry to hire new teachers. Most of the representatives in that district weren't taking interviews at the time, especially in the areas of teaching I was qualified for. There was a backlog of teachers who had just graduated from college and were looking for positions; and I figured out that state funding for schools was pretty paltry thanks to our governor at the time, the one and only Jesse "The Body"

Ventura, whom my friends and I had dutifully voted for when we were sophomores in college. (Hey, who wouldn't want an ex-wrestler as a governor?) Anyway, I was getting the cold shoulder from many schools in the area. And worse, having a social studies license was like showing off you had a Ford Pinto. There was absolutely no room for social studies teachers. The few districts I inquired with gave me a sympathetic look and said, "Well, we're really not looking for social studies or history teachers at this time. . . ." Instead, Minnesota schools were looking for teachers licensed in secondary math and science. I was not in a good spot!

I also noticed quite a few of my cohorts at the job fair. As I talked to some of them, I realized I wasn't putting in the required effort to find a job. Many of my peers had already had on-the-spot interviews. I even saw some of them in the middle of interviews as I walked around the fair. I didn't feel prepared for an interview, though. I wasn't dressed well, with jeans and a hoodie; and they were looking presentable for their interviews. They were being aggressive, and I wasn't. I didn't even have a résumé or a cover letter at that point! The envy and exasperation were starting to build up.

What was odd to me was the numerous recruiters from other states who were begging prospective teachers to apply. Three states that stuck out to me were Arizona, Alaska, and California. They were practically standing on the tables to attract attention. A perk they were promoting to get teachers was a $10,000 starting bonus when you were hired. That didn't sound bad to me. But being stubborn, I didn't want to move out of the state at the time. What if I hated what I was doing and was stuck out there, with nobody I knew? Some people can handle that, but I didn't want to.

I was trying to figure out what it would be like to teach in California if I didn't get a job in Minnesota. I knew that it was extremely expensive to live out there; and with the salary I would probably be getting, regardless of a signing bonus, I would have to live with multiple roommates in a tiny apartment. In Alaska, I was envisioning myself living a solitary life that wouldn't fit me.

I also noticed all the overseas teaching positions in places like Germany, Brazil, and China, just to name a few. I didn't know anybody who had taught abroad, so I wasn't that interested in going overseas. I did have friends who studied abroad, and I had even visited one of them in Ireland. We'd had a blast, but I had always known I would come home in a few months. I just didn't want to work and stay for practically a whole year in another country.

Today, if I could offer one piece of advice to new teachers, it would be to start your career by teaching abroad. I now know numerous teachers who have done this. I even have friends who started in the business sector only to leave and teach abroad, and they said it was one of the greatest moves in their lives. You get a chance to see what education is like across the world and how it's different from the United States. You can also bring back best practices that are not taught in our institutions, develop an understanding of a culture that's vastly different from ours, and appreciate working with a new population of students. (As a matter of fact, I know teachers who have been teaching in the States for fifteen to twenty years and want to go back abroad. But my sense of adventure was nowhere to be found during that time in my life. Woe is me!)

I came away from the job fair disheartened. I walked out of that convention center with my eyes downcast and my shoulders slumped. The prospects weren't good for me because of the lack of openings and my sheer laziness. I also hadn't taken the Praxis exam, so I had felt that it wasn't worth it to try out for a job. But I had to figure out how to get myself into a position to interview for a teaching job.

The résumé was the important first step. I had no idea what went into a professional résumé. Luckily, the U of M had services to help us put that and a cover letter together. I hated it. It's never fun to put together your life's work and wonder if it's good enough, if it's going to stand out against your competitors. I also hated doing the cover letter because I hated coming off as bragging about myself. I felt like everything I was writing was a lie, even though it wasn't.

In the end, I was proud of my résumé. Thankfully, my work with the YMCA's Fresh Force and Kids' Safari helped fill it out a little.

I also had to ask for letters of recommendation. I think I had to have at least three of them, and this was the part I didn't want to do. In addition to writing about myself and pretending to talk a good game, I now had to ask people I didn't know what they thought about me. So I went to Kids' Safari to ask my former bosses there, and they gladly gave me permission. I wasn't worried about what they would say, since we'd been on good working terms. I also needed to get the principal's recommendation from my student teaching site at Echo Park. This, I was a little bit wary about. But when I called, the principal thankfully remembered me (or at least pretended to). And when I asked, she said yes, for which I was grateful.

Chapter 8

TWI: TESTING WHILE INTOXICATED

G raduation was finally here. I was completely done, aside from taking the Praxis exam. I ended up doing the whole cap and gown ritual with the group that was graduating from the teachers' program. Even though we were all relieved to be graduating, most of us were still in limbo, and our nerves were on edge about where we would find our first teaching position. Not only that, but it was a stressful time for everyone who was just coming out of college. I was seeing friends either from my area of study or a completely different major getting their first professional jobs, while I was stuck in slow motion. I even saw friends in the business sector moving to New York City or Chicago while I was still trying to find my career.

The Praxis exam finally came in early June. It would have been ideal if I'd done it in March so that if I'd passed it, I could have been more aggressive in trying to find work. But since I hadn't finished school at that time, I'd decided against it. I was nervous about this test, just as anyone would be for their entrance exam for any profession. Granted that it wasn't the bar exam or a med school exam, but this was our exam. And, of course, it would take six to eight weeks for the results to come back, which would further my excuses for not aggressively applying for teaching positions.

I was living with Ren at his house in Saint Paul and decided to go down the street with a few of my friends the night before the Praxis. What would a couple of beers do, especially when the exam was taking place just a few minutes' drive from where I lived?

Whenever my friends and I went out, it always seemed to go this way: I believe it was a Wednesday night. Of course, we were at our favorite watering hole, owned by a couple of guys our age. (Their dads were restaurateurs, and I think the dads just gave their sons this hole-in-the-wall in hopes that they would be productive and stay out of trouble.) Of course, the sons joined us, and we started throwing quite a few back. And the whole time, my mind was saying, *Blair, you have the Praxis tomorrow. You NEED to get home!* That voice finally broke through to me at 2:00 a.m. My exam was at 8:00 a.m.

Waking up was, as usual, hell after a night like that. I realized that I had a monumental hangover and I had to take a test—and if I failed, I'd have to wait until next September and pay another fee to take it again. I was already scraping the bottom of the barrel as a poor college graduate, so I didn't want that to happen. I was hating myself. Would a couple of fun social hours possibly ruin any chance I had of getting a teaching job next year? What an idiot I was!

I was also running late, so I had to hurry and get dressed. I have no sense of style; and since I was hungover, I put on the sloppiest clothes I could find. The outfit was a shabby green sweatshirt and jeans that were ready to fall apart at the seams. I barely had the coherence to brush my teeth. There was no time to take a shower. So I got into my car, knowing that if I was pulled over, I would probably fail a field sobriety test. And since I was heading to the College of St. Thomas, where the exam was being held, that would be quite the scene. A prospective teacher, getting pulled over at seven-thirty in the morning for drunk driving! My parents would have been proud.

St. Thomas was Saint Paul's largest university, and I had little clue where the room I was supposed to take the exam in was located. I had ten minutes to get there, and I felt as if I was going to have a panic attack. My heart was racing, and I was breaking into a cold beer sweat. And there's nothing worse than having this feeling compounded by a pounding headache and a riotous stomach from the previous night. I wanted to give up, lie down, and die right on the sidewalk. Luckily, at the last moment, I spotted the building I was supposed to be in for the exam and struggled up the stairs to the room.

When I walked in, pretty much everybody else was in their seats, getting ready to start. They turned and looked at me, and I bet they knew right away. It was as if I had I'M A DRUNK Sharpied on my forehead. I knew I was sweating, and my eyes were bleary. I sheepishly walked up to the front desk where the proctor was and mumbled my name. The proctor had this look that said, *This is the future of our educators?* And when I grabbed my supplies and turned around, I saw half smiles and looks that doubted my success all over everybody else's faces. I sat down at a hard, cold desk, ready to vomit at any minute and desperately needing a Gatorade. I hadn't studied for the test, and I didn't even know if there were study companions for it. So on top of the overwhelming nausea, I was pretty sure that I was woefully unprepared.

The Praxis was designed to see what you knew about teaching in general. It started with questions on content knowledge in your field. For the elementary license, it seemed fairly easy. Even in the condition I was in, I felt like I understood what the rudimentary questions in grammar and literary elements were asking me. But I also started to think that maybe it was a little too easy, and my bruised brain just wanted to get the exam over with.

There was also a math part of the content knowledge section, where questions about math factors, areas of shapes, and missing variables were asked. I have to be honest: I have zero recollection of this part of the exam. Math and I have been mortal enemies throughout my life, and this was a subject area I was certain I wasn't going to teach.

The next part of the test was an assessment of student work. Around this time, I thought I was starting to hallucinate. The words were moving on the page, and I was starting to break into another cold sweat. I began to think that every student example on the test was okay with me and deserved a passing grade. I was starting to hate myself tremendously for the foolish decisions I had made the previous night. I tried to remember every rubric I'd put together in the classes I'd taught during student teaching and applied the test examples to them as best I could. But I felt like I wasn't passing the test at this point.

The last test section I remember covered classroom management. This section provided a long description of a situation that could occur in a classroom and asked how you would solve the issue. In my case, it was something about a girl who had refused to cooperate with the teacher, and the question asked me what I would do to solve or diffuse the issue. This was my weak spot, as I had always struggled with this aspect of teaching. By this time, I was cranky, so I gave the harshest answer on how to deal with the student. It probably wasn't an acceptable answer at all. It was along the lines of removing the student from the classroom—which, as I stated before, I'd never thought to be a good move. By this time, I was one of the last students to complete the exam. I thought the other students were pitying me as they were leaving. I could feel their last shameful glances toward me as they walked out.

I slowly got up and had to steady myself as a wave of lightheadedness came on. I walked up to the proctor, gave her a weak smile, shakily handed her the test, and headed out of the classroom. Strangely enough, I felt that I could at least breathe then. I was still tired as hell, though. I couldn't wait to get home and lie in bed in complete depression and failure. It was about time to figure out what I was going to do for the rest of the summer and what was going to happen in the fall.

HOORAY! (MAYBE?)

After the exam, I kept working at Kids' Safari, where I was at least being active and continuing to work with kids. I also continued working at my old high school job at the grocery store. By the time I'd get home each day, the last thing I wanted to do was look for a job, especially with my exam results still pending. What was the point? It would be embarrassing to submit résumés and get interviews only to find out that I'd failed the exam. I was afraid that principals would find out I failed and remember the next time I applied—when, or if, I ever passed. They would have second thoughts about hiring me, for sure!

Over the next few weeks, I didn't think about the Praxis much. It was out of my control, and I didn't want to burden myself with it. I had a couple of friends who were also waiting on their results, but we didn't bug each other all that much to see who had received their scores yet.

By late July, the results came in. This time was now definitely too late to get a teaching position, as most of the interviews had finished by now. I went to the mailbox one day—and lo and behold, the results were in.

They were in a thick envelope, and I imagined all the ways the contents would tell me how I'd failed and that I should never be a teacher. I could see Professor Buggey's face when I opened it, cackling at me as I was trying to process my failing marks. I was shaking as I opened the letter, which I had never done before in my life. I had to calm myself down. I told myself that if I passed, I wasn't going to get a full-time position anyway—it was too late! And if I had failed, I could always scrounge up whatever money I had saved from the summer and take the test again in the fall. Maybe I would actually take it sober next time.

Eventually, I got the damn envelope open and unfolded the wad of papers. There was a moment when everything looked like it was written in Russian, as I had to focus on how the information was presented. And to my surprise, I had gloriously passed with flying colors.

I couldn't believe it! Unbelievably, I scored higher in math than I did in the reading portion of the test. In fact, I had almost maxed out on the score range for math. There had to have been some miscalculation. As for my general content knowledge of elementary education, there was a score, but I had no idea how it scaled up. But it looked like it was in the eightieth percentile—and I'd take that! I wanted to run out of the house and scream, *I PASSED THE PRAXIS, AND I WAS SUPER HUNGOVER WHILE TAKING IT!* Instead, I just sat down and let the relief wash over me. However, that was short-lived.

Now that I had my scores from the Praxis, it was time for the mad dash of submitting résumés. The only way to find a job at this stage in the game was if somebody had unexpectedly quit for some reason. I was stubborn in my ways and wanted to remain in the southern suburbs of the Twin Cities—which astronomically reduced my chances of getting a job, as those positions were looked at as prime teaching spots. I was still unsure if I was capable of teaching in inner-city schools.

After making a handful of submissions, I heard nothing. It was still early, so I wasn't too worried. I started to lose touch with my cohorts after graduation, so I didn't know if any of them were successful in their job search, either. The term "gap year" would have been nice to have at that time. I could have used it as an excuse for not having a job yet, especially whenever I ran into a friend who was already hard at work with their career.

"So, Blair, you haven't found a job yet?" they would ask me.

"Nah," I'd say. "I haven't really been looking. I'm sure if I tried, I'd have one by now. But I've been thinking of taking a gap year. I've had an overload of classes and been in school for all these years, I just need some time to do my own thing for a little bit."

As July turned into August, I started to accept that I wasn't going to get a teaching position. I decided to expand my search into the outer edges of the suburbs. Social studies didn't seem to exist, as that hadn't even surfaced during the two months I'd been looking. I was starting to wonder why the heck I had gone for that useless specialty. Why not science?!

In desperation, I called Tom about any positions opening at Echo Park. He told me the bad news: they'd had to cut some teachers because of budget cuts.

It was looking more and more like I was going to be jobless by the time the school year started. By the end of August, I gave up looking. I'd had exactly zero interviews. It was time to face the notion that I was going to have to substitute for the year.

Chapter 9

THE SUBSTITUTE

Substitutes. What do students think of when a substitute is in the classroom? Freedom! Trouble! Chaos! Movies! No work! Acting out! Playing tricks! At least, this was what I'd thought when I had been a student and our teacher was out for the day. It was a day to not take anything seriously. Since I hadn't been much of a troublemaker growing up, I'd enjoyed watching others create trouble when there had been a sub. Sometimes I'd participate, but not all the time. Sometimes I would feel sorry for the sub. My classmates could be ruthless. They would stand up and openly mock the teacher when they had their back turned. Sometimes there were verbal spats between a student and the sub that crossed the line. Other times, students refused to listen to the sub and chose to do whatever they wanted, and the sub would just give up and let them be. My friends would sometimes brag about how they made subs cry because they had behaved so badly.

We'd also had our favorite subs. If the classroom teacher announced that they would be gone the following day, we would beg them to get a specific sub we all liked. We'd want a particular sub because we knew we'd get away with a lot of mischief and the sub wouldn't report it. Another reason we'd had favorite subs was that, at times, they were better than the regular teacher. One time, I had this sub in grade school who everybody loved because he was a master storyteller. He was always funny, and it seemed like we learned quite a bit more from him. We respected these subs as much as (if not more than) our classroom teacher. I believe we even told the classroom teacher this once. Needless to say, we didn't see that sub again. Who knows? The sub could have moved on to better things as well.

My friends and I had also had subs who were there all the time. So much so, in fact, that they had started to mesh with the regular teachers. They knew the routines, and it was hard to get away with anything because you knew there was a good chance you'd see that sub every day for the rest of the year in some capacity. They knew how to discipline in the classroom, and they knew the administration and how to reach them in the main office. These were the tried-and-true substitutes. They even knew your first name, because you may have had them throughout your career in primary or secondary school settings.

The strict substitutes were the worst ones of all. They were viewed as mean and were usually retired teachers. They were often more strict than our actual teachers, and there was absolutely nothing we could get away with in class. These subs came from a generation where physical punishment was acceptable in their heyday. We also knew they were always going to have a list of names written down for the teacher after class. Students would plead with these subs to not put their name on the list, because they knew that their mom was going to get a phone call about it the next day and that there would be an interrogation from the classroom teacher, which could result in a loss of recess time— which was the worst! Certain students might as well have had their name stamped on that list, because no matter what, they couldn't help themselves. Back then, I'd always thought these retired teachers had a hobby of coming back just to terrorize students. I didn't know how they could have enjoyed doing that day in, day out.

Not all retired teachers were this way. My friends and I enjoyed some of these subs, because they were at the stage where they knew they didn't have to deal with an unruly class again if they ever got one, so they never got uptight with students.

Whenever I walked into the classroom and saw a sub, the first thing I'd think of and pray for was a movie day. I wanted as little work as possible—and, obviously, so did most of my peers. Whenever we had to do actual work, we made sure to complain loudly about it and try to persuade the sub that our classroom teacher wouldn't usually have us working so hard.

SUBBING: ROLLING IN PEANUTS

Now, as an adult, it was my turn to be the substitute teacher. I was more frightened of this than becoming a regular teacher. For one thing, I had no idea where I wanted to sub. I also would never have a set classroom and would never get to know the students consistently. Finally, I would most likely feel the disrespect I'd seen substitutes go through—and I wasn't too thrilled by that.

When deciding where I wanted to sub, I had my full choice of schools because I was in the city/suburban area. Since it was now late August, I had to hurry up and decide where I wanted to go, because there were orientations to attend on how to be a substitute in certain districts. Since I already had my education license, I didn't have to be so restricted in what I could teach, either.

The three districts I chose for subbing were all related to me in one way or another. I had the Prior Lake-Savage school district, because that was where my sister, Carrie, was teaching, and she could promote me to other teachers if they needed somebody to fill in. However, there was also the threat that if I was god-awful, word would get back to Carrie—and I didn't want her to feel embarrassed for me.

Another district was the one where I grew up. It had all the familiarity, but I was reluctant to apply there. I wasn't too pumped about getting a call to possibly sub in my former schools. I didn't want to teach where I had been raised, because it would seem that I didn't want to move out of the area and be adventurous, which was partly true. The other reason why I didn't want to sub in my home district was, again, out of a fear of failure. What if I subbed for an old teacher of mine and completely bombed out? I felt like I would forever be stained in my hometown and I would never go back to sub there again because I would be too ashamed. However, I applied anyway. I figured that if I did well, they would want to hire the local kid back, right?

The third place was the district where I had done my student teaching. It was what most student teachers did when they couldn't get a job after graduation. Also, it would give me a leg up on the hiring process when they started hiring again in the spring.

Another concern I had about subbing was payment. Being a sub isn't the most financially rewarding job in the world. It's extremely hard to make a living from it. You need other supplemental income if you want to make ends meet. Luckily, I was living in my brother's house where he was giving me, shall we say, a brotherly idea of rent. I was grateful for him, because it was either going to be him, my parents, or living in a small apartment with a roommate. And at the time, the wage for a substitute position was roughly $100 to $110 per day, depending on what district you were subbing for.

I had to figure out the minimum number of days I needed to sub to cover bills I had to pay, like loans, my car, and rent. I had a section in my daily calendar labeled Rent with five squares below it, then a section labeled Car with three squares below that, and the same with a section called Loans. That brought me to a total of eleven squares. So I made sure I subbed at least eleven days that month. After each day I subbed, I would check off one of the boxes. Once I had eleven squares checked off, then I was golden on paying for my absolute essentials. The rest would go to groceries, clothes, and whatever fun a substitute teacher could have.

One area I knew I wasn't going to pay off was health insurance. I felt like I was young enough and in good enough health that I didn't need to have it. Substitute teaching doesn't supply health insurance unless you are a long-term substitute or have been hired as a building sub. I eventually called my insurance the "look both ways" health insurance.

Knowing that I wasn't going to make that much money, especially if I took into account the holidays when subs weren't called on, I needed to get another job. I was done with my campus job at Williams Arena, since I had graduated; and trying to work at Kids' Safari after school would be difficult, because different school end times wouldn't permit me to get over there on time. Most substitute teachers had jobs that were outside of the education field, like being servers at restaurants, where they could earn extra income in tips and shifts could go late. Other teachers stuck to education vocations. I decided to stick to the latter so that I could put something else on my résumé. I ended up taking a position at Sylvan Learning.

Sylvan was an interesting place because it was a tutoring center, and

I had never known that places like it existed. I knew one of my brothers had to get help in test prep, but this wasn't what I thought it would be. I'd thought it would be more of a one-on-one setting. But at Sylvan, you had a small U-shaped table with a small group of three students. Each student had already taken a diagnostic test in reading, language arts, and math. Then there was a building lead who would prescribe what each student would learn based on that diagnostic test. The prescribed curriculum would come from Sylvan's curriculum. My job would be to follow the prescriptions and teach what was prescribed to the students, each of whom would be at their own level.

Once the students were seated at the table, I would have to decide which student could start right away with independent work, then move on to the student who needed more instruction. It was rare for students who were sitting together to have the same lessons. Almost always, each student had something different to learn from the others.

Working with Sylvan also enhanced my awareness of how to teach certain subject areas and the content each one came with. I became aware of what each grade level should have within its content area. I worked with age groups ranging from first grade up to high school, so it was great to see the full range of behaviors and how to work with different maturity levels. I also felt sorry for some of the kids. You could tell they were coming straight from school, where they were most likely struggling, and now they were stepping into yet another educational arena. They were mentally exhausted at times, and this would come out in their behavior from time to time. For the most part, though, the students did well and were self-motivated.

There was also a reward system at Sylvan. Students could attain chips, depending on how well they worked and how much they accomplished. They could then use the chips to buy knickknacks, toys, treats, or gift cards.

Overall, I would say that Sylvan's system was good for its students, as we did see gains. However, there were underlying issues that didn't address students who were struggling with undiagnosed learning disabilities. Being a young teacher, I didn't know how a private learning company should deal with this issue.

HERE COMES THE SUB

I didn't consider that September was going to be slow for subs. It's not flu season, and it's also the time when teachers will do everything in their power not to miss class. So for the first few weeks, I didn't get phone calls. During that time, I picked up a few shifts at Kids' Safari and worked at my new Sylvan job. It wasn't until late September that I would get my first phone call to sub.

Before the Internet was implemented in the school systems, you'd receive a phone call in the wee hours of the morning, mostly around 5:30 to 6:00 a.m. This was somewhat annoying, especially if it was on a day when I wasn't going to sub. My brother *hated* it. Some districts had an automated system that would tell you the grade and the school where you'd be teaching. I liked those phone calls because I didn't feel so bad about denying them. But as soon as you denied one phone call, you'd get another right afterward. Other districts would have a district employee—or even the school secretary—call you. If it was a job I didn't want, like a kindergarten spot, I would feel bad about saying no to it. And if you said no too many times, the district employee or secretary would reconsider calling you for future sub jobs—and that could ultimately hurt your employment chances should a spot open up for next year.

After I would get the phone call, I would get ready. I always had everything set aside for the possibility of subbing, even if I knew there was a good chance I would not be working that day. Start times would vary from school to school and district to district. Sometimes you'd start as early as 7:15 a.m. or as late as 9:15 a.m. I loved starting later because I could sleep in a little longer and not have to feel so rushed.

I was always at my most nervous in the morning. In my nonwork life, I'm late for almost everything, to the irritability of my friends and family. However, work is a different story. Everybody has the nightmare of being late for something or completely missing it. Mine was like that for work. Whenever I was called in to sub, I would arrive forty-five minutes or a half hour early. This wasn't necessary at all. Most subs come around five to ten minutes early. And whenever I would enter a school, the secretaries would have a perplexed look and jokingly comment about me being early. The hallways would be eerily quiet because the majority of the staff wasn't there yet. I would also get strange looks from teachers that said, *Why is that sub here so early? Did something happen?!*

My main reason for being there so early was that I was afraid there would be no plans or materials laid out by the teacher. This did happen a few times, and I would have a mixture of emotions, including annoyance and panic. Luckily, I could ask another teacher from that grade level about what I could do. We would have plenty of time to get a secondary plan ready, which was mostly to put a movie in—which was fine by me! Easy money!

Another reason I wanted to be there early was kind of strange. I was absolutely afraid of failure during my first year, so I wanted to make sure I had almost everything memorized and the materials looked over so that I knew what potential problems could arise. This was helpful not only to myself, but also to the students. I wouldn't be bumbling around, wasting their time by trying to find a way to help them with a problem. With this extra time, I would also visualize what the day would look like. I would go by each instruction and try to visualize how long it would take. What would the students do if they finished too early? What would they do if they didn't finish at all? What would happen if I didn't do everything that was asked for in the sub plans? I knew teachers would get pissed if you didn't finish the lessons they had planned out for you that day—and I didn't want to have a teacher pissed at me! A teacher got upset at me at least once because I hadn't graded any student papers. That was ridiculous! I hadn't seen any specific instructions about grading those papers!

Sometimes I would get to the classroom and all there was to do was watch a movie, which usually focused on what they were studying. So I had no prep. I would just sit at the teacher's desk and daydream, maybe look around their classroom for cool ideas I could use for my future room (a very important tip for you youngsters) or see if there was a teacher I knew who I could help out. But mostly, I just daydreamed.

If there were no plans, I had to improvise quite a bit to keep the students engaged, and I didn't care if I did a good job or not. If the teachers were going to leave me half-assed plans, then they shouldn't expect me to accomplish everything. In this case, I had to do a song and dance. One time, there was half a worksheet about the immune system that students had to complete for science class. I knew the assignment would only take a few minutes to complete, so when teaching the lesson, I had to expand the lecture and bullshit my way through it. I had to act like I knew something about the topic, even though I was making it up.

I liked working for teachers who had great, detailed plans. These plans would last for the hour and were engaging for the students. They would also write down the names of students I should watch out for or who could help out at a moment's notice. Whenever this scenario happened, I would try to reach out to this student and be friendly right off the bat. It didn't work all the time, but sometimes they would be receptive.

Hello! Please Like Me!

When I first started subbing, I didn't know how to act around the staff. I pretty much did what I'd seen most subs do: keep to myself. But I did encounter some nice and welcoming teachers. There were the teachers who would come in the morning to say hi and see if I had everything down. Some of them were personable, and they would ask me where I had gone to school. "How's the job hunting going so far?" they would always ask.

"It's going pretty slow," I would admit. "I don't really have anything yet." This would be followed by a pitiful smile and a nod from the teacher. At the end of the day, they would make sure to say goodbye and even ask for my contact information for when they would need a sub.

I would rarely run into teachers who were churlish or mean. Most teachers were just indifferent. We would walk past each other and give a perfunctory nod. The only situation where a teacher was upset with me was the time I didn't grade the work that had come in. Who knows if other teachers were upset with me? Teachers love to talk about bad subs after they leave!

Aside from all the calls, getting to each school, ingratiating myself with the staff if the opportunity arrived, and the art of getting ready for class, everything changes when the class comes through that door. Each class represents a different dynamic in attitude, behavior, and management. Sometimes you can tell within the first few seconds. There seems to be a certain aura or atmosphere a class can bring even before the first student speaks up. These are the times when you say to yourself, *Oh, this class seems to be nice, or, Shit, I don't like the feeling of this group. It's going to be a LONG day!*

When you have classes who are eager to help, willing to comply, and engaged throughout the day, you can feel like a super sub, and you want the regular teacher to be out for a prolonged illness or vacation so you can sub for the class forever. These classes seem to have positive leaders and don't give any oxygen to negative ones. Whenever you need help locating something, the students are right there to help you find it. They also seem to laugh at anything you say. You may have to redirect a student once or twice, but that's usually for something minor—and it's a fraction of what you'd normally do in a typical class. When the students leave, they even remember your name, say goodbye, and tell you that they want you again as a sub. I would leave the most gushing report to the teacher about how great the students were and would practically beg for them to call me if they ever needed a sub again. Then I would leave the building with the biggest smile on my face, since the day hadn't even seemed like work! Those were the best days. And then there were the bad days. . . .

OPEN SEASON

Having a bad day as a sub is common. Elementary classes were the worst, as I would be stuck with these students for most of the day. One would think that because these students are younger, they would have more respect for the teacher. But that isn't always the case. The young troublemakers have their ways of setting the class off-kilter and making it a long day of teaching.

There are many ways a day of subbing at an elementary school can be cast off into the abyss of madness. One is the lone-wolf scenario. In this case, the class is generally compliant, but they're afraid of the one student who is the class's authoritarian of trouble. This student will be argumentative to the point of yelling and will sneakily bully their typical targets, whether through subtle physical jabs or constant put-downs. This student also can't sit in one place, which is more pronounced at this grade level. In elementary school, the lone wolf is usually undiagnosed with some form of learning disability, and that exacerbates the problem.

Where I struggled was knowing how to discipline this student. If I tried to discipline them, they would be defiant by either stating, "You're not the real teacher!" or saying they're not going to listen to you. This would set the class even more on edge, since the tension would become thicker. And the more the student acted out, the more I was coming closer to kicking them out of the classroom. I hated doing this because, as a young teacher, it made me look like I couldn't control the students. But when it had to be done, there would usually be a few minutes of negotiation to give the student one more chance to stay in the classroom. And when they couldn't accept the terms of settling down and following directions, I had to have them sit in the hall. I hated it. However, once the lone wolf was gone, the class would seem relieved, and the day would go on. On a rare occasion, there would be another lone wolf waiting to replace the alpha, and the process would repeat itself. It was tiresome! Then, once the class left, I was hesitant to write down names because I felt like I didn't have control of the class. However, since there were only one or two students, I didn't have a problem with this.

One lone-wolf situation happened in a fifth-grade class I was subbing for. The teacher had left detailed plans and hadn't indicated which students to keep close tabs on, which was normal. However, once the students came in, one boy in particular—I'll call him Sean—started acting out right away. When I was going through attendance and calling out names, he would say "Here!" for every name I called. The students would get a kick out of this. Even after I told him that it was enough, he continued. When it was time to transition into the first math lesson, Sean got up and started doing handstands against the wall. The students were egging him on then. When I tried to direct him back to his seat, he would reply, "Make me." The class did the collective *ooooh*, and I felt my skin turning red from the neck up. After telling Sean that I wasn't going to "make him," he said, "Fine," and just continued to do his handstands.

At this point, I had to tell Sean to leave the classroom—which he, again, responded with, "Make me." I decided to get on with the class because, frankly, I didn't know who to reach out to. I didn't know which students I could trust to get a teacher or administrator. The noise he was making had to stop. Eventually, I left to grab a teacher from the next classroom to have Sean removed. I felt humiliated that this was happening, but the teacher was extremely helpful and understanding. After that situation, the students went back to normal. Probably knowing the report the teacher was going to get from me, they didn't want any extra trouble.

The worst-case scenario is a full-on riotous class. These days are traumatizing to a sub and cause thoughts like *Maybe I should get into a different career* to creep in. After those days, I just wanted to go home, have a beer, and crawl into bed. I probably would have taken the next day off, too.

In the elementary grade levels, a full-on riotous class is the worst, because you have them for the whole day. It's doubly worse if the weather is bad outside and the students have to stay in for recess. Discipline was the hardest. It was playing a game of whack-a-mole. I would try tricks like threatening no recess, writing names on the plans to the teacher for tomorrow, calling the principal, and—the worst talent I have—yelling.

It was as if nothing seemed to matter to those students, though. At the end of the day, they hated me, and I hated them. I could feel the distrust and tension in the air. With every order I gave, I felt as if the students were going to loudly protest. I could see the disgust on their faces, with furrowed brows and frowns mixed with shouts of, "This is not how our teacher does it!" Those days were few and far between, but even having just a couple of them within a few weeks of each other can be a dagger to your optimism as a teacher.

The one class I'll never forget subbing—the one that made me feel like I had just come out of jungle warfare, crawling and bleeding to my car, and that was only for a *half day*—was kindergarten. I got the call at my usual time in the morning and accepted it without knowing what I was teaching. I was blindsided when I was told it was a kindergarten class.

"Hi, Blair," the secretary said. "We have a half-day position open for you this morning. Would you be able to come in?"

"Sure!" I innocently replied without asking about the grade level.

"Great! It's a kindergarten class. We'll see you soon!"

Shit!

A bolt of apprehension shot up my spine. I am not good with primary students—at all. It wasn't that I hadn't taught classes with primary students; I had done that when I was at the U of M, but under the guidance of another teacher. I just never had the patience to deal with primary-age students, especially if I was going to be in charge of them!

Reluctantly, I accepted it, because I didn't think it was going to be that bad. (And besides, it was only for half the day.) Of course, I planned on getting there a whole forty-five minutes early just to get reacquainted with a primary classroom and see what kind of plans and teaching a primary substitute teacher would have to do.

As I stepped into the classroom, I was amazed at all of the play manipulatives, from clocks and fake money to coins, building blocks, and more. Then I noticed all the cubbies for each student. One cubby was for books, another for math supplies, and yet another for their writing and coloring. Cubby containers, all over the place! There were posters for everything around the room with word walls, calendars, math facts—you name it.

Finally, I went to the teacher's desk to find out what I was going to be teaching. I was shocked. There were about ten to twelve different activities that had to be taught just for a half day. Not only that, but there were also the administrative tasks of making sure jackets were put away, doing attendance along with the alphabet, checking the lunch situation for the day, and getting into the morning meeting/sharing circle. This was going to take a lot of visualization for me to focus! Where would I sit or move when doing a certain activity? What would a male kindergarten teacher sound like? Where were all of the supplies so I wouldn't have to scramble all over the place?

Once the students came in, it was like an army of ants. They were so small! The little tykes had boundless energy right away. They came in like a whirlwind of gabbing and laughing. And apparently, I was their first substitute teacher. They looked at me with great wonder and anxiety, like I was some wizard or representing stranger danger. Thankfully, their teacher prepared them by letting them know the day before that there was going to be a different teacher the next day, so they had been expecting me.

Right away, the students came up to me in what seemed like army divisions. They needed help getting their boots off or unzipping and hanging up their jackets. This was a lengthy process; and even though there were only around fifteen students, one student seemed like five with all the needs of a typical kindergartner. With that ratio, it seemed like I had seventy-five students in the classroom. I was already out of my league.

The rest of the day, I was just trying not to drown. I sat down and got into the morning meeting, and one of the students immediately started to bawl. I didn't notice until a sweet young girl came over to let me know her classmate was crying. So I went over to this student and asked what the matter was. She said she missed her teacher already.

Oh boy. I had to do some convincing and let her know that the teacher would be back tomorrow. Apparently, that student had missed the prepping for the sub.

The next part of the class involved a read-along that involved singing. I had never had to sing in front of students before—and this was going to be a challenge, since I was possibly the worst singer in the Five-State Region. But then I thought, *What the hell? These kids are just kindergartners. They're not going to know whether a person is a good singer or a bad one!* So when I started the singing part, the students all started to laugh, which kind of surprised me. So I stopped the story and asked why they were laughing. One student said that I sounded funny. Another commented on how I was doing the singing wrong and how I wasn't singing it like their regular teacher did. At that point, two other students started to cry during the read-along. I was starting to wonder if every student was going to cry while I was there.

After the read-along, the class had to do some writing and an art project with string. And this was where everything came undone.

I had about a third of the students start their letter-writing (to this day, I'm not even sure if I had them do it the way the teacher wanted them to do it) and another third start with the string art, which turned into an unmitigated disaster involving glue and scissors. There were globs of glue on the tables, on the floor, on students' clothes, and in their hair. Using the scissors, the students could hardly cut the string, so I found myself doing the majority of that. The final third of the students just went off to do whatever they wanted. That included getting up to sing and dance, picking their noses, going off to look at a picture book (I was cool with this), or making a mess in the play area. It seemed like these students had already developed a keen sense of making excuses when I pleaded with them to go finish their writing. They wouldn't even look at me, and they would tell me that they were already done with their writing or art project. How do you argue with a kindergartener?

Around this time, a student came up to me with a look of horror on his face. He let me know that he had gone to the bathroom in his pants. I should have known this was going to happen. It was one of the situations I had failed to visualize earlier that day! Thankfully, another student knew what to do in these situations, and they helped their classmate get to the nurse's office or wherever they needed to go.

Each transition into another activity was like trying to corral all the cockroaches in New York City. I'd never imagined how short of an attention span a kindergartner could have, especially when you're not equipped to know how to hold that attention span. As I would try to help one student, I would be interrupted ten seconds later by another student who needed attention about going to the bathroom, wiping their nose, or reminding them that their teacher was going to be back tomorrow. (The students either seemed to forget this or were becoming increasingly alarmed that this stranger was going to be there forever.) Some of them even told me that they wanted to call their mom for some reason or that they felt as if they were going to be sick. It was one after another, like a carousel.

The last part of the day was some sort of free time. I was seeing the light at the end of the tunnel then, and I didn't care what the students did as long as they were still alive by the time they headed out to lunch and I was out the door. This part of the day was pretty much the same, but I did have some singing obligations, where some of the students wanted me to sing along with them. Maybe my singing voice wasn't that bad, or they just wanted something to laugh at.

The minutes on the clock couldn't have moved any slower. There was a silver lining to the day, though. It seemed that I hadn't damaged all of the students, because when it was time to walk down to the lunchroom, I got a few hugs from the little minions and a couple of comments like "I liked it when you sang!" and "You sound funny!"

The day was finally over. It was around noon when I went back to the office to sign out. Right away, the staff must have seen the look of a beaten-down soul as I entered the office. I still remember the knowing smile they each had on their face and the relief I felt when I handed over the keys. Then I walked back to my car in a daze, knowing I had worked only a four-hour shift but feeling like I had taught three full days without a break.

After that day, I pay the utmost respect to all the kindergarten teachers out there. You need to have the patience of a saint and be one of the most versatile teachers out there.

Chapter 10

No Place Like Home?

I was halfway through the year of subbing when I started to look for long-term sub positions. I was fully prepared to sub for the rest of the year, but whether I was going to do this for another year was a different question.

One day during the winter, I received a phone call from my hometown of Lakeville. I thought it was going to be a regular sub call, but I was surprised that it was from my former elementary school teacher, who was now the principal of my old elementary school, Christina Huddleston Elementary. She asked me if I was interested in interviewing for a long-term sub position at her school, which would start at the beginning of February. A sixth-grade teacher was going on maternity leave, and they needed somebody to fill that position. Immediately I was excited at the prospect of finally having a steady job that would have some benefits. So I agreed to the interview.

Just as I hung up the phone, though, a sudden wave of dread crept over me. I was going to be interviewed by my third-grade teacher, where I could potentially be working with teachers who had had me when I was a student and would know all of the trouble I had caused, the embarrassing moments I'd had, and what a spectacularly average student I'd been. Right away, I thought about the possible doubts certain teachers might have about me coming back and being a long-term substitute. Were they going to remember all the things I'd done, good (which wasn't much) or bad? Like the time when I'd spread an awful rumor about my friend that ended up getting him suspended for days? Or were they going to remember that I'd been an unremarkable student who liked to do the minimum? I remembered the classes I was in through the years at that school and how they had been filled with troublemakers—and how my best friend, who still was a good friend of mine, had been one of the biggest troublemakers. I was a follower of that gang. Hopefully, those teachers had forgotten about all that. And we all grow up, right?

I also had another problem with going back to the school where I'd grown up. I didn't want to become a Lakeville lifer. Nothing was wrong with that town; it had actually been a nice place to grow up. But I didn't want to be one of those comfortable hires just because I had grown up there. I would have felt that it was a charity hire, and that would have felt cheap. I always wanted to be somewhere where I had no attachments, where I'd get a job based on my own merits and not because of the token of being local.

In the end, I couldn't back out of the interview. There were thousands of subs out there who would have killed for the chance to be interviewed for consistent work where they didn't have to wonder when or where their next job was going to be for the next day. Also, I knew there were plenty of teachers who taught where they had grown up. So why was I so different?

When I told my brothers that I had an interview for a position at my old elementary school, they laughed. And when I told my old childhood friends that I had an interview at Christina Huddleston, they also laughed.

"Why would you want to go back there?" they would say. "They all know what you were like!"

"I need to get my foot in the door for a regular job," I would rationalize. "I have to do it."

"Oh man, I remember Ms. Seig," one of my friends said. "She HATED me, but Mrs. Gilmore was the best."

"I wonder if Mr. Fink is still there with his Finko-Bucks," another friend recalled. "Remember those? The money he'd give you for an end-of-the-year auction? Remember Chris stealing them out of his desk that year? You gonna do Clinto-Bucks? HAHAHA!"

My parents also thought it was funny that I was potentially going back to teach at Christina Huddleston. However, I was sure that my mom had some of the same concerns I had, as she'd had to deal with some of those teachers as well as the principal to address the behavior trouble and academic laziness I'd exhibited while I was a student there.

"Oh, Blair, do you think they are going to remember you?" she said at one point. I knew she was hoping they wouldn't.

You Can Never Leave Home

I was nervous about the interview. It wasn't like I had my heart set on the position. But having a job to open the door for a future permanent spot, to help me gain experience, and to actually have a steady income with benefits would be great.

On the day of the interview, I walked into the school wearing my best shirt and tie (and I didn't have much to choose from). When I entered the building, it was as if nothing had changed at Christina Huddleston. The hallways and the office still had that brownish-orange carpet, and the walls were still comprised of that brown cinder block. Two secretaries were there, although they might have been different secretaries than the ones who had been there when I was a student. And there was Mrs. Schmidt, my third-grade math teacher, now the principal of the school, waiting for me.

There was one thing about Mrs. Schmidt that I remembered from back in my school days. I had been in the medium level of her math students, and the one thing she'd said to me that had stuck was, "Blair, it's amazing how each quarter you start off so slow, but then you always finish strong." That amounted to me being the average student for the rest of my career. I didn't know, even at that age, whether that was meant to be a compliment. She'd certainly had me pegged as a professional procrastinator. So when I walked in for my interview, she was exuberant about seeing me and gave me a big hug. I was surprised that she remembered me, because I wasn't exactly a student who had stood out from the crowd.

I thought it was going to be just me and Mrs. Schmidt for the interview. But it turned out that the whole sixth-grade team was there for it. I didn't know how interviews quite worked out yet. Nonetheless, I was surprised to see the team there. To my relief, the three other teachers weren't from my past, so at least they didn't have any prior knowledge of me to cast doubt on whether I could do the job.

I don't remember much about the interview. But I do remember them asking if I was familiar with the FOSS science curriculum. I was, since my classmates and I had used it during our science practicum at the U of M. I was asked a few questions from the sixth-grade team, and they seemed like a fun, young group to teach with. One of the teachers was the one I was going to potentially replace. After the interview, I actually felt confident—and relieved. This had been my first interview for any teaching position, and I thought there was a good chance that I wasn't going to get it for that reason. I figured that I probably needed more experience in interviewing. Still, I felt that I had done all right.

The next day, Mrs. Schmidt called me at my brother's house and told me that I'd gotten the job. I was truly shocked! There had to have been some bad interviews for me to have gotten it. I told my brother that I'd gotten the job, and the same thing he'd done when I'd announced I was interviewing for the job happened again: he laughed. My friends also laughed again, but they were also intrigued to hear what it was like back at our former school and who was still teaching there.

"Remember when they smoked in the teachers' lounge?" one of my friends asked. "Blair, are you gonna do that, too?"

"I'm pretty sure they stopped that a long time ago," I answered.

And, of course, my mom was happy for me to reach the new heights of a long-term sub. Yet I was still having the thought that I'd never leave my hometown. This was a problem for me; I thought I'd be seen as somebody who was afraid of branching out and being adventurous. I was going to be a townie, and I didn't like that. Also, there was still the thought of completely bombing my work in front of teachers who I'd had and who were potentially still at that school. Would I bring them shame by making them think I had learned nothing from them?

I had about a week to get ready to sub for the class full-time. The teacher gratefully asked me to come in to observe the class and get used to the curriculum we would be teaching.

The next time I walked into that school, a staff member told me that I was to meet the teacher in the staff lounge. I remembered that lounge because on occasion, when my friends and I had been students, we had smelled the cigarette smoke as we'd passed by in the hallway like it was no big thing, so remembering where it was located was easy. When I opened up the door, there was a greeting committee with a lot of the teachers from the school, including three former teachers: Mr. Weber, my latchkey school golf coach, as well as Ms. Seig and Mrs. Gilmore— both of whom I'd thought had been ready to retire when I'd been a student! The biggest surprise came when I saw a huge blown-up poster of my second- or third-grade picture on the wall. There I was, with straight black hair, freckles all over, and a goofy smile with my two front teeth missing from when one of my other older brothers, Ryan, had knocked them out in front of his friends. A proud moment of growing up, that was!

I felt almost overwhelmed with emotions to see so many teachers here to welcome me. I hadn't thought they were going to remember me at all, or at least even care that I was going to be teaching at their school. I felt speechless. It was my introduction to what it was like to have a welcoming staff for a full-time position, even if it was for long-term subbing. My three former teachers came up to me, and we talked for a while. They were completely different from when I'd been a student. . . . Well, maybe not. Mr. Weber had always been calm and cool, from what I remembered. But I froze at the moment I saw Ms. Seig. She was the strictest teacher I'd ever had—and I'd had her twice! She couldn't have been more different now. "So how are we going to keep you in line this time?" she asked. "Welcome to the dark side!" She remembered almost everything about me from when I'd been a student, from the friends I'd run around with to my parents. I was impressed!

That moment also taught me that teachers are not what they appear to be outside the classroom. Mrs. Gilmore had always been one of my favorite teachers, and she was just as sweet when I joined the staff. It was a day I would never forget. But now I knew I couldn't screw things up, or this welcoming party would have been for naught!

I Can Do This . . . I Think

That first week observing the class I would be taking over was invaluable. It gave me a sense of how the students were behavior-wise and of the curriculum that was being taught. For this class, I would be teaching language arts, science, and social studies. The homeroom class I would get would only switch out for one class. For example, I would be teaching two sections of social studies, while a different teacher would be teaching two sections of math.

The regular classroom teacher was Mrs. Moore, who was due to have her baby any day. That meant that I had to be ready to take over the next day or the moment she started having the baby. Just observing for that week, I could tell I was going to have some pretty big shoes to fill. She was a master at teaching.

It started with her classroom management. Mrs. Moore had clear expectations, and the students dutifully abided by them. There was no side talking or goofing around. She did this with easy authority. She never came down hard on students or yelled, but she had a steady guidance about her. I could tell there were some troublemakers in the class, and she had a discussion with me on how to work with the students who liked to push the envelope.

Mrs. Moore was also a completely different teacher than Tom. She was more by the book and seemed to be more data-driven. She used the curriculum to a T, which was something I was going to have to get used to. But I was getting the hang of it, and I found it easier than having to rack my brain and resources just to come up with content for one lesson.

One of the curriculum sets they were using was the FOSS science kits. I'd had to go through these and teach them during the science minicourses at the U of M. Later, I would have to unleash what was probably one of the most dreadful disasters with that FOSS system at Christina Huddleston.

That week, I also had a chance to observe how the other teachers at the school worked with their students. One interesting point I noticed was that one of the teachers, Scott, had a classroom management technique I'd never seen before. He had one of his students in charge of a clipboard with all the students' names on it. Whenever there was an issue and a student was acting up while Scott was teaching, the student who was in charge of the clipboard put a check by that student's name.

Scott had a tightly run ship, just like Mrs. Moore did. However, his technique reminded me of when I'd been in elementary school and my friends and I had always gotten our names on the board if we'd done something bad. If we continued to misbehave, we would get a check (or more checks) after it. The next day, the board was wiped off, and you'd start anew. I remembered seeing the same kids' names on that board. Scott's method wasn't that much different; it was just a little more discreet. I also noticed that his students didn't want this happening to them. They stiffened up whenever their name was written down, and I didn't notice any talk-back. I kept a mental note that this was something I might want to try.

The other teacher was Mrs. Chancey, who was only a few years older than me. Her class was a bit more loose and freewheeling than the other classes. This gave me a sense of relief, as it was probably something akin to how my class was going to run. However, she still had a unique way of running it, where most of the students were still engaged in what they were doing. They also had a high sense of respect for her.

I knew I was walking into a situation where I was joining a team of three strong teachers. I was hoping desperately that I could pull off this transition seamlessly to where they wouldn't be cleaning up any of my messes and the students wouldn't be too screwed up by the time I was done with them.

We finished the week without me having to take over, as Mrs. Moore made it through without going into labor. That gave me the weekend to prepare. It was one of the most nervous weekends I've ever had.

I took home the class list just so I could remember the students' names without having to look them up. It was also a technique of Mr. Nelson's back from my student teaching days. On top of that, I pretty much brought home all of the teacher manuals on all of the subjects so that I could plan. This would be my first time planning for teaching where I was going to get paid. As I mentioned earlier, the manuals were nice because they scripted everything I had to do. For example, read part one of the story on Monday and assign this, read part two of the story and assign that, do vocabulary and spelling work on Wednesday, etc.

I had my blue planner book, which had a row for each day of the week and a square for each subject hour of that day. I found out that it wasn't going to have enough room—because I was planning everything down to the minute! So I also had a Teacher's Daily Reference Planner that was about 200 pages, and I used that space to write down every stinking detail. That weekend, I even had index cards to write down specific things I wanted to say! This obsessive-compulsive behavior would later follow me when I finally got my full-time teaching job.

That weekend, I also went over the grade book. I wanted to be consistent in my grading, and I wanted to see which students were struggling. The grade book was your typical red vinyl-covered book where you'd write down the names on the left side, label the assignments you'd corrected along the top, and write in the students' scores in the itty-bitty squares. As you may have guessed, this was the time before grading by the Internet. So if I lost this book, I would be screwed. I had seen this happen quite a bit when I was a student. Some of my peers had stolen grade books; and in other cases, teachers had lost their grade books. I'd even had a science teacher in high school (who was also our baseball coach) who had lost his grade book, so he just asked everybody one by one what they thought they were getting in the class. This had happened with two weeks left in the school year, too! Plus, the red grade book wasn't conducive to somebody who had bad handwriting. You had to write so small in it!

By the time Sunday hit, I was a wreck. I was triple-checking everything just to make sure I had everything in order. Did my plans make sense? Did I remember all of the students' names? Did I remember what the schedule was? I even had to go out and buy new clothes from what I called "the new teachers' clothing store," or Kohl's. I'd gotten so used to wearing pretty much the same three outfits, because I was never at the same school for more than two days.

By nightfall on Sunday, I felt worse than I had when I'd been a kid on the night before the first day of school. At least back then, I could blend into the walls and not worry about being seen. But in this situation, there was no avoiding it. I was going to be the show, and I had to lead. I knew my coworkers and the principal weren't just going to ignore what I was doing. I was even too nervous to eat anything. My stomach was in knots. There was one thing that did help me, though. I found myself going into a type of meditation where I visualized what I was going to do over and over in my head. My brother could even tell that I was nervous. He pretty much stayed away from me and didn't want to be in my space.

As you could probably imagine, I slept horribly that night. I was wondering if it was normal for all first-year teachers to go through this, even if it was just for a long-term subbing position. I was thinking that maybe after a few years of doing this (and if I even had a job), I wouldn't have to constantly feel these nerves year after year. I twisted and turned all through the night. What if the students started calling me names right when I entered the room? What if I couldn't control the classroom, and Mrs. Schmidt had to come in and help me out through my humiliation? What if the team and the staff knew I wasn't up to the job? What if I woke up late because it took me the better part of the night to fall asleep?

Eventually, I did grab a couple of hours of sleep; and the alarm clock, which I'd set for a good hour before I had to get up, sprang to life. I was groggy, and my stomach was churning. There was going to be no breakfast that day, as there was no way I could stomach it. I didn't have to be at the school (which was a half-hour drive from my house) until 7:30 a.m., but it was only 5:00 a.m. I didn't want to go to bed, because I knew that if I did, I was for sure going to sleep late and not make it on time for my first day. So I took my time at home with getting ready and making sure I had everything I needed and in order.

I ended up getting to the school at 6:15 a.m., which was way before any other teacher was in. When I walked into the classroom, it was odd to know that this was going to be my classroom for the rest of the year. As the minutes passed, the teachers started to come in, and some of them popped their heads in. "Hey, good luck today!" they would say. "Is there anything you need?"

"No, no," I would say. "Thanks, though!" My mouth was dry as chalk, though, and my mind was spinning in all different directions. I bet the other teachers could tell I was trying to do my best to exude confidence and suppress the look of terror on my face.

By 7:15 a.m., the students had gotten off their buses and started rolling into the classrooms. Oddly enough, my nerves started to fade away—not completely, but at least I knew I wasn't going to start hyperventilating!

I took some time to reintroduce myself, and I could tell the students were holding their end of the bargain by engaging in the planned activities and lessons. It was as if we were both feeling each other out. The students would tentatively participate in the activities I had. There were no complaints or eye rolls, nor was there a whole lot of blurting.

When it came to the actual teaching, I felt like I was lecturing too much on the account of trying to maintain control of the class. The students looked either bored or were just studying my teaching style. When it came to independent work time, though, they didn't do too bad. I didn't lose the class or have to do any damage control. When the students left, it was nice to know I would be back the next day and I didn't have to write any notes for their regular teacher.

However, my obsessive-compulsive self reemerged, as I would go through a routine of meticulously setting up for tomorrow's classes. That meant making sure I had laid out the materials for each class and the worksheets that needed to be copied. Of course, I had a prep hour, but I wanted to save that hour in case something went wrong so that I could adjust or tweak something and do it better the next time.

I also developed a case of analysis paralysis by trying to visualize what would happen during the next school day. So at the end of the day, the students had left around 3:15 p.m., but I ended up staying until 5:00 p.m. All the other teachers had left. This would also become a trend. I would often be the first teacher to show up and the last one to leave. This wasn't because I wanted to be the greatest teacher in the world, but because I had an unreasonable fear of failure and was incredibly inefficient in preparing my work and using my prep time during the day. I didn't mind this. I kind of liked the silence, but I knew this wasn't normal.

Chapter 11

LONG-TERM TROUBLE

A s the days went by, the students' true colors invariably appeared. I knew there were a couple of students I needed to
look out for, just from observing the class and the discussions I'd
had with Mrs. Moore.

As I shared earlier, I didn't like removing students from class if they
were being disruptive, because I didn't want them to miss the content
I was teaching. I also felt that if I did remove a student from class, it
would go down as a sign that I was losing the classroom, and I felt like
the students could sense that. So I reverted to verbal warnings—like
"Jason, go out into the hallway, *now!*" or "Jeff, if you keep this up, I'm
going to have to have you leave the room!"—and that wasn't going well.

As I also shared before, I wasn't the most effective yeller. Some teachers can snap their voices into high decibel levels with the flip of a switch,
but I'm not equipped to do that. The students realized this as well—
and a few of them realized they could take advantage of that fact.

Initially, I was struggling with a boy named Michael. He was trying
to be the class clown. Sometimes it worked, and he was quite funny.
But other times, he went way over the line, and I had to deal with it.
He wasn't quite a book-smart student, because he struggled with reading comprehension and was a master at work avoidance. Whenever
I looked at the back of the classroom as the students worked on an
assignment individually, he would be leaning back in his chair with his
hands behind his head and without a care in the world. So I would walk
back to check on him, and he would have little to nothing completed.
When I told him to get going or asked if he needed any help, he would
always respond, "I'll get going, Mr. Clinton," or "Nah, I'm good." In
group work, he was a drag to his classmates, as he would get them off-
task by simply talking the whole time and they would fall way behind.
Michael's writing was also atrocious. I would cringe whenever I got

anything back from him, because I knew it was going to take extra time to decipher whatever he wrote. But he was good at being people-smart.

Verbally, Michael was a little more mature than most of his classmates. He could easily join a conversation with adults at that age, and the students looked up to him. But whenever he got bored, he would look for ways to entertain himself. That would sometimes include him thinking to himself, *How can I get Mr. Clinton super annoyed and have all the students think it's hilarious?*

Even though there were times when I wanted to let loose on Michael, I knew I couldn't. It wouldn't work. It would have been nothing to him, as he was also a challenge in other classes. What I found worked best was talking to him after class. I realized he had three older brothers who were well-known throughout the district (for good or bad), and he was influenced by his siblings. Right away, we had a connection, because I had grown up with a similar dynamic with my brothers.

Oftentimes we get a messiah complex with our older siblings, and we want to be just like them as we're growing up. Younger siblings often say to themselves, "Whoa, I can do what my brother is doing someday!" And that could be something that was either good or bad. So if you had older brothers who were good students and respectful to other people, chances are you may have wanted to be like them. Michael's older brothers were good-looking kids, and very popular. They were a carefree bunch, and he wanted to be just like them. It was something he couldn't deviate from. Talking about his brothers, what they were doing, and what he wanted to do became helpful to both Michael and me. He knew that I understood where he came from, so he could trust me and focus a little better—not all of the time, but enough that he was improving in class and became a more positive leader for his classmates.

Then there were the students whom I just couldn't reach.

One student who stuck out was a boy named Joey. He was one of the first on my radar when I was observing during that first week. He would hardly get anything in on time, was failing most of his classes, and had this smoldering, loathing look about just being in school. After I noticed his hygiene and his propensity to wear the same dirty clothes each day, I profiled him (perhaps unfairly) as coming from a family who was struggling to make ends meet. By the time Mrs. Moore left and I was in charge of the class, he started to act out.

Joey would openly and defiantly not do his classwork. He also made it known to the whole class that he wasn't going to do it because it was "stupid." I would often get into a verbal struggle with him about this, and that would lead to the class getting distracted by it. Somehow, he had some sway over a couple of other students, and they would join in on his mutiny.

"This is so dumb!" Joey would repeat. "Why do we have to write all this down?"

His followers would then echo his sentiments: "Yeah! What good is this going to do?"

I didn't know how to handle this, and I couldn't grasp why he was struggling to comply and why others would follow him. I also didn't know how to create a lesson he would understand and be comfortable participating in. The more he got his followers to follow suit, the more agitated I became. He was the first student I kicked out to go sit in the hall. And whenever I had a chance to talk to him about his choices in class, he would just stare at me and not say anything.

As the year went on, Joey's behavior started to unravel even more. He began acting out in almost all of his classes and was becoming more unruly. He was the first student with whom I almost lost my temper, and that was a feeling I always despised. Eventually, I had to contact somebody from his home—and I had a horrible time doing it. I found that I disliked calling parents on account of their child's bad behavior. To me, it was a sign that I didn't have the wherewithal to control their kid. But it turned out that I wasn't the only one to call Joey's home.

What I found out was telling: Joey lived with his mother, and that was it. He'd had trouble with school all his life. All I did was tell her what he was doing wrong in class; I didn't have the tools to discuss how we could work together to improve. That was something else I wished the university had taught us: how to work with students who come from backgrounds that need immediate attention. Instead, my conversation with Joey's mom was an empty phone call.

"Hi, Mrs. Phillips," I said. "It's Mr. Clinton, Joey's homeroom teacher."

"Oh, what did Joey do today?" his mother listlessly asked.

"Well, Joey had a difficult day working with his classmates and was pretty much disrupting the learning of the other students today."

"Okay, I'll talk to him about it when he gets home," she answered robotically.

The next day, it was as if Joey wasn't even aware I'd had the phone call with his mother. He would go right back to disrupting the class.

I wasn't sure how to identify students for special education at that time, either. It was clear that Joey had something identifiable, but I didn't know how to approach it. We didn't have a way to identify and help students who may have had learning disabilities and start them on a tiered learning intervention, though.

The battle with Joey and his followers lasted for months. It was getting to the point where I needed help from other teachers to get the students reengaged with what we were doing. And it takes a *big* piece of humble pie for me to ask teachers what to do if I'm struggling with classroom management. It even got to the point where Scott, the sixth-grade teacher across from me, had to talk to my class about respecting me as their long-term sub. One time, as we were switching for our one class, I overheard him talking about me to the students and how they needed to respect me, as I was now the teacher. I felt heat rising up my neck, as now it was known that the other teachers knew I was struggling. I was utterly embarrassed.

Not only was teaching Joey and some of the boys a challenge, but some of the girls caused problems as well. Okay, maybe just one of the girls. First of all, when it comes to working with preteen girls, there's a huge difference between men and women, especially among first-year teachers. And in my case, I had been mostly surrounded by men and boys while growing up. Women, I feel, know how to work with girls at this age, as they better understand their needs. And most girls at this age feel more comfortable with a female teacher, since they're entering a turbulent time in their life, with many changes going on. So having a young, ignorant long-term male sub wasn't going to bode well. There was a time or two when a student needed to ask for a female teacher, as they were going through their first period. They must have intuited that I would be helpless about this, and they were right.

But those challenges weren't what had me miffed. It was dealing with behavior issues. I knew what to expect from boys when it came to behavior. Theirs were straightforward and easier to deal with, even though I was struggling with this. The girls were much more intricate and frustrating for me.

One girl in particular kept butting heads with me, and it was pissing me off. I stupidly assumed that the girls wouldn't be like the boys, that they would be more mature and accept responsibility more readily. If they acted out of line and I had to reprimand them, they would more likely stop the undesirable behavior immediately. Boy, was I wrong. Cassandra was a gifted athlete but struggled with academics. For some reason, she couldn't accept that she wasn't doing well, and her grades were falling off a cliff. She blamed me for this by complaining to me about how other students got better grades than she did and that she felt I was targeting her—for reasons I had no idea about! I didn't know how to take this, and it got worse as the year went on.

I finally received a phone call from her mother on this matter. She was upset that Cassandra's grades were cratering. We had a nice discussion about what we could do to help Cassy improve her grades by checking in with her while she was doing independent work. However, that didn't seem to go over well, as she resented me coming over to help her. It was as if she didn't want to be singled out for having difficulty. So her grades didn't improve.

As it turned out, Cassy's father was also a substitute teacher in the district and had been for the last decade or so. How did I find this out? He was a regular at the same bar where my dad was a regular—and he brought up some criticism about me to my dad. He felt as though I didn't know how to handle a classroom, and his daughter wasn't growing as a student. The nerve!

When my dad told me this, I was livid. Then I wondered if Cassy's father had interviewed for the job I currently had. It wouldn't have been too much of a stretch, since his daughter was in the class, and sometimes teachers want to teach their kids. I was also concerned because I know how bar gossip works, and he was probably spreading this talk to everyone else who was there. I had to find a way to bury it and not let it get in the way of my teaching. However, it was hard not to look at Cassandra and see both her and her father talking conspiracy about me! In the end, I couldn't disagree with his analysis. But give a new teacher a break! I was working my rear end off!

MASS MURDER OF FISH

It can be hard for us teachers to forget lessons we taught that went horribly wrong. At least I think it's hard for most teachers. But for me, they are great moments in learning our limitations—and in asking ourselves, *What the hell was I thinking??*

During my long-term subbing at Christina Huddleston, one lesson I had to do with the FOSS science kit involved goldfish. With this exercise, I had to go to a pet shop and buy a certain number of goldfish for each group of two students. The students were to do some type of observation with the fish.

The day before we had to start the activity, I went to PetSmart after school to buy dozens of goldfish. I felt awkward about this. I wanted to make sure to tell the seller that I was a teacher and not some goldfish nut. Then I went back to school and placed the fish in plastic containers for each group of students so that they would be ready for the next day. Now, I wasn't a fish expert by any means. In fact, I'm awful at fish care. One time in college, I was supposed to keep my friend's exotic fish alive while he'd gone on vacation during spring break. Now, it still gets cold in Minnesota during the spring; and my roommates and I were cheap on the heating bill, as you can imagine. Well, the expensive fish couldn't adapt to a house temperature of fifty-five degrees, and it ended up dying. That was the last time I ever watched over any pets!

Back to the goldfish: In hindsight, I'm sure I committed numerous missteps right away with keeping the goldfish alive, like putting too many in one container, no filtration system, and the incorrect water temperature. But when I left the fish in the classroom, I had no way of knowing this, as they looked healthy to me. The next morning, when I walked into the classroom, I went over to check on the fish. To my horror, almost half of them were dead. They were floating on the top of the water. What a horrific moment for the fish that were alive. I had to go through each container, pick out the dead fish, throw them into the trash, and tie up the bag so that they wouldn't start to stink. When the students came in, I adjusted the number of fish for each group. Thankfully, the students had no idea this had happened. I didn't want them to see me as more incompetent than I already was!

It got worse after that. Our class didn't have science until the end of the day; and as the day progressed, more and more goldfish died. By the time science class started, the students got into their groups and were disgusted to find out that another third of the fish had died. "GROSS, GROSS, GROSS!" they would cry out. "Mr. Clinton, half of my fish are all dead!" And being a new teacher who was already struggling with classroom management, this situation was getting out of hand for me. Some students were grossed out, others wanted to give the goldfish a funeral, and still others were just plain disappointed. And while I was bewildered at how all of this was happening and questioning myself about the missteps I'd made, I had students from each group go to the bathrooms and flush their dead goldfish. *Big* mistake!

That night, I had to recoup the loss of the goldfish so that we could complete the lesson appropriately. I made another stop at PetSmart to buy another batch of goldfish. By this time, I was feeling ridiculous about the number of fish I was buying and the amount of money I was spending out of my pocket for this stupid lesson. Thankfully, it was a different seller this time, and I acted as if I hadn't just killed off scores of fish. By the time I got to school, there was yet again another batch of dead fish. I threw the fish in the trash again and made my apologies to the janitors about the situation. I was at a loss at what I was doing wrong. I was feeling hopeless—and like a murderer.

The next day, the same situation occurred again, and the students were starting to question my decision to buy fish for this lesson.

"GROSS! The fish are dead—*again!*"

"Mr. Clinton, do you want us to flush these down the toilet, too??"

"I don't think this science experiment is going well, Mr. Clinton."

I was at my wit's end. I sent the students whose fish had died—which was almost everyone—to the bathrooms to flush them down the toilet. By the time they got back, I just wanted to finish the lesson so that I didn't have to look at a goldfish ever again. I'm sure it was a haphazard ending to the lesson, but it was finally over. I had students bag up any fish they wanted to bring home. I was relieved when it was over. At least I knew there would be a good chance I wouldn't be teaching a sixth-grade FOSS curriculum the following year. My goldfish-killing was done.

The next day, when I got to the school, I was called down to talk to Mrs. Schmidt. It would be my first scolding by a principal. Apparently, when I'd had the students bring the goldfish to the bathroom, I'd had too much faith that they would put the fish in their final resting places and obediently flush them down the toilet. But it wasn't so. Some of the students didn't even flush the toilets when they put the dead fish in, creating a minor horror for the next student who used that toilet later in the day. Can you imagine a first grader going to use the toilet, and it's full of dead goldfish? Some students didn't even put the fish in the toilet; instead, they put some in the sinks and left them there. Some even put the fish in their friends' or enemies' lockers. Worst of all, there were so many dead fish that the toilets had started to back up.

Mrs. Schmidt let me have it. "Blair," she said, "the janitors said we could have had thousands of dollars' worth of damage if they weren't able to get all the fish out of the toilets."

"I'm sorry, Mrs. Schmidt," I sheepishly admitted. "I didn't really think of another way to get rid of the dead fish. I'm sorry."

I was embarrassed! I wasn't particularly angry at the students, because I should have known what was going to happen. If I were that age, there would have been a fifty-fifty chance of me putting that goldfish in a friend's locker. This moment taught me that in times of crisis, like a mass burial of goldfish, it was better that the teacher handle it and not leave it to unsupervised sixth graders. I confessed this to Mrs. Schmidt, and she pretty much gave me the figurative pat on the head and let me go back into the classroom. When the students came in that morning, there was no reason to be mad at them, since I had created that chaos. I just wanted that chapter of misery behind me!

Chapter 12

GROW UP!

Another life lesson I learned during my long-term subbing was that I was going to have to make some lifestyle changes. I had just turned twenty-three years old, and I was still in the partying stage of my life.

I was still living in Saint Paul with my brother Ren and another friend who was temporarily renting at the house as well. There was (and still is) a well-known bar called The Nook that was just down the street from us. This place was also the scene of the crime before I'd taken my Praxis exam. They had the greatest burgers and the best deals on beer within walking distance. Best of all, we became good friends with the owners, Mike and Ted, who were both our age. We were all like-minded as well as somewhat wild and nonsensical at this point in our lives, and we believed we were invincible. So whenever Ren, my friend, and I went to the bar, there was a good chance that we were going to be there for awhile and come home late, full of beer.

On this particular night, which was a weeknight, I was with my regular group of friends at The Nook. It was just to have dinner and a beer or two and then head home. One friend who was with me that night was doing landscaping at the time. The other wasn't doing much; he may have been in between jobs then.

After we finished our dinner, we went on to have a couple more beers and watch the baseball game that was on. Then Mike and Ted came in and joined us for conversation and to watch the rest of the game—and they brought out a case of Blatz beer that we were going to drink for free! At that age, and where my checking account was at the moment, I couldn't pass up a night of having a couple of beers when more were being offered for free.

As the night went on, we were getting a bit more bravado as we reminisced about college and lied about how awesome we used to be and how much we missed those days. I was starting to feel buzzed, and I knew I was way over my limit and was going to have a headache the next day. I had to get home!

Just then, my friends started talking about how much and how fast they could drink beer—which, to tell you the truth, had been a hidden talent of mine when I was at the U of M. I wanted to join in on the conversation, but I knew I had to go or else one of those guys was going to start a competition. As I was getting up to leave, one of my friends mentioned that I'd been a champion at slamming a pitcher of beer back in school. I kindly acknowledged it and was trying to make my way to the door when the bartender challenged me.

"Hey, Blair!" he shouted. "You and me. Let's go!"

I told him that I couldn't because it was already past my bedtime and that I had to be at school early the next day. He started to beg for me to stay, and so did my friends. But I was determined to beat this attack of peer pressure!

Just then, one of my friends went to the jukebox and started playing Queen's "Another One Bites the Dust." This song had been my rallying cry when I'd needed to buck up during parties; and when the bass line started, my friends all cheered, and I stopped in my tracks, right when I was about to go through the exit.

I looked back and saw that the bartender was already filling two pitchers. I was getting anxious about this. I had school the next day, but I couldn't back down in front of these guys! I had a reputation to uphold! So I walked back to the bar, still wearing my work clothes from the day, and rolled up my sleeves. It was time for business.

I hadn't slammed a pitcher of beer in some time, so I was nervous about how this was going to shake out. Plus, I was going up against a bartender who was a seasoned vet in the art of drinking. Mike, Ted, and my friends stood there in great anticipation. Freddie Mercury was blasting his vocals in the background. On the count of three, I grabbed that pitcher and lifted it with two hands. The beer started rushing down my throat as I was trying to keep up with the gulping. I drank it in fifty seconds flat, easily destroying the bartender. I had won.

As I got up to leave, Ted grabbed my shoulder and wanted to try me.

But it wasn't just Ted—it was all of the guys. I couldn't go away without defending my title! The alcohol was officially pumping up my artificial bravado. I went to the jukebox again to play the same song. But as I got up, I walked in a diagonal line. I knew this wasn't good. But I got the song going, and the bartender filled up five more pitchers. The beer was probably something like a Coors Light. At the count of three, we all started slamming our pitchers. I didn't know what my count was this time, but it was faster than all four who dared to usurp the king!

After I set the pitcher down, I got up without saying anything and walked out. My job was done there, and I knew I was going to be in trouble the next day. I barely completed the short walk back to the house. I went straight to my room, checked the alarm, and went to bed.

The next morning, when I got up, I didn't feel hungover. I was tired, but I thought I was feeling fine. Little did I know that I was still drunk. That was why I didn't call in sick.

By the time I got to the school, though, the hangover had come over me like a tsunami. I was having horrible pains in my stomach, an incredibly dry mouth, and a monster headache. A cold sweat was forming down my back. Worst of all, I didn't have any Tylenol to subdue the upcoming onslaught of sickness. The room started to spin a little. The lights, for some reason, were affecting me, as if they were too bright, and this intensified my headache.

The students started filing into my classroom, and it felt as if my brain was starting to short-circuit. I was having issues with my speech, rambling like a drunk (because I still was) and being incoherent. I had trouble recalling the students' names. I wasn't even done with the first hour of class when I had to go to the bathroom and was sweating profusely. So I had the students start some independent work, then snuck off to the bathroom. I had never left the class by themselves before, but it was an emergency. I've been known for having an iron stomach, and I don't vomit all that much. Instead, it comes out the other way.

As I was in the bathroom, I was incredibly upset with myself over what I was putting myself through, and I wasn't even close to finishing the school day. While I was there, I sat with my eyes screwed shut and my damp head in my clammy hands. It was only the first hour.

When I got back to the classroom, I could already tell that the students had a wary gaze on me. Either that, or I was feeling overly embarrassed about the spot I'd put myself in.

"Mr. Clinton, where'd you go?" one of the students asked then.

"Oh . . . ah . . . I had to ask Mrs. Chancey something for our social studies class coming up."

As the hour went on, things got progressively worse. My head was pounding. My stomach was roiling with the alcohol and the greasy burger and fries. I continued to sweat away the alcohol, and now I was developing the shakes. I noticed this whenever I would pick up an Expo marker and try to write on the board. My handwriting was extra sloppy that day.

During the second hour, my stomach was making sounds I'd never heard before. I had to make another emergency bathroom run in the middle of class. When I got there, I looked in the mirror and saw that my complexion was ghost white—as if I wasn't white enough! I tried to get in a few gulps of water, as dehydration was surely settling in. When I got back to the classroom this time, another student asked me if I was feeling sick. I couldn't completely lie this time around, so I said that I thought I may be coming down with a cold or that maybe I'd had something bad to eat the night before. I hoped the students wouldn't bring this to the attention of the other teachers when they switched classes. I didn't want anyone checking in on me!

I don't know how I made it through the rest of that day. I ended up having to go to the bathroom three more times during the classes I was teaching. So, yes, during every class I taught, I left to go to the bathroom. Teachers hardly ever go to the bathroom while conducting a class. I was worried that the teachers had noticed I was making my way to the staff bathroom down the hall every hour. I was going to have to tell them that I thought I had food poisoning or something. If they found out the truth, I was sure they would have been nice enough to take over my class and let me go home. But I was also worried that they were going to smell the alcohol coming out of every pore of my skin. What would happen to me if they found out? I had no idea.

By the end of the day, I was exhausted and had probably drunk eight gallons of water. My shirt had sweat spots forming at the armpits. My hands were completely unsteady, and my head felt like it had gone through a twelve-round match. I had students asking if I was going to be in class tomorrow, since they thought I was sick. I told them I had no idea. If it was up to me, I would have taken the whole week off. But since I was a long-term sub and was trying to make an impression with everyone, I didn't want to miss a day.

I sat at my desk until all of the students were out of the hallways, then slunk away as best as I could without anybody noticing. When I got close to the principal's office, I speed-walked by. Then I got in my car and drove back home to Saint Paul. Once I got home, I hit the bed and slept until the next morning.

A Lesson Learned

That day when I was pretty much drunk and hungover at school scared me. It made me feel like I wasn't taking my job seriously. Since then, I've often been jealous of friends who could tie one off on a weekday. I would like to participate, but now I know that one beer can lead to another, and I would be back to where I was that day when I was long-term subbing.

That's the End of That!

The school year was coming to a close by then, and I felt as if I was trying to land a single prop plane in a Category 5 hurricane. I just wanted to land the plane so that I could survive and move on. Some days were good, and the students were engaged in learning. Other days were what my former college instructor would call a "three-margarita day" (which is ironic, since I just finished spouting off about not drinking on weekdays).

I had one writing research lesson left to do, which was comparing and contrasting. Surprisingly, it went fairly well. I had the students pick whatever topic they wanted to write about; and I found that if they had the power to choose, they were more interested in doing the research that went with it. I also found that Michael, who was still struggling academically but had become less of a wisenheimer, was interested in comparing hot rods. I didn't even care about his grammar; I just loved the content he was getting out.

On the last day of school, I was happy to be done. I knew I would remember some of the students who had given me a dose of reality on how to manage crisis situations in behavior management. I also knew I would remember the ones who had done their best while I'd tried to navigate becoming a full-time teacher.

I felt mixed about how my job as a long-term sub had gone. The teachers at the school said I'd been given a tough class to handle—but that was sometimes told to a sub as a cover for why they weren't good at the job! However, I had enjoyed temporarily teaching at my former school. The teachers were welcoming and helpful throughout my time there. They didn't avoid me like I had the plague. They had even invited me out with them to happy hours, at which I had a good time listening to their conversations and their thoughts about teaching and getting to know the other side of the teachers I'd had while growing up. I also ended up having a good relationship with the principal, Mrs. Schmidt, even though I'd had that goldfish incident; and she said she would try to help me get a job for the next school year.

As the last day of school approached, I knew I would miss the students. Even the ones that had given me all the trouble in the world—well, maybe not that much. And I had to give them credit; many of them had been helpful and willing learners. Sometimes I felt bad that they'd had such an inexperienced teacher to close out their elementary career.

As the final bell rang, all the students cheered and raced out of the classroom. I did the same thing when I was their age at this very same school, and it brought me big joy to watch them go out. No matter how bad or good a student is, you want them to succeed. That was what I was hoping for as the last of the students skipped out and said goodbye. Some even thanked me, which was a surprise to me. I was going to miss them—and my consistent paycheck!

Chapter 13

SUMMER OF THE UNKNOWN

The summer was officially here, and I was in trouble. Throughout the time I'd been teaching at my former elementary school, I had done the minimum with looking out for jobs for the next school year. There were reasons why I hadn't been diligent in my search. First, I'd been busy with the long-term subbing; and whenever I got home each school day, the last thing I wanted to do was school-related activities. Second, I'd been naive enough to think that Lakeville or Apple Valley, where I'd been a student teacher, was going to hire me because I had connections at both places and had done an okay job there (or so I thought). So I thought that if I could get a job through connections from my hometown, I could get hired there as well. But what it came down to was that I was just plain lazy. I updated my résumé and my cover letter, but the crucial days of March and April had already slipped by without me submitting anything to other districts, and I wasn't looking online to see what positions were open. As mid-May approached and the end of the school year was coming up, I figured I should get my information out there. But I was pretty much too late.

I asked Principal Schmidt once again about the possibility of being hired at Christina Huddleston. "Yes, Blair," she answered. "I will definitely consider hiring you. But as of right now, we're planning on freezing on hiring new teachers."

I knew this had been coming, as every district in the area was coming up on a budget crunch. So my prospects weren't looking good. I also asked Carrie if her district had any openings. She shared the bad news that, once again, nothing was coming up. I still had the opportunity to apply for a position out in the boonies, but I didn't want to do that. I wanted to stick around the areas I was familiar with.

So I was heading into the summer with my two jobs at the Kids' Safari and Sylvan. Once June started, school hiring would pretty much go radio silent. One thing I knew for sure, though, was that I wasn't going to sub again.

I decided to not sub again as soon as I'd gotten the long-term position in Lakeville. Now that I'd had the taste of a constant paycheck and some semblance of health insurance, I didn't want to go back. I was done with the days of budgeting my money down to the penny, worrying about getting sick, and having to pay through the nose for medical care. I was sick of trying to figure out where I was going to be teaching every day. I was also tired of not having the same students consistently and having to reintroduce myself daily. Some of my teacher friends were going to have another go at subbing for the next year if they didn't get a job. A few were even going into their third year of subbing after college. I wasn't going to do that.

As the summer rolled along uneventfully, I had to look at what I could get with a teaching degree. Some of my friends with business degrees were starting to get into entry-level jobs, working in cubicles for whatever company they could find. I figured I could try this. It wasn't like I was going to be an engineer or start my own business anyway. I didn't have any capital for the latter, nor the background knowledge of the business world!

The only thing I was finding were positions with credit card companies that were looking for people to do cold calls, with the promise of moving them quickly up the ranks to be managers. I knew friends who were doing this, and they said it was awful. "All I'm doing right now is sitting at a desk, trying to get people to buy something, but they just hang up on me," they would tell me. "It sucks."

But I figured I wouldn't be making cold calls my whole life, right? So I was starting to think that hooking up with a big corporation wouldn't be that bad. People usually made good money, work was consistent, and I thought it would be a generally stress-free environment. It wasn't like I'd be consistently doing a song and dance in front of thirty-five sixth graders. I might even enjoy the peace and quiet of cubicle life.

The recruiters of these companies were relentless. They were on full-sell mode to try to get me these jobs, which were comparable in pay to what a starting teacher was making. "With you being a teacher, this position is perfect for you!" they would say. "We are definitely looking for people with personable skills! Our manager was once a teacher, and he is now making six figures!" I tried asking my friends if they knew much about management and what it was like, but they were all in entry-level positions, getting bossed around.

At this time, I was also asking Sylvan if they had any permanent positions opening up. I had looked online and seen some corporate positions available, but I didn't know if I was qualified. It turned out that I was—but I would be going up against a horde of other teachers who were looking for corporate positions as well. Plus, I wasn't that high up in the Sylvan system. I was just a tutor; I wasn't even a lead of the building.

The summer was coming to an end, and I had to make up my mind. Kids' Safari was closing up to get ready for the fall, so I wouldn't have any work for the next couple of weeks. The idea of becoming a teacher was now almost completely out of my mind—until I got a call two weeks before the school year started.

Chapter 14

I'M COMING, WHETHER YOU LIKE IT OR NOT

B y then, I was just about to make up my mind to join the cor-porate world and leave teaching behind. I wasn't too down about this, as I had found out that a lot of people don't necessar-ily get a job out of college with the degree they graduated with. This had happened with a few friends of mine who had graduated with sports management degrees but were getting those entry-level business positions instead. However, things changed when I re-ceived a call from my sister's school, Five Hawks Elementary, part of the Prior Lake district. The school year was imminent, and a sixth-grade teacher had pulled out of her position because of a contract situation from her previous job. The secretary asked if I wanted to interview immediately for the open position. I was shocked—I hadn't had one inquiry for an interview, and now I was getting one a week and a half before the school year started?! I immediately said yes and made myself available for whenever they wanted me. It was going to be on Monday, when their workshop started for the school year.

I wasn't that nervous, because I now saw that I could get jobs outside the education world as a backup. Well, not a job I'd always dreamed of, but jobs with the potential for mobility and getting a steady paycheck. So if this interview went poorly, I could get a job somewhere else.

Carrie was excited about the possibility that I'd be teaching with her—at least I thought she was. It was hard to tell. We were twelve years apart in age and had pretty much had separate lives. I didn't talk to her much about my subbing experiences, so she didn't know much about how I was as a new teacher. I did ask her what questions they might ask, who was going to be in the interview, and if she thought I'd have enough time to get the class ready if I got the position. She was a real help in letting me know what to expect.

That weekend, I had to get everything ready again: my résumé, my cover letter, and my references. I also made sure that I had my best shirt and pants ready—which was becoming hard to find, as they were getting stylistically older and worn out. I was set for Monday; I just had to wait.

When Monday approached, I had to be interviewed in the middle school, because the beginning-of-the-year workshops were going on there. The secretary told me where I had to go, and I entered a small office with the principal of Five Hawks and three other teachers.

I wasn't as nervous as I had been when interviewing for the long-term sub position at my former elementary school. Sure, it would have been embarrassing if I didn't get the job, since my sister worked at the school. But the way the other teachers interviewed me put me at ease. Two of the three teachers were only a few years older than me; and the third teacher, Tim, was about ten years older. I actually knew Tim a little from when I had visited Carrie at Five Hawks from time to time. This, of course, was another bonus, as I felt this would give me a little bit of a leg up on other interviewees, whether that was fair or not.

The teachers asked me about my teaching philosophy. I used the latest lingo in education speak while answering their questions, making me look smarter than I actually was. They weren't giving any sideways glances that said, *This guy is a lost cause,* so I took that as a small victory. I didn't stumble too much over my speech, either. They asked a few questions about classroom management and student engagement, however. I struggled through those, as I didn't have a clear-cut answer.

In the end, I left the interview feeling mixed. How many people were they interviewing in such a small window of time? There was no way they could have rounded up tens of people to interview just over the weekend, right?

The answer came on Wednesday, when the principal, Mr. Boone, called me. "Hey, Blair. Congratulations! We decided to offer you the sixth-grade teaching position."

"Oh! Wow! Hey, thanks a lot!" I was shocked, even though I knew there had been a chance I would get it.

"Does that mean we can see you at school next week?" Mr. Boone asked.

At first, I was elated. Then the crushing nerves set in. I barely had a week to get the class set up and get to know the curriculum. I didn't even know the students who were going to be in the class! Out of pure gall and stupidity, I answered, "Uh, yes. Could I just clean up the week with other interviews I have?" This was a lie; I didn't have other interviews lined up. I just wanted the time to consider whether I really needed this job. To my surprise, they let me have the weekend to think it over.

OKAY, I GUESS I'LL DO IT

My nerves were starting to set in as my decision and the first day of school approached. That weekend, I accepted the job at Five Hawks, as they needed an answer right away. However, I was subconsciously looking for a way out of it. I was getting cold feet about teaching as my career, even after I accepted the job. It was kind of like the spouse who got married and already was having serious doubts about their relationship.

Since I had also found out that I could have a whole list of other careers, I was wondering if teaching was the right fit for me. Part of it was greed. I knew that teaching wasn't the greatest-paying job in the world, and everybody sort of pitied you for that—and I hated people pitying me for anything. With a chance to work in sales, I felt like my potential for making money could be unlimited. But I was naive on that front, since I hadn't even gone to business school and didn't even know if I had any talents in that area. Also, I felt like I would be stuck in the teaching profession for the long run, and it would be too late if I ended up not liking teaching and wanted to go in another direction.

To make matters worse, I got another unbelievable phone call from the Lakeville school district, where I had just subbed long-term. I wasn't there to answer the phone, but this time it was from another former elementary school teacher, who was now a principal at a different school in the district.

The message was a shocker. In the message, Mrs. Miller (the principal) called to offer me a sixth-grade teaching job because the teacher who was supposed to teach that year—a thirty-year veteran—had died over the weekend due to an allergic reaction to a bee sting. I could tell by the strain in her voice that she was desperate for a replacement. She said she had also talked to Mrs. Schmidt for recommendations, so Mrs. Schmidt must have given my name, which was gracious of her. This message came on a Saturday, so now I had a decision to make between two teaching positions when I hadn't even had one interview in the previous year and a half.

I felt horrible for Mrs. Miller. I could have been the hero of the day and come in to teach amid the despair at that school. Even my parents knew who the deceased teacher was. Then I thought of all of the kids who were expecting to have that teacher in the classroom on that first day—and all of their parents, too. Some of those parents might have even had her as a teacher when they were kids, which was a common thing in that area. I imagined that these parents were thinking their child would be taught by a venerable, wise teacher with many years of experience—and who had been suddenly, under tragic circumstances, replaced with a rookie.

Not only was I worried about what the students and parents were thinking, but the staff must have been going through some major grief as well. According to my parents, the now-deceased teacher had spent the majority of her career at this school. Teachers who have taught for a long time in one school pick up familial roles—like a mother or father, or an aunt or uncle—to most of their coworkers. She was one of those teachers whom other teachers would approach for career and personal advice. And now she was gone.

Aside from the emotional devastation her death was going to leave, I would have to contend with the physical space of her classroom, which would have all of her posters, decorations, photos, and personal items. I would have to help erase all of that with her family members or former coworkers. That would be a morbid task. As I talked with friends and family, they suggested that I not take the job, as I'd be walking into a difficult situation—and especially if I had already said yes to another teaching position.

I did want to teach in Lakeville, just because I was already familiar with teaching in that district. Plus, there was a part of me that wanted to help them out in this horrible situation. But selfishly, I didn't want to deal with it because I had another job offer with fewer emotional strings attached.

By Sunday, I had to make the decision: Lakeville, Prior Lake, or the corporate route. I went with the Prior Lake job. I had no idea what would happen in the corporate world at all. It could be a life of just sitting in a cubicle forever, and I would probably come to hate myself for it. Besides, most of my friends in that space were already telling me how much they hated their bosses and how dreadful cold-calling was. Also, as the saying goes, there were three reasons why I'd decided to go with teaching: June, July, and August. Not a lot of adults have their summers free. Little did I know that those three reasons would draw the ire of so many friends and family as they continued to slave away at their jobs. Sure, I'd be making less money, but there was always going to be a beach waiting for me in the middle of a summer workday!

I called Prior Lake to officially accept the position on Monday morning and went in to get ready for the year right afterward. The conversation was short. Mr. Boone was happy to have a body for the classroom. I was relieved to finally put that decision to bed. I also, sadly, had to call Mrs. Miller about her offer and apologetically decline, saying I'd just accepted the Prior Lake offer, which had come first. We had a good talk during that brief conversation, and she said that Mrs. Schmidt had nothing but good things to say about me. So Mrs. Schmidt must have forgotten all about the goldfish and other rookie mistakes I'd made. Since then, I've always wondered who took over that class in Lakeville and if it had been a smooth transition.

HERE I AM! WHAT DO I DO NOW?

That Monday, I surveyed the bare classroom. I had a week to get it ready, along with learning about the students and the curriculum I was going to teach. What would I have done without my sister! She was teaching fourth grade at the time, but she'd taught sixth grade for about ten years before switching. Carrie came through in the clutch with a plethora of posters, including literary element definitions, plot-line information, and ancient civilization infographics. She also had decorations like bulletin board borders and lettering for the classroom. There were other office and classroom supplies I needed, so I had to make countless trips to the teacher supply store and figure out what to buy for more bulletin board borders, calendars, and dry and boring supplemental worksheet books. I also made my way to OfficeMax for what seemed like every conceivable office item. I needed markers, Sharpies, dry-erase markers, erasers—you name it. I quickly found out how expensive it was to be a first-year teacher with your own classroom. Thankfully, Carrie probably saved me hundreds of dollars just with the novels she lent me.

Decorating the classroom and deciding how you want the desks set up can be taxing on your brain if you let it, and I was fussing too much over it. I was wondering where I should put my morning meeting easel, the calendar, the bookshelves (not that it mattered, since the only books I had were from Carrie), and so on. Since I was going to be at the elementary level, I wanted to make sure my room was appropriately decorated to impress the students' parents. We had back-to-school night coming up, and I wanted to put the parents at ease by showing at least some decorations and posters had gone up, rather than a bland, unwelcoming classroom.

The worst part of decorating was that we didn't have an appropriate poster maker. Today, we can print PowerPoint slides as large posters through our media center. But back when I started teaching, if you wanted a poster, you either had to do it by hand (which I couldn't do, because my artistic ability was nil) or use die-cut letters (which took forever!). You would cut the construction paper in half, then find the die cut and put the paper into a press with a lever. Most times, it wouldn't cut all the way through. And when you were done with the die-cut letters, you would put them up individually on the wall, only to notice you had missed a letter and have to go back to the other end of the school to die-cut that last letter. It was a complete waste of time!

That was the majority of my Monday and Tuesday that week. The decorating was intermittently broken up by meetings. These meetings were important, as I was finding out what I was going to teach. It turned out that I would be teaching language arts, social studies, and math. This was fine with me. I would finally get to teach in the areas I was more comfortable with, aside from math. I would be switching with my coworker, Tim, for social studies and science. This was a relief, as Five Hawks also used the FOSS system for their science curriculum. But now I didn't have to teach it and risk leaving a bunch of dead goldfish around. And for social studies, I was going to teach our ancient civilizations curriculum twice a day.

Around midweek, the principal informed me which class I was going to get. It turned out I was going to get the gifted and talented class, better known as the Synergy group. I was pumped! Throughout every experience as a student and a practicing student teacher, I had known the gifted and talented group of students to be nerds and eager to learn. They would probably be willing to be patient with me, as I was a new teacher.

When I told Carrie that I would be teaching the gifted and talented group, she was concerned. "They gave you the Synergy group?!" she exclaimed.

"Yeah!" I answered. "Why are you so upset? They're the most behaved group!"

"They should have a more experienced teacher with that group."

I was somewhat dumbfounded as to why Carrie would think this. She never explained why. I just told her that this would be a breeze and that I could handle these geeks. Boy, was I wrong.

MEET THE PARENTS

Back-to-school night was coming up, and I was a wreck about it. I knew that some of the parents were aware that the teacher they thought their children would have was no longer teaching at Five Hawks. So I was anxious to see how they would feel about me after our first interactions.

During back-to-school night, the parents and students would come into the classroom, and I had to give a half-hour spiel about myself and what I was going to teach. I had never done a back-to-school night before, other than when I'd been student teaching. But I was just an afterthought back then. This would be the first one where I would be leading. I was happy to have the Synergy group, but I was terrified of their parents. Parents of gifted and talented students can be ruthless. I knew it was going to be hard to convince them that I was the right teacher, as the majority of these parents had been through the best schools and universities themselves. They were going to be skeptical of everything I did and wonder if I was going to do whatever it took for their child's best interests when it came to their education. I had no idea if that was going to happen on back-to-school night.

That Thursday, the day of our back-to-school night, I still had a lot to do to get my class ready. I felt like time was starting to close in on me, because we also had various meetings throughout the day. This was the second-to-last day of the workshop before our students would come in on the Tuesday after Labor Day. I needed to make sure the highfalutin parents would be at ease.

I had only been through one back-to-school night. I knew that other districts had vastly different methods, but the main point of this night was for parents to get to know the teacher, the curriculum, and the rest of their child's classes. So I needed to know how to introduce myself (or, rather, sell myself) to these parents. This was going to be diffi-cult; I'd had almost zero full-time teaching experience, and I'd never taught a gifted and talented class before. What could I sell them on? The focus would have to be on where I'd gone to school and perhaps on my teaching experiences in Minneapolis, as sparse as they were. Maybe they might come away impressed by that.

The other topic on the agenda was the curriculum. This was a bit easier. I could study a little for each subject. I knew that our language arts would be a thematic unit of character, so I just had to memorize that. For our social studies class, I just had to memorize a few of the important units. That was easy, since they were ancient civilizations of Mesopotamia, Egypt, Greece, Rome, and (for some reason) a 1960s unit we taught at the end of the year. I had to teach lower-level math, so I wouldn't see many of those parents until they were free to go and visit other teachers. I even skipped out on lunch that day and stayed during the three-hour window after the workshop to write down what I was going to say on a note card and then visualize what I was going to say and how I was going to move. I did not want to screw this up!

We also had to have a syllabus ready for the parents. I was surprised about this, because I'd never seen them during my time as a student teacher, even with Tom. Of course, I was familiar with them from college, but I'd never thought you needed to have them at the elementary level! Thankfully, we came together as a sixth-grade team and produced a template we all could use and fill in the blanks for what we wanted to say about our courses, the materials needed, and the expectations for our classes. Also, I was doubly thankful that Carrie had one pretty much written up from her days of teaching sixth grade. Oh, the joys of mooching off your sibling!

I will say, if it hadn't been for Carrie, I wouldn't have had a great beginning at Five Hawks. I was too much in over my head to feel like I was asking too much of her. I had to make sure I was going to survive this first week. It seemed like she didn't mind helping me, either. This was the first time I had ever interacted with Carrie in a serious way. We were getting to know each other more as brother and sister as well.

PowerPoint wasn't used that much in the classroom back then. There was no Epson projector we could use, and we didn't even have a TV in our rooms. (That would be coming the next school year.) So we had to do the presentation by using textbooks as props, and everything else was verbal.

As back-to-school night was getting closer, I was getting more anxious. Not only that, but that day was also a scorcher outside, and the air conditioning wasn't working well. I didn't notice the temperature in my classroom because it had been by and large empty for most of the day.

Finally, I had everything in place for the night. I had the syllabi on each desk for the parents. The classroom was as decorated as it could get and looked like it had a teacher who had been teaching for a couple of years, thanks to Carrie. Plus, I was dressed in my go-to Kohl's khaki pants and a shirt and tie. I was surprised that a couple of my coworkers gave me a ribbing about wearing a tie. "Hey, looking fancy for tonight!" one of them commented. "Did your sister help put your tie on?" I didn't notice how casual they were dressed for the night. Maybe I was overdoing it.

Once the parents started trickling in, I felt awkward. I wasn't used to having parents coming in and respecting my classroom. I'm also not one for making small talk other than just coming up with the same old welcoming pleasantries, and I felt I was struggling that night. Now that I've been in the trade for a while, I'm much better at doing this. But in my first year, I didn't know how to break the ice with the parents. I was worried about what they were going to think of my presentation.

By the time all the parents and students were there, the room was packed. I had four rows of paired desks, yet there weren't enough desks for everyone. Thank goodness I had extra syllabi. As I began to speak and make introductions, I realized I'd forgotten my note cards on my desk—and I didn't want to have to walk back there and get them. I would have looked like an idiot, as if I needed the cards to remember what I was going to say. Based on the looks they were giving me, I felt like the parents were thinking, *Well, shit. My child has a rookie teacher. Let's see what he's got.*

This school district was an up-and-coming urban sprawl lake district. Wealthy families were moving into this town, as Carrie had told me how it was starting to grow. Other families had lived here for a few generations. When I'd been growing up, Prior Lake was the next town southwest of us, and it was just a little farming town then. Now it was a wealthier suburban area, and the townies had faded to the back. But they were still there when I started teaching. The families I had in my room that night looked more like they were the successful type, as they were sharply dressed. They had high aspirations for their kids, since they were in the Synergy program. So I was getting these studied looks from these parents.

Well, hell. Once I started talking, I felt like I was rambling. I didn't have my note cards—which was probably good, since I would have been the only teacher in the history of back-to-school nights to have note cards. Still, I had no idea if I was making any sense. And worse, the room was getting *hot!* After only about fifteen minutes, it had become stiflingly humid. My mouth was also turning into the Mojave Desert. I was hoping I wasn't developing that white film on the corners of my mouth like my former science teacher had, which we'd all thought was disgusting. I was also starting to sweat, kind of like my hangover day from the previous year. I just wanted this to end.

When I was finished, my mouth was bone-dry and I had about five minutes left to kill. So I asked if there were any questions from the parents. There was an uncomfortable silence as they just stared back at me. I didn't see any reassuring smiles, only the kind of stares a comedian would get from the crowd if they were awful or had just told an inappropriate joke. So I ended it by inviting the parents to have a look around the room if they wanted. The majority of them just got up and started talking to each other. Their children by and large had had class together for years, since the gifted and talented students hardly ever moved out of their group from grade to grade. I was relieved that this part of the night was over, but I still felt vexed that none of the parents came up to ask any questions. I just kind of stood there and watched the parents and their students interact.

When it was time for the group to leave, I started to get the parents from the other classes I was going to teach: my lower-level math class, and the social studies class I would swap with Tim. I liked this format better, as it was more informal talking to the parents one-on-one. And compared to the Synergy parents, they didn't seem to put on any airs. Each family looked like the one I had grown up in. They wore regular clothes and had a blue-collar vibe of just getting off their nine-to-five job. Their conversations were more informal and relaxed. Not that the Synergy parents were snobby or anything; it was just the general feeling I'd gotten.

Finally, the announcement came that back-to-school night had reached its conclusion, and it was time for the parents and students to make their exit. I was relieved. Of course, Carrie came right away to see how everything had gone. She was probably happy that I hadn't messed anything up too much and wasn't a weeping mess in the corner. She also warned me that this group of parents would be difficult, because the demands they had for their kids would be the same demands they would have for the teacher. Good thing I hadn't thought about it before that night. Otherwise, I would have been a sweaty mess and probably stammered through my whole introduction.

READY FOR TAKEOFF

The next day, after back-to-school night, I came in just to make sure that everything was right, the same way I'd prepped when I'd had my long-term sub position. This is something that I continue to do to this day, and it's what most teachers do. We don't want any surprises on that first day. While I was getting things ready, my paraprofessional, Colleen, came into the room. She was going to be helping some students who had an individualized education program (IEP). This surprised me, because I'd thought that since I had the gifted and talented group, there wouldn't be any students who were on an IEP. I didn't know at this point how to deal with IEPs or what they entailed. It was something we had never been exposed to during college.

When I met Colleen, I also found out that she had a son in my class who was in the Synergy program. The student she would be working with, though, was a different student on a behavior program. Colleen was extremely bright and proper. I was nervous about this, because she seemed like a well-connected woman in the community, and now I had her in the class with her gifted son. I had a feeling she was going to be keen on me making sure I would be the best teacher to raise her son educationally. I was wondering how she felt about having a completely green teacher teaching this group. At this point, however, I was still naive, and I thought these kids would be patient and well-behaved. I thought it would at least be easier than the group I'd subbed the year before!

As the weekend hit, I had friends who wanted to go out to a lake, a cabin, or downtown. It was Labor Day weekend, after all. However, I was too uptight to go anywhere. I just wanted to hang out at home and clear my mind. I didn't want to go anywhere, party up, and overserve myself, only to come back that Monday night and be frazzled the next morning. I knew I might have been taking it to another unwarranted level of cautiousness, but I was nervous. This would become a pattern of mine on Labor Day weekend throughout the years. I just didn't want to do anything but have a Zen mindset. (Yes, I realize it's a bit over the top, and most teachers can get past this strange thought process.)

Also, during this weekend, I still had to plan out what I was going to teach for the week. I still used my blue planning book with the days and hours grid on each page. However, I was still being too maniacally specific about what I was going to teach. I was writing down everything to the minute, including transitions to bathroom breaks. My planning pages were filled to the brim, with writings smudged with eraser marks because I kept changing my mind about what I was going to teach.

In reality, the first-day plans were all about taking care of administrative things, like going through the school handbook, introducing myself, and playing icebreaker games with the students. All of this took longer than I thought it would. I had to thank Carrie again for helping me come up with ideas for classroom icebreakers during those days before the students arrived. I was horrible at planning icebreakers. I didn't have a huge catalog to rely on.

Monday night approached, and I was nervous as usual. I talked with Carrie, who was like a mama bear, seeing if I was all set to go. I was as prepared as I thought I was going to be. As usual, I had my clothes ready and ironed, everything organized in my backpack, and two different alarms set for probably about an hour earlier than I needed to get up. I settled in for a fitful night of sleep before the first day of my full-time teaching career. While lying in bed, I had visions of my students and me asking myself how they would behave. I couldn't stop thinking about their parents and how I was responsible for their education. Lastly, were these school nights going to be like this for the rest of my career?

Chapter 15

STUMBLING OUT OF THE GATE

Finally, the first day of school arrived. I don't know what it's like for every teacher out there on the first day of school. Are the students going to be a fun class to teach? Are they going to be the class a teacher will never forget, for good or bad? Or is the teacher going to feel like quitting by the middle of the year?

Every year, teachers get a list of the students they'll be teaching for the year or semester. The only students you hear about are the ones who have wreaked havoc as they moved up through the grades. We can ask previous teachers about how they handled these students in the past, but I don't try to do that. The most I do today is seat the challenging students close to me, but I like everyone to start with a clean slate. Who knows? They might have changed over the summer.

Sometimes at the beginning of the year, rumors swirl that the whole incoming grade level of students will be difficult to handle. Usually, these rumors percolate toward the end of the previous school year, when you have a chance to talk to the teachers in the grade below you. I would often get mixed reviews; some teachers would say that the grade level was difficult, and others would say it was a good group.

Once in a blue moon, I hear about what I call the "menace" class. If you're a sixth-grade teacher and you start hearing about how horrible a class is when they're in the *third* grade, you may have a menace class in the pipeline! "Watch out for this group you'll get in a couple of years," the elementary teachers would say. "They are hell on wheels!"

This has happened to me and my sixth-grade teacher colleagues once or twice. When the menace class was making it through the ranks, some of their current teachers would be so exasperated that they would start rethinking their careers. By the time the menace class was finishing fifth grade, my coworkers and I would be worried. It was going to be a troublesome summer, trying not to think about that next group.

As for my first year, and my first day, I didn't have the luxury of knowing anything about my students. I didn't have the time to do any type of research. Back then, there wasn't much data on students, as there wasn't an emphasis on standardized testing. That was starting to change dramatically, though, as President George W. Bush was just passing No Child Left Behind and schools were now on the hook for passing state standardized test scores. Thanks to that law, today there's a boom in data collection. For better or worse, we can have multiple diagnostic test scores available at all times.

As far as knowing the behavior concerns of my students, I could only glean a few details about a couple of students from Colleen, my paraprofessional. She gave me a heads up about one student, Steven, whom she would be helping. She also gave me a warning about a couple of other boys who were just your typical goofballs. I thought these students would be too intimidated to try anything silly now that they were in a gifted and talented class. They would be way outnumbered and feel like idiots if they acted out.

DEAR FIRST DAY OF THE REST OF MY LIFE, PLEASE DON'T SUCK

When I got to school on that first day of the new year, I was, of course, the first one there. The first order of business I had was to get our morning meeting ready. The morning meeting was when the class and I would gather in a circle in the front of the classroom and have a sharing or icebreaker game. These meetings in sixth grade are different from the meetings in primary grades in that more teaching comes from that concept. By the time the students are in sixth grade, they have pretty much grown out of it, but it was mandated by our school to do it.

Well, there I was on the first day, writing like a third grader, doing his best to get his letters on the lines. It honestly looked like I was taking about thirty seconds to write each word. It was horrible. By the time Colleen entered the room, the first thing she did was read the message.

I felt my skin turn red with embarrassment. When she was done, she just turned and stared at me for a few seconds, then looked back at the chart as if she was considering if she should critique me right away. She decided not to, and I was glad for that.

Around 9:10 a.m., the students started to enter the building. Here they were, the first students of my full-time teaching career. As they entered the classroom, I directed them to the seats where they would be sitting, and away we went.

First, we started with simple seating charts. Then I introduced myself, which took a bit longer than I expected. Next, I had the students do a little activity (which I stole from Carrie) that involved making "me bags." Basically, each student was to take a brown lunch bag and design it with simple construction paper and markers to represent one thing that represented them. It could be a hobby, family, or whatever. Then they needed to think of three small items to put in that bag to bring to school and talk about when they introduced themselves to their classmates. I had them write sentences about what they might say. Thankfully, this activity took a ton of time!

Afterward, we played some icebreaker games like Two Truths and a Lie and a type of interest Bingo, where the students had to go around the room to find classmates who had interests based on their cards. The rest of the time was spent going through the curriculum, the syllabus, and other mundane administrative duties. I repeated some of this with the other classes I switched with.

The day pretty much went without a hitch, and I'm sure I sounded like a bumbling fool. But no major catastrophe went off, as it's hard to have a chaotic first day of school no matter how many years you've been teaching. The icebreaker activities Carrie had given me had gone well. This made me feel pretty good overall. The other two classes that came in did well, too, although I noticed my lower-level math group was a bit squirrely.

At the end of the day, I was tired. I never realized how much talking a teacher did on the first day of class. My throat was scratchy, and my jaw hurt from yapping at the students all day and going over everything. It would turn out that by the end of the week, a lot of the teachers—including myself—would have almost no voice from the amount of talking we had to do.

It was also a good time to talk to my team and compare notes about students who stuck out. If there was a student you noticed right away, or who had been chatting away while you'd been talking, you knew you were going to have a long year with that student. However, after this first day, we didn't have any particular student we were worried about. Boy, that was about to change!

The rest of the week went pretty well. However, some behaviors were starting to pop up, especially with Colleen's student, Steven. What we quickly learned about Steven was that he had been diagnosed with ADHD. At the time, I wasn't familiar with it. I remembered a young student who had it during my special education observations in college, though. He'd had to wear a lead vest that would wear him out throughout the day. That was the severest intervention, and I don't even know if that's allowed anymore. Steven didn't wear the vest, although it would turn out that on 90 percent of the days, I wished he had been wearing one.

My fatal mistake with the Synergy group was that I had thought they would be the most compliant group in the school. I had assumed they would be sitting quietly, constantly listening to every word I said, and doing the work I asked them to do eagerly. But I was wrong. Now I knew why Carrie and other teachers were wary of me getting the gifted and talented group. After the first week, when the rubber meets the road as far as teaching a curriculum, the students were bored out of their minds. And as teachers know, when there's boredom in the classroom, shenanigans are not far behind.

For language arts, I was going strictly by the book. Whatever was laid out that week, I was going to teach it. However, with the Synergy group, I found that I was going to have to come up with something more engaging. The students were used to having teachers create supplemental projects that would challenge them. Since what I was teaching was on grade level and wasn't engaging, they felt like the work they were doing was beneath them and started to grow discontent about doing habitual busywork that was easy for them. I wasn't expecting this, as I'd had the misconception that they would be content with busywork. They would usually complete their work before the allotted time I thought it would take them to finish it. This created a problem with the other half of the class that wasn't part of the Synergy group, who were grade levels below the students in Synergy. I mean, it wasn't even close. It was like they had given me the top group of students academically and the lowest group in one class. So I had to figure out a way to get everyone engaged for the same length of time. This was going to require a massive amount of differentiation, which I wasn't familiar with at all.

With the students' misbehaviors starting to permeate, I found myself staying at school way late to try to make that differentiation happen. Since it was 2003, the Internet was starting to become widely used by teachers, and we could find resources for teaching to help boost our lessons. Websites were starting to come out with lessons targeted for specific grade levels and specific areas of study, like finding lessons on figurative language or main ideas. However, there were nowhere near the number of resources that are available today.

With the Synergy group, I had to try to align what I was teaching and find something extracurricular. So I spent hours and hours after school, trying to come up with daily improvements to the lessons that were prescribed in both language arts and social studies. It turned out that when the students left to go home around 4:00 p.m., I would be at school until six or seven at night, trying to find something extra. And boy, did I try some lessons that were complete disasters.

One of those lessons was to get my Synergy students to write more. I found one online where the students would write letters to delivery truck drivers. What the hell was I thinking? And why do that lesson with that group?? I could have easily had them correspond with other students in other countries, which would have been more interesting to my class. But instead, I picked this?! Needless to say, it was an instant bust. Maybe it had come to me late one night, when my brain was fried and I just needed a quick lesson. But I still look back at that decision now and shake my head.

As I stated, some of the other teachers were wondering why I got the

Synergy group. It turned out that two other teachers on my team were also new. So the options before I was hired had been two veteran teachers, and the school ended up giving the Synergy group to the woman who had to back out at the last second (and whose class I had taken over). I found this out from Tim, the other veteran teacher who didn't want the Synergy group.

Our school also had a Synergy liaison teacher who would take the group and do enrichment activities with them—and who was, I believe, also supposed to work with the classroom teachers who had Synergy. One would think that this Synergy liaison would have helped me a bit more to create engaging lessons and learn how to effectively teach this group. But this didn't happen much—at least not as much as I needed it, looking back on it now. Our interactions were brief, as she had other schools to work with. So whenever I received lessons from her, they weren't on topic with what I was teaching. They seemed frivolous and inane, like puzzles you'd see on a Mensa test. What I really needed were lessons that were supplemental to the curriculum I was teaching.

As I was trying out the new lessons I found online, I would get suspicious looks from the Synergy students. Some of them were starting to become indignant, because they thought I was being punitive by adding all these projects. It wasn't getting any better with the class of kids who weren't in Synergy, either. They were getting further and further behind, and their grades were falling. So they were starting to not care anymore, because they didn't know what I was doing and they felt their grades were too far behind to improve. I felt a mutiny coming with a rising chorus of complaints like "Why do we have to do this?" and "This is dumb. I don't know what I'm ever going to do with this!"

MEET YOUR FIRST MATCH

The complaints about my lessons were the first time I had a chance to see the true colors—good and bad—of my students. Aside from handling Steven's outward behavior issues, I was dealing with students who were displaying quiet passive-aggressive behaviors of choosing to let problems escalate, like not doing independent work or delaying their compliance. These would come more from my gifted and talented students. The one who stuck out to me the most was the "queen bee" of our class, Allison.

I felt bad for Allison. It turned out that her parents were going through a divorce. She was also the attraction of all the boys in the school and was probably at an eighth-grade level both physically and mentally. She could make a boy in my class cry at the drop of a hat. All I had to do was ask, "John, why are you crying?" He would sob, point to Allison, and claim she had said something mean to him.

"Allison, what did you say to John?" I would ask.

"All I said to him was, 'Be quiet!'" she would retort. "I don't know why he's crying!"

I would go back to talk to John, and he would say he was all right. Then I'd look back at Allison, who would have this sneering smile directed at her friends. I'd never seen a little girl hold such powerful venom in my life! Elementary school was becoming a joke for her, and I could do little to change her mind about that. She also had a keen grasp on sarcasm at that age and was applying this skill liberally to the whole class—even me. It never warranted severe reprimand, but she certainly wielded it effectively for her age!

I tried my best to make the class a challenging place for her educationally, but it was difficult. Her attitude at times was pretty toxic; and some of the students would look at her to see which direction she wanted to take the class, whether positive or negative. The other girls in the class always deferred to what Allison wanted. So the passive-aggressive behavior from the class that I mentioned earlier? She was best at deploying it.

The interesting part about Allison was that she had her own insecurities. As the Synergy teacher, I was to coach the Math Olympics team, and Allison was one of four students to make the team. As a team, we would practice once or twice a week after school to get ready for the state regional contest. When Allison found out she was on the team, she didn't want to be on it because she was going to be the only girl. This surprised me. At first, I thought she didn't want to do it because she thought it would be too stupid for her. So I begged her to be on the team because this was the chance where I saw she could finally be challenged in school. Somehow, I convinced her to try it.

During team practice, I noticed how focused Allison was when it came to complex math problems. She was determined to solve them and even debated over them with the boys, who were completely intimidated by her. Since I was certainly no math whiz and found it ironic that I was the math coach, I would have the team teach me how to solve these problems. That was when I saw Allison shine. She would get into the zone and focus on how to explain a complicated question. She thrived on this. This was the real method of teaching I should have employed for the whole class: have my students get into debates and discussions about the topics and themes I was teaching, then have them teach me what they learned. I do this now, but back then, I was viewed as the point man for learning—and I may have stifled voices who wanted to contribute.

Our math team did ridiculously well, taking second out of thirty-four teams. We celebrated at the end with a trip to a pizza joint, and it was great to see Allison have fun with members of a team she wouldn't have otherwise acknowledged or hung out with. We laughed and discussed the questions that were asked. It was the first time the boys felt like they were on equal footing with Allison; and I saw Allison start to relate to these boys, like they were okay to hang out with and find common interests.

Tread Lightly, Rookie

I also had a student whose mother worked at the school, and that would be my first of many. And if you've ever been a new teacher in this position, you know you want to win over the parent and not give a bad first impression that may create rumors of incompetence that land you in the principal's office.

This particular student was enjoyable. He also knew his mother was the secretary, who was only just down the hallway. However, he did love a little mischief now and then; and when he sensed that he was in a position to take part in the troublemaking, he would do so. It was hard to get mad at him. He tried hard in class academically, but he also had a group of friends who weren't in the Synergy group and wanted to create some chaos. I was always timid about telling his mother what he was doing wrong in the classroom. I assumed she thought I was lacking control of the classroom, and she could easily come back with that argument—and she would be right. So I regrettably went through the year as if her son was doing a magnificent job. It must have been obvious that I was wearing the biggest rose-colored glasses of all time. I just wanted everything to be all right.

In the end, I never knew how his mother, the secretary, felt about me as a teacher. She neither complimented me nor criticized me—and I'd take that! No news was good news to me!

THOU SHALT NOT SPEAK OF EVOLUTION

There was one mother I managed to infuriate, however. This had nothing to do with what or how I was lacking in classroom management. Instead, this had to do with religion—by accident.

It started when I was teaching social studies to my Synergy students. At the beginning of the year, I was talking about the ancient civilizations we were going to cover, from Mesopotamia to the ancient Romans. I don't quite understand how I started on this rant, but I believe a student asked me how long humans have been on Earth. I proceeded to answer the student's question to the best of my ability and brought up the notion of evolution in passing. Another student then asked a question about evolution, and I explained it—again, as best I could—based on what I had learned about evolution. It was something that I had taken as common knowledge of what science had uncovered about our roots in Africa. It was only a thirty-second explanation (if that), and then we moved on.

It was less than twenty-four hours before I got a call from the principal. "Blair, we got a call from a parent about something you taught in your civilizations class," said Mr. Boone, "and we need to have a meeting about it."

I had no idea what he was talking about. "Really? What for?"

"I'm just going to have to have her explain it to you. I believe it's something about religion."

I felt like Mr. Boone had no idea what the complaint was about, either. I was trying my best to figure out what exactly I had said that was so offensive. So we set up a meeting for the next morning. Needless to say, I didn't have a good night's sleep.

This was my first experience of meeting with a parent who was upset with me. I was dismayed, as I had been teaching for only about a month, and I was already in trouble with a parent. Was it going to be like this for the rest of the year?

To my relief, the principal didn't sit in on the meeting the next day. I felt more comfortable having to explain it to just the parent and not two people. Anyway, this parent came in with her daughter, who was a sweet, hardworking girl. This made me even more surprised and confused about what the problem could be.

Well, the problem was the evolution issue. It turned out that this girl came from a family of devout Christians who were nonbelievers in the theory of evolution. Her mother wasn't happy, to say the least, that I exposed her to that way of thinking. Now, being a first-year teacher, I wasn't about to get into an argument about what science had uncovered about human evolution, like the findings of Lucy in Ethiopia and the early bipeds of *Australopithecus.* I wasn't even an expert on this topic. But it's kind of hard to avoid the truth of it, since you can watch any show from the Discovery or History channels or pick up a copy of *National Geographic.*

The mother was adamant in her argument, though. "You *cannot* be teaching evolution to students who do not prescribe to it religiously!" she said at one point.

I didn't want to upset the mother. I was amazed that her daughter was in Synergy when they were ignoring the basic fact that evolution exists. But as I said earlier, I wasn't going to push it. The mother was also deeply involved with the school district through volunteering. So I assured her that I had no intention whatsoever to teach the topic and that it was just mentioned in passing. I also apologized for not being cognizant of other beliefs my students might have. By then, I just wanted the damn meeting to be over. I was more pissed about their ignorance than me being embarrassed. I wasn't even embarrassed anymore! I felt like I had done nothing wrong.

When the meeting was over, I didn't think I convinced this parent that I would keep evolution out of my teaching. Whenever I met with her throughout the year, I felt like she distrusted me, as if she was thinking I was the spawn of Satan. In the end, there was nothing I could do about it. I knew I wasn't even going to come close to teaching evolution in our ancient civilization curriculum, so I'd let her worry about it.

I felt bad for her child, too. I felt like she was being denied basic scientific knowledge based on her family's insistence on religion. She seemed to change after that and had an air of suspicion whenever she had a question or needed help from me. She also became timid when she asked for help, and she seemed to question what I was doing more often. I felt like I had to work to earn her trust all over again. I didn't think I was going to be able to do that, though.

What was ironic about the whole evolution situation was that two or three years later, the school purchased a brand-new social studies curriculum where we were going to teach ancient civilizations again. What was different about this curriculum? It had a whole unit on evolution, from *Australopithecus* to the Neanderthals. I laughed out loud when we were presented with this curriculum. I wished we'd had it when I'd started! I wondered if there would be a parent uprising about this. But throughout the life of the curriculum, I didn't have one parent complaint. Funny how things work in teaching sometimes.

I Can't Get Anything by Them

Another embarrassing moment was when one of my students asked where I was getting the extra curriculum to teach the class. As I stated earlier, the original curriculum that was prescribed wasn't enough to keep my Synergy students engaged. So I had to find whatever else I could to spice things up—and being a new teacher, I didn't have that much in my arsenal. Naturally, I had to look toward the Internet for ideas.

Once I had a project that I thought would work for the class, I would implement it almost immediately. However, only a few months into the year, I had a student come up to me and point out, "Mr. Clinton, how did you come up with this lesson?"

It was an odd question, but I didn't want to say, "I looked it up online." That would have made me look lazy. So I was vague and said, "Oh, it's just something I had."

After this, the student replied matter-of-factly, "Interesting. I looked it up last night and found it online."

I was shocked by this. First of all, what student goes online to see where a teacher gets their lessons from? Second, why would a student be interested in learning the origins of a lesson in the first place? The student was, of course, a smart Synergy student who was quiet and unassuming, but I was kind of upset! I felt like she was cheating, and now she knew I was being lazy.

Since then, that incident has been a nagging memory every time I look for extra help for lesson ideas online. I can't help myself from changing or tweaking lessons that I find to make them my own. Maybe I feel guilty about not even attempting to teach but relying on other people's expertise. It's common for us to take ideas from one another, though; and it's irrational of me to think that nobody should do this. But I can't help it.

CONFERENCES . . . UGH

Trying my best to swim upstream through the beginning part of the year was difficult. I didn't know if I was doing well with the students, and conferences were coming up. This would be my first time conducting conferences by myself. I had been involved during student teaching, but I hadn't been leading the conferences then.

I was, of course, apprehensive about what would happen during these conferences. Would parents criticize me for not challenging their students and insist that I was in over my head? Would they be indifferent and have nothing to say? Would we just stare at each other during the time allotted? Would some parents give me compliments? I had no idea how this was going to turn out.

I wished my peers and I had had a minilesson on conducting a conference during our time at university. I wished they had told us what to do if we had defiant or angry parents. Learning how to show student data during conferences would have been helpful, too. Maybe even showing us how to outline a twenty-minute conference and what actions, words, or conversations were necessary would have been valuable, at least for me.

As teachers know, the conference format is different from school to school, and they can change quite a bit. I don't think there's a perfect system, as it seems that we change our conference formats frequently at my current school. As for my first year, we had to have a twenty-minute session for each student and their parents. We had three days in which to schedule them, which was done by the parents filling out the three most desirable times for their conference. This was pretty easy to do, but not every parent sent back their requests with their child. So I had to try to get a hold of them to see what times would work.

I felt that twenty minutes was way too long to meet with parents. I had no idea what I was going to say to the parents of the students who had no problems. And while I knew I wouldn't have trouble filling up the twenty minutes for students who were creating madness in my class, those meetings were still going to be uncomfortable, for sure. I don't enjoy confronting parents with bad news.

I remember how tedious it was to get ready for conferences back then. The first part was getting the students' grades ready so I could explain how well or awful the child was doing. I was relying on that old red grade book with the small grading spaces, adding up all their scores and coming out with a grade that way. I always had to double-check to make sure I didn't add up anything incorrectly and end up with a different grade. Man, what a waste of time that was!

After that, we had to fill out a form that would show each student's progress grades. This would be helpful to guide the conference and converse about it to eat up the twenty minutes. With students I knew I was going to have difficult conversations about, I needed to know what I was talking about and exactly where they were struggling. I didn't want to come off as somebody who just gave out bad grades for the fun of it. I hated getting grades ready. I was always staying even later at the school a couple of days before conferences just to get those grades and reports done!

After the grades, it was about getting the classroom cleaned up and presentable. Carrie told me, "Make sure to keep a box of Kleenex nearby."

"Why would I want to do that?" I asked.

"You're probably going to have parents or a student who will start crying," she replied.

Now, Carrie is a master at shaming. She has been known to get a parent or two—and especially her students—to tear up. She also doesn't put up with any excuses from students or parents. I took her advice by putting out the Kleenex. I was honestly thinking that I was more likely to need them.

When the conferences started, I had extreme cottonmouth and forgot to get any water. I was booked solid my first night, and it was hell. It was four hours of nonstop conversations. The parents were there for their twenty-minute slots, and we had to use up all of those minutes. Sometimes I felt like I was just talking gibberish to the parents and students whom I had no issues with, because there wasn't anything to talk about after five minutes. Sometimes there was this awkward staring between us as we waited for someone to say something.

The conferences went pretty smoothly. I had students who I was concerned about, including Steven. He was an interesting case, as he came from a wealthy family. I had a good connection with his father, who used to be a college hockey player at the U of M. The family was genuinely concerned for Steven, but it seemed like I was just another broken record, telling them how Steven was misbehaving even with the paraprofessional in the room. I felt useless because I didn't have any solutions other than the same old "We'll keep an eye on that," or "He has the potential, but he just doesn't use it." His parents just looked tired; and I felt helpless, being just a first-year teacher. I didn't have a whole lot of tricks in the bag of things I could say. I also didn't have a toolbox of interventions, like having a behavior check-off sheet we could go over at the end of the day or reminder Post-it Notes to help Steven monitor himself. I felt ineffective.

I also had Allison, the queen bee, in with her mother, which helped me realize where the attitude was coming from. As I shared earlier, Allison's parents had just divorced; and I could tell her mom was seeking a new life for herself. She was dressed a bit too slinky for a student conference, which was affecting Allison, in my opinion. It could have been that her mom was focusing more on her newfound single life than on what her daughter was going through. It's interesting how teachers start to become crack psychologists during conference time—or how we can be horribly wrong in our judgments.

The same went for my struggling students who weren't in the Synergy program. It was starting to become obvious to me that the apple didn't fall far from the tree when it came to struggling students and their parents' experience with education. In most instances, it was just the mother who showed up to the conference, and the student's dad was out of the picture. Other times, both parents would show up, and I could tell they might have been struggling to make ends meet, even in the prosperous district I was teaching in. (It's not like this with all struggling families, though. You do have students who rise above the troubles they're going through at home.)

I did have a conference with the mother who was furious at me for "teaching" the concept of evolution. To smooth over the edges, I gushed about how well her daughter was doing, hoping to ease the tension. The girl's father was there, too, and he was a nice gentleman. But the mother still had this look of suspicion that was boring straight through me. I couldn't wait for that conference to end!

I had one more difficult conference that stood out, and it was with the student who had caught on to the fact that I was copying my extra lessons from the Internet. It turned out that her mother was a science teacher at the high school—and boy, did she grill me with questions about whether I was challenging her daughter enough, whether I was keeping her engaged, and what was I using for extra curriculum to get the most out of her. I was kind of taken aback. I almost wanted to stop the conference and say, "Look, lady. I'm a first-year teacher, and I'm working my balls off! I'm here till seven o'clock most nights! You've been a teacher for at least fifteen years. Cut me some slack!" That obviously wouldn't have gone over well, and I don't think it would have made a difference in the conference with her. This woman was just concerned for her daughter's education, as she should have been; and I think that she thought I wasn't up to the task of being a Synergy teacher—which I totally understood as well!

By the end of the first night of conferences, I was tired. I just wanted to stay at school until the next morning. I didn't want to drive back to Saint Paul. I did survive, though. The first night also gave me ideas on what I could do differently for the next two nights of conferences.

Once the other teachers and I were finished with the three nights of conferences, I was invited by a group of them (thanks to Carrie!) to a tradition they usually had: going to a small hole-in-the-wall bar in a town south of Prior Lake that I didn't even know existed. Prior Lake was the outskirts of the suburbs, and this town was just on the outskirts of Prior Lake. It might have been somebody's house whose downstairs had been converted into a bar. Anyway, the beer was cheap, so I wasn't complaining. I sat with those teachers and considered myself a peer among them for the first time, listening to stories of their conferences that were similar to mine.

This also gave me another glimpse into teachers' lives beyond the classroom. I talked to them and learned about their interests outside of school, the families they had, and their thoughts and opinions about education. It was a treat to unwind with them.

Yes, conferences are a necessary evil. After that first encounter with parents for conferences, and each subsequent conference afterward, I would say that I've been lucky. I haven't had a conference go completely off the rails, nor have I had to stop one and get the school's administration involved. Yes, I've had conferences with parents that did go badly and would leave a bad taste in my mouth for days or even weeks. But now I've come to somewhat enjoy them, as sometimes it's the only time I get to see the parents and let them know that I really do care for their child, no matter how much they may be driving me up a wall.

I'm lucky to be where I'm at school-wise when it comes to these nights as well. In our district, the majority of parents show up, depending on the topic we teach. I had a friend who taught in low socioeconomic areas, though, and those teachers have to do everything in their power to get parents into conferences. It's no fault of the parents, however, as they're often dealing with difficult circumstances.

As for the format of conferences, I'm happy I'm in the secondary level now, and I don't have to schedule twenty-minute conferences anymore. However, it seems that the format keeps on changing. Sometimes we don't have parent sign-ups, or we'll have parents sign up for a five-minute session, which is nowhere near enough time to have a sufficient conference. I have no idea if there's a perfect way to do conferences that will satisfy everybody. That's a committee I gladly choose to not take part in.

STRIKING OUT

Now that the first conferences were over, I had to look forward to the observations from my principal, Mr. Boone. I knew there was no way I could skirt these observations like I had with Professor Buggey when I had been student teaching. I had been observed before, but only informally by some of the professors back at the U of M. Now, these observations were going to be used to see if I was even proficient at my job and to decide whether the school would keep me, so a lot more was at stake here.

Overall, there were going to be three different observations throughout the year. These observations would look at various criteria the district was pushing new teachers to use in their teachings. These criteria (or domains) would include planning and prep, classroom management, instruction, and personal responsibilities. Obviously, I was worried about the classroom management part.

I did have one angle working in my favor: Mr. Boone was a new principal at our school. I automatically assumed he was going to be an easy grader for us new teachers—at least that was what I was hoping. We seemed to get along fairly well, too. Every time he saw me in the hallway, he would greet me in a warm, almost too-enthusiastic way. It wasn't that I hated it; I just wasn't used to somebody greeting me that way. I often thought he was way too nice to everybody, almost like he had a primary grade teacher attitude, which was what I think he had been before crossing into administration.

We set up the first observation a few weeks beforehand, and you bet I was circling that date on the calendar and fretting over it. Even on that Sunday night of weekly planning, I was trying to come up with something that would knock the socks off Mr. Boone and find something extra-engaging for my students so that they wouldn't act up. It always seemed like each day leading up to these observations, I was changing my plans. I would have something planned for figurative language, then overthink that it was too much independent busywork for him to find the lesson acceptable. So then I would try to incorporate some form of group work into it. I knew Mr. Boone was big into group work!

The day before the first observation, I finally settled on an idea for a story we were reading through our basic curriculum for language arts. It had something that included cutting out turtles and some reading strategies for the book. The students were going to work in groups for this project, and I thought that I had it all nailed down and that Mr. Boone would be super impressed with this cooperative learning activity.

I was wrong. When the principal came in, we finished reading the story from a day earlier, and I didn't go over the parts of what we had read from the previous day. Instead, I just wanted to dive into this turtle project. It turned out to be complete chaos. This one was on me, as (along with not reviewing what we had read in the story) I didn't go over the directions of the project very well. I had students who were completely befuddled as to what to do. "I don't get what we are supposed to do with the turtle," they would say to their groupmates.

My face was turning red. "You're supposed to write the figurative language example in the turtle!" I repeated again and again.

I also had other students who thought that cutting out turtles from construction paper was completely beneath them. "This is like something we would do in second grade," one of them said. If Mr. Boone hadn't been there, it probably would have been worse, as some of my troublemaking boys knew they were being watched a little more closely and didn't want to get into trouble. Regardless, it was a bad lesson, and I knew I wasn't going to get good marks on the criteria we were shooting for, which were planning and prep. But I also knew Mr. Boone was going to have something to say about my classroom management.

We were scheduled to have a post-observation meeting the next day. I was hoping with everything in my power that something would come up for Mr. Boone where he would have to reschedule and then (hopefully) forget that we even had a meeting. But no such luck. When he sat down, he asked me, "Well, Blair, what do you think worked well in that lesson?"

The only thing I could say was, "Well, I think the concept of the lesson was a good idea." I mentioned nothing of the lesson itself, though.

Mr. Boone seemed to agree politely, then asked what I thought could improve. I confessed and told him just about everything from that lesson could improve. He agreed with this wholeheartedly and gave me a good talk about the lesson. While he was talking, his tone changed from the cheery principal to a serious, skeptical tone about my teaching methods. He told me that I needed to do a lot of work to become proficient in classroom management. "I noticed numerous students were doing a lot of side talking that had nothing to do with the lesson," he said at one point. "I also noticed that the majority of the students were not engaged in the assignments as well."

I agreed with him on this. There was no use arguing. I felt like I wanted to sink through the floor. I managed to look at Mr. Boone, and he didn't look like the cheery principal I'd come to know. The smile was gone, and he had this stare of pity.

I was depressed after that meeting. Somehow, I managed to get the principal who thought everyone was fabulous to start thinking that I wasn't cut out to be a teacher. I had to figure out what to do.

I did remember what my cooperating teacher, Tom, had told me once about creating lessons: Just hit singles, and don't worry about hitting home runs. I had tried to hit a home run in front of Mr. Boone, and I had struck out swinging on three pitches. To minimize the possibility of misbehavior, I needed to just have regular lessons that weren't going to throw off the class. Maybe this was something I was going to have to do for the rest of the year.

My Kind of People!

Even though I was having trouble trying to effectively challenge my Synergy class in language arts and social studies, there was one class I was unbelievably having moderate success with: my lower-level math class. I'd been worried about this class when I first started to teach them, because people generally think students who struggle at school have behavior problems. That wasn't necessarily the case with this class.

First of all, the group I was teaching was relatively small (around twenty students or so) compared to my regular classes, which had around thirty to thirty-five students. This gave the class more breathing room and didn't seem so claustrophobic. Second, I was preparing for this class just as I was for my Synergy students. We had the curriculum for it, but I found that the students needed more visualization and manipulatives with their math. So I either had to go out and buy more manipulatives, or I had to create them myself. I even made fraction circles and cut them out by hand. What a pain in the ass that was! I was coming to the end of my budget to buy all this extra stuff, so I had to get creative. I'm sure there was a way parents could have done this, but I was too stubborn and ignorant to find out. Plus, most of my ideas seemed to come at the last minute, so there wasn't time to ask for money for supplies, I had to get everything myself.

Anyway, there was something about teaching these students who needed extra instruction when it came to math. We didn't have to rush through everything, and they seemed genuinely grateful that we weren't going at breakneck speed as they probably were in their other classes. Maybe I enjoyed teaching these students more than my gifted and talented students. These students actually needed the instruction. Most of these students were at least two grades below where they should have been and struggled with even basic multiplication facts. They didn't pretend to know everything, whereas my other students were looking for me to get out of the way and let them do their own thing, which I was having trouble accepting. Maybe that's why I love what I'm doing now as a reading interventionist, teaching students who hate reading.

I also hate saying this as well, but I felt as if the students in the lower-level math class weren't going to get any more screwed up at math than they already were. There was only one way to go, and that was up. I felt like that took a lot of pressure off me when I was teaching them. It also felt like the stakes weren't so high back then when it came to students who were in remedial classes.

Being a secondary school teacher, this class was a one-hour breath of fresh air. I think all secondary teachers can relate to having that one hour of class when we know there won't be too much trouble. This was the class that I should have had Mr. Boone observe me in!

JUST GET THROUGH IT

As the year went on, I was just trying to survive. I was grateful for the lessons that Carrie had given me, but I was still staying late at night to differentiate the curriculum. Every day was a challenge, trying to work with the divide between my Synergy group and the students on the opposite end of the spectrum. But onward we went.

I had my two other observations with Mr. Boone, too. They were a little bit better, but not much. I took out a bit of the extravagance of the lessons so that there wouldn't be so many instructions for the students to get confused over. In these observations, I stuck more to the prescribed curriculum. These met more of Mr. Boone's expectations, and I knew they wouldn't blow up in my face. If I just had the students do the independent busywork, they would keep more to themselves; and I wouldn't be marked down as badly as I had been during the first observation.

However, classroom management remained a problem. Halfway through the year, as the winter doldrums hit, it was starting to get toxic in my Synergy class. It seemed like the students who hadn't been troublemakers before were starting to join the fray, and I was becoming ornery. I didn't want to ask Carrie for help because it would seem like I was failing. In retrospect, I should have asked for advice from several teachers. I also should have asked for time to observe veteran teachers to see how they worked with their classes and how they used their classroom management. But my stubborn pride was getting in the way.

During this first year, I was way too preoccupied with my planning and may have exhibited some OCD in trying to get the perfect lessons. I was even skipping lunches just to make sure everything was right where I wanted it to be. My sixth-grade team would get on my case about skipping lunches. If I had listened to them and relaxed a bit, maybe I wouldn't have been so uptight and tense during that first year. Students are good at figuring out when a teacher is that way, and they can often exploit it for their own pleasure by seeing what they can get away with. They clearly noticed I was preoccupied with my lessons and not necessarily with them.

Not all of the days were bad, though. I did have some good days with the students, and there were times when we had good discussions in class about certain topics. I found out that I enjoyed teaching ancient civilizations during the social studies class. There was information in that curriculum that the Synergy students didn't know, unlike in language arts, where they felt they knew everything I was teaching and therefore became bored and discontented. With ancient civilizations, I found activities and games from these time periods that the students enjoyed doing. Carrie even had an ancient Olympic Games curriculum ready for me from when she had taught sixth grade previously, so I used it for the ancient Greek unit of my class. The students especially loved this; they designed their own city-state flag, and I looked up games the ancient Greeks played, which included running and throwing activities as well as children's games such as hoops and a type of jacks game called knucklebones. These were implemented in the lessons, and winners were awarded golden wreaths to wear on their heads. My troublemaker boys really were into this!

As for language arts, the one piece that students thrived on was creative writing. The challenge for me was to adequately teach them how to organize and write. It took almost the whole year for me to become proficient in teaching writing organization. Once I could give them a formula for writing, especially after teaching a unit on descriptive writing, the Synergy students took off. Yes, there were some gifted and talented students who would have rather had tests all day than express their feelings, but it was good to challenge them and get them out of their comfort zone.

As for my non-Synergy students, I was starting to get a handle on the differentiation, so they didn't have such lofty expectations. I still wanted to challenge them in the same way, so if they went over what was expected of them—great! I just wanted them to write a lot. I didn't care how many grammar mistakes they made, but editing was a pain.

By the end of the year, I took a cue from my coworker Tim to lay on the projects and work so that the students didn't have time to sense that summer was approaching. Luckily, I did have some end-of-the-year projects that needed to be done, and I was getting somewhat better at forming groups for the students to work in.

Finally, the last day of school arrived. I was glad it was coming to an end. The day before, we'd had our sixth-grade field trip to the amusement park Valleyfair, which was a good send-off for the students. But on that last day, the last seconds of my first year whittled away. The students were excited to get out, of course, just as I was excited to put this year behind me. As the final bell rang, the students ran out to the bus, and I could finally relax my shoulders and breathe. Of course, when I went out to the hall to say goodbye to the students with the rest of the teachers, there was Steven, dancing in the communal sink in the boys' bathroom. I wasn't going to miss that!

After that last day, I didn't know if I was going to be back for the next school year. I'd never known of anyone getting the boot after their first year of teaching. Most of my friends who had completed their first year of teaching were already coming back for the second year, except for one. But that wasn't related to her teaching abilities at all—in fact, she was a tremendous teacher. She had been teaching in Minneapolis; and in a surge of urban sprawl, people were leaving the city and flooding the suburbs. Her school was losing population, and she got pink-slipped. If I recall correctly, this happened to her a couple of times at the end of each year. She ended up leaving the city and heading out to teach in the suburbs, where she currently is today.

I was already thinking that because Carrie taught in the same school, they wouldn't fire me. Or would they? I know it was crass to think that way and pretend I had the right to teach, but that was how much doubt I had in my teaching skills at that time. The only way I thought I could come back was because of connections, not my capability. Sad, huh? I felt like I clearly needed to improve, despite knowing I was going to be back. I didn't want to be known as only teaching there because of my sister.

It was the day after the last day of school when I had my final meeting with Mr. Boone. I was nervous as hell. When he walked into the classroom, he wasn't smiling—which usually was a bad thing, because he smiled all the time. We both took seats at a small table that was in my classroom. I was sitting directly across from him, trying to keep my composure.

"Hi, Blair," Mr. Boone said. "Well, let's get right to it."

Oh God, I thought. *I'm fired.*

"We're going to bring you back for next year."

What?! A huge relief came over me then. But Mr. Boone let me know that I had a lot of things to work on—most notably, of course, classroom management. If I didn't improve in that area, there probably was no way I could come back for the school year after next.

Even though I should have been elated that I was going to be back next year, I was feeling irresolute about my teaching and disappointed in my meeting with Mr. Boone. I knew I had to change my approach big-time. I decided right then and there that I had to get help on how to control the classroom. I ended up buying a couple of textbooks on the topic to read over the summer. One was called *CHAMPs* by Randy Sprick. I took that reading seriously and was looking forward to implementing new classroom management strategies during the next school year. The book centered on better ways to improve classroom conversation, help, activity, movement, and participation.

There was another change coming that would benefit my teaching. There were rumors swirling around that the sixth grade was going to move up into the junior high school, and the ninth grade was going to move into the new high school. These changes would be voted on during the upcoming election. That meant we were possibly going to move into junior high, effectively making it a middle school.

Catching a whiff of this, my sixth-grade team and I thought it would be good practice to start specializing in one area of teaching, since that was what we would be doing in the middle school. This was great news to me! It meant that each of us would be tasked with teaching one topic all day. To fill the complete schedule out, we all had to add a half hour of language arts to our schedule, which would have been independent reading. Still, to teach ancient civilizations all day, and not be stuck with the same class of students? Sign me up! Our team was perfectly fit for what we were going to teach, as most of the four teachers in our group had a secondary license in English, math, or social studies. Tim didn't have one, but he liked teaching science anyway.

This was going to also make my summer easier by tenfold. I didn't have to prepare at all for language arts during the whole summer. I could just focus on making my social studies lessons stronger.

COULDA, WOULDA, SHOULDA

There are numerous things I should have done to have had a more successful first year. The first one that comes to mind was utilizing the Synergy teacher more often. I knew that she was busy with other grades, but I should have been more demanding of her time to come and help me plan for my group of Synergy students. She also would have been a tremendous help in planning differentiated lessons for my students who weren't in Synergy. It wasn't like it was her fault that I didn't do a good enough job, but I do wish they had given me a bit more slack, especially considering all the warnings and questioning looks from veteran teachers about having me teach the gifted and talented group.

Another area I should have taken advantage of was asking for outside help. We had a district reading specialist who was fantastic at her job, and I should have asked her how to work with certain units of my language arts curriculum. I was also in mentor-mentee meetings for first-year teachers, and I should have been more engaged with those groups by asking questions about certain teaching strategies.

Aside from trying to get help from outside of the school, I also should have gone to my colleagues and the school's administration for help. I knew I had my sister, but like I said earlier, I didn't want her to think I was having trouble with my job. It was foolish of me to think that. I should have asked Carrie for more advice on strategies for classroom management. She was a pro at it. Even to this day, we have different teaching styles that are at opposite ends of the spectrum, but classroom management is her specialty. I also should have observed other teachers, especially the fifth-grade teachers who had a wealth of experience. I even should have worked with my principal a little more. Instead of just having him come in and observe me flopping around on "home run" lessons I would create for him, I should have had him critique my teaching in my other classes. Maybe he would have seen something that worked and then told me to stick with that.

Finally, I wasted a lot of time after school trying to come up with elaborate lessons when I should have just kept it simple. Sure, the curriculum itself wasn't going to be enough when it came to my Synergy students, but little tweaks should have been adequate.

It wasn't like my first year of teaching was a total failure and disaster in which I irreversibly damaged all the students I taught. There were moments when I drove home thinking we'd had a good day. I do think that most teachers are hard on themselves in critiquing their own work—and maybe I am, too. Sometimes we expect perfection with sunshine and lollipops. But that isn't always the case, and we have to be good with that.

Chapter 16

SUMMER'S HERE!
WHERE'S EVERYBODY?

That first summer off was sort of surreal. I was the only one of
my good friends to have a summer break. All of them were
now at their full-time jobs, just starting out. It was a strange feeling,
as if I was the only one in the world who wasn't working. I still had
my job at Sylvan, but I was working only about thirty hours a week,
and I wouldn't consider it hard work by any means. I could pretty
much set my own schedule.

On my first day of freedom, I fired off an email to all of my friends
about my new summer daily schedule. It went kind of like this:

6:30 a.m.: Wake up
7:30 a.m.: Get out of bed
7:35 a.m.: Make and eat breakfast
8:00 a.m.: Go back to bed
9:30 a.m.: Get back out of bed
9:35 a.m.: Watch *SportsCenter*
10:35 a.m.: Watch something else
11:30 a.m.: Have lunch
12:00 p.m.: Take a nap
1:30 p.m.: Watch the news
2:30 p.m.: Eat a snack
3:00 p.m.: Take a shower
3:30 p.m.: Think about what I should do next
4:00 p.m.: Have another snack
4:30 p.m.: Power nap

The amount of hate mail that I received was enormous:

- "You suck!"
- "I hope you choke on your cereal!"
- "Why don't you do something constructive, like clean the house?!"

This became a standing tradition for the next few years, always followed by substantial hate mail within an hour of me sending it. Later, I would just send pictures of what I was doing on that first day off: a picture of me lying in bed late in the morning, a picture of me watching TV on the couch, or a picture of the snack I was about to eat. It may get old for my friends, but I never tire of it!

In all seriousness, though: during that first summer, I wanted to be better prepared for next year's school season. I was grateful to only have the social studies curriculum to prepare for. So I used the free time to plan out a framework for the year. I also used the *CHAMPs* textbook and other resources to research best practices for classroom management.

Other than that, it was a pretty uneventful summer. I did start to have a sense of uselessness by the time August rolled around. The days were just an endless cycle of the same nothingness. I felt as if I wasn't contributing anything worthwhile to society. It also wasn't like I was making bank off my first-year teacher salary and could take an exotic vacation. So I was getting pretty bored with summer.

In the final weeks of August, with the week of teacher workshops looming, I started to get anxious, kind of like a kid does before the start of the school year. Was I going to be a better teacher? What kind of students was I going to get? I was excited to start, knowing that I was better prepared than last year, when I didn't even have the job yet. The night before we had to go back for the workshop, I was sad to see summer go, but I was definitely ready. My friends were even giving me grief that I had to go back to work and were wondering if I was going to accidentally oversleep.

YES, THEY LET ME COME BACK

The workshop week was ten times less hectic than it had been the previous year. I had time to set up my classroom for what I was going to teach. The meetings with the other teachers and staff felt natural, and I didn't have that deer-in-the-headlights look all the time. I felt more relaxed around my coworkers, as I didn't have to ask and harass them for every little thing like I had when I'd been hired the year before. I even went out to lunch with my team rather than staying in like a shut-in. It was nice to have more time to discuss how we could be more of a team by aligning our expectations and how our daily schedule was going to work within our sixth grade.

As a team, we also reviewed the students who would be in our "homeroom" class so that we could figure out who we were going to have each hour. It was nice to be in the elementary school at this time, because if we had a question about a student, we could go right to their fifth-grade teacher from the previous year. As the end of the workshop week approached, I felt ten times more confident than I had the previous year. I had a year under my belt with the curriculum, rather than having less than a week. I also felt like I'd learned from my mistakes in classroom management and had better strategies to deal with that for this year. So I was eager for the school year to start.

Even the back-to-school night was way more relaxing. I knew the curriculum in and out, so I didn't have to have those stupid note cards to remember what I was going to say. I didn't have the Synergy group this year, either, so I didn't have to worry about the expectations of this group of parents compared to last year's. And when the parents came in that night, I didn't feel like I was being scrutinized like I'd been the previous year. The parents were easier to talk to, and I didn't have that much of a problem with the small talk. Thankfully, the room wasn't as stuffy as it had been the previous year, so I could discuss the curriculum and relate it to what we had done the previous year. I made sure to highlight the projects (the ones that wouldn't blow up!) that would be coming up for the year. When the night was over, I thought the parents looked pleased as they left with smiles and nods. I felt excited to get going as I walked back to my car that night.

Chapter 17

BACK BIGGER AND
BETTER . . . HOPEFULLY

T he second year started smoothly. The students adjusted to the new schedule accordingly. We'd begin the day with our homeroom morning meeting, which was about a half hour. During this time, we would sit in a circle where I would introduce myself and we'd have a summer share. We'd also use this time for get-to-know-you icebreaker games. After that, we would start the transitions into the other classrooms. Being an elementary school and implementing this experimental schedule, we didn't have bells go off at the end of every hour, as it would have been a distraction to the other grades. So we had to agree within our team on a time to release the students to the next class. Agreeing was easy enough. However, there were times when we'd let our students out a little early, and they would be waiting at their next class while the other teacher was still trying to finish up their class. That was the only drawback of the schedule for me. It wasn't a big deal, though.

At the end of the day, the students would come back to their homeroom for a half hour to have an extended language arts lesson. When our district reading coordinator heard that we were doing this plan of consolidated subject teaching, she was immediately concerned that we weren't including enough reading time for the students. At the time, I didn't see what the big deal was, considering that the students were reading in their other subjects. But she wanted to have our day be text-heavy. So we planned an extra half hour of independent reading at the end of each day.

The students seemed to like this transition as well. The other teachers in my team and I noticed that the sixth graders didn't like the elementary level, because they were starting to feel like all the activities associated with being an elementary school student were childish. Having a schedule mimicking what they would be doing next year in middle school gave them a sense of maturity.

Our team liked this schedule, since we were able to see all the sixth graders. This was immensely important, because in our team meetings we would discuss students who were struggling. The team meetings just consisted of us four sixth-grade teachers getting together in one of our classrooms. If Gary was having success working with a student in his English class, he could share strategies with the rest of us. We also liked how we weren't stuck with the same class of students for the whole day. And it was refreshing for the students to see a variety of teachers and not be stuck with any one teacher with whom they might have had a problem.

As for teaching one subject, I noticed that I was getting better as the day wore on. If I thought something didn't go over so well with the first class, I would easily adjust and change that for the next class. However, I noticed I was being more specific with the content as the day went on and giving more instructions on how to do each activity—to the point that I was wasting time. So my last class of the day didn't have as much time to complete an assignment as the first class did.

Classroom management was also easier for me. I had picked up a few tips on classroom management from the textbook study over the summer. Plus, I took some workshops on the topic at the beginning of the school year. Having the students rotate in and out also proved to be better for managing behaviors, because they didn't have time to get comfortable or bored and start looking for ways to create havoc. Along with using new strategies to monitor behavior, I was more confident in my teaching. And when the teacher is confident and knows the content, the students tend to feel like the teacher is in complete control of the class. So they may feel less inclined to cause trouble.

By improving on classroom behavior, I was better prepared for my observations. The first one came a month into the school year, and I was actually looking forward to being observed. And for my first observation, I made sure to pick a time with my least troubling class, even though most of the classes were pretty good.

When Mr. Boone came in to observe, I naturally did way better than I had during my first-year observation. I still kept my lesson close to the prescribed curriculum and didn't try to hit that home run. It also helped that I had a different set of students who weren't too critical about what was being taught, like my Synergy group had been the previous year. And let's be honest: I had set the bar pretty low the previous year.

Mr. Boone gave me much better marks on my observation checklist. However, I still needed to improve on controlling the class and not having them side talk so much. I couldn't be perfect at everything! Here's an interesting story about Mr. Boone, though: At the beginning of the school year, during the all-hands staff meeting, he admitted to the whole staff that he'd received poor results from the end-of-the-year survey. This surprised me, because I thought everybody loved him as a principal. But he was new, along with me. So I didn't know how well the staff had gotten along with the previous principal. But I was shocked at the outcome of the survey and how forthright he was about it and owned up to it. It was a huge relief to know it wasn't just me who needed to work to get things right.

Conferences were less stressful as well. Just for our grade, we didn't have to have the twenty minutes allotted for each student we'd had the year before. Since we were sharing all the students, this would have taken too much time. So we decided to mimic the middle school again and just have a first-come-first-serve conference with no real time limit. This especially went in my favor, as most parents are not too concerned about how their child is doing in social studies. I would get half the parent phone calls or emails about student performance compared to the other teachers in my sixth-grade team. In fact, social studies is probably considered less important than the other three core subjects of math, science, and language arts. Some students were struggling with the content. But in talking with the parents, I could be more specific about what their child needed to work on, since I didn't have to keep track of three different core classes.

The whole year was going swimmingly. I no longer had thoughts of possibly changing careers, nor was I doubtful that I would be back for the next school year. There was just one minor incident that prohibited me from finishing that second school year, though: I broke my leg.

The incident occurred while I was playing in a softball league with some of my coworkers. Our team name was the 719s, which is the number of our school district. I was playing first base, and there was a pop foul ball that was going beyond the base for about twenty yards. Now, in my defense, it was starting to rain—okay, it was sprinkling—and I was backpedaling to catch the ball. Somehow my foot got caught on some turf and twisted, and my ankle separated from my leg. Then, almost simultaneously, the weight of my body shattered my fibula near the separated ankle. I heard the crunch of the bone, and I knew it was bad. I crumpled right there on the foul line. The guy who hit the ball was rounding first base; and as soon as he heard the break of my leg, he shouted at my teammates to call an ambulance. Unbelievably, I still caught the ball.

As I was lying there, I managed to peek at my leg—and I noticed that my foot was pointing in the wrong direction. I didn't look back down there after that. However, I did manage to look across the diamond and spot my coworker, Gary, who was playing third base—and laughing at me. I didn't think that was very nice.

The pain wasn't as bad as I thought it would be; I'd seen this type of injury happen to athletes on TV. It might have been that I was in shock and disbelief. When the team gathered around my pathetic, crumpled body, I could tell by the looks on their faces that it was bad. They all had either a look of amazement or disgust bordering on nausea.

Thankfully, we had a high school sports trainer on our team. "Okay, Blair," the trainer said. "I'm gonna pinch your toes, and tell me if you can feel them."

I wasn't too thrilled with that, as I could clearly feel what was going on down there. But I said I could, and he looked relieved, which made me relieved. I was actually in a joking mood when this went down. I was joking to Gary that it looked like I wasn't going into school the next day—or the next week, for that matter. I also apologized to my team because we would have to forfeit the game due to them not being able to move me from the ballfield. Like it mattered anyway. We were a lousy team, and what was one more loss?

Finally, the ambulance showed up, and the paramedics placed me on the gurney. They wheeled me out of the complex, and again I was embarrassed by the number of people staring at me. When we got to the ambulance, the paramedics almost spilled me to the ground by taking a sharp turn trying to get me into the meat wagon. They asked how much pain I was in on a scale of one to ten so that they could get me the right amount of painkillers. I wasn't in horrible pain, but I gave them a ten anyway. The effects of the medication seemed to work on the way to the hospital, as I was feeling pretty good!

I was scheduled to have surgery, but they had to wait for a week to do it. We only had four weeks of school left; and the doctor didn't want me to go back to teach right away because they had to put some heavy metal in my leg, and they didn't want that disturbed. We made a deal where I could go back after two weeks. Until then, I had to get a sub to fill in.

After my surgery, I had to live at my parents' house because the leg I'd broken was my driving leg. So I needed somebody to drive me around! My dad loves to cook; and he was probably grateful that somebody else was at the house, distracting him from my mom's nagging. We would sit in the garage, watching the neighborhood, him drinking his beer and me being spaced out from the Percocet. When it was time to go back to school, it was like I was back in grade school but better. My dad would make these huge sacks of lunch for me to take to school. When he dropped me off, I'd have my backpack of school papers, my crutches, and a grocery bag of lunch. I think I gained at least twenty pounds during those weeks with my parents.

One other part of the broken leg saga was that I dared not tell anyone that I was on those painkillers. The doctor ordered a few weeks' worth of Percocet for me to take, and I could see why people would get hooked on it. I didn't know if I would have been in trouble if the administration and staff knew; and I didn't want to spend any more time away from school, especially at the end of the year. Thankfully, when I was done with those medications, I didn't have the urge to go back to them!

As the school year ended, I was sad to see the students go. Even though I can hardly remember the students from that year, I remember them as being an easygoing, fun group.

Over the summer, I had time to reflect on whether our system of specializing in one core subject had worked. Even though it had been easy to prep and teach the course, and I had developed confidence in my teaching because of not having to worry about so much prep work, there had been times when teaching was kind of boring. For each class, I had to repeat the same things over and over. Yes, I loved teaching ancient civilizations, but it was becoming monotonous. I was kind of missing language arts.

Thankfully, the district was thinking that we should go back to teaching at least two subjects. We kind of knew this was coming by the last month of the school year. Our district reading coordinator was still not convinced that the students were getting enough reading time, and I agreed with her. The following year would be our last year in the elementary setting. The new high school was being built, and moving the sixth grade up to the middle school was becoming a reality.

Chapter 18

REACHING MEDIOCRE STATUS

The last year of our elementary school days was unique. First, my team had to switch classrooms. Tim and I were moved to the lower level of the school, which was sort of like a basement. There were only four classrooms down there: the art room, my and Tim's rooms, and a high-level emotional behavioral disorder (EBD) classroom. My new classroom used to be an old kindergarten room and was twice the size of any classroom in the building—and unbelievably, it had its own enclosed bathroom! This worked out great because to get to an actual bathroom, the students had to walk for what seemed like a mile. But it could also be embarrassing for any student who might have had explosive diarrhea, since most of the class could hear what was going on in that tiny bathroom. So I think most students held it in.

The EBD room was right across from us, and it had about three teachers for ten students. During workshop week, the lead teacher, Kim—who is still with me at my school today, and who I consider one of the finest teachers—came to warn me about possible "disruptions" her students could cause throughout the year. She was right. In fact, Kim came into my class to talk about her students at the start of the school year. She told my students that they might hear some bad language and the slamming of doors and to be accepting of that. After that speech, my students did well whenever there was an issue in Kim's class. There was a safe room on the other side of our room where her students would run to, and we heard just about every swear word known to humankind coming from there. My students remembered what Kim said, though, and carried on as if nothing was happening.

I will say, though, that moving rooms was an enormous pain in the ass. I'm lucky in that I've only had to do this a couple of times in my career, but I've known teachers who have continuously bounced around from room to room. Every time a teacher has to move, there's a never-ending search for empty boxes, and every little item in the classroom has to be packed. It's also a time waster when you have more important things to do to get ready for the school year. You could be meeting with your team members about the curriculum or your students, but instead you're spending hours finding a perfect spot for your Expo markers or breaking your back while trying to move the box you overloaded with all your novels.

As the school year began, I had to get reacquainted with the language arts curriculum. This time around, I asked our reading coordinator for some help in teaching reading more effectively. She was a great help and advocated the idea that the students needed to keep their heads in the text, meaning that we had to up the ante on reading, especially since standardized test scores were becoming more important to schools. Our coordinator was also valuable in teaching how to get more writing in, rather than focusing solely on the dry curriculum that our basic set was offering.

We also had a new social studies curriculum coming in. This curriculum taught about evolution—and I couldn't wait to get all over that! I was secretly hoping I would have a parent come after me about teaching it so that I could finally show that the state's standards even backed up what I was teaching—and yeah, evolution happens! The rest of the curriculum had the same information we had taught in the last ancient civilization curriculum, so I was pretty set in my preparation.

The social studies curriculum was also different in that it was offering new technology: PowerPoint! I was lucky that we had a TV in the room, and I could hook my computer up to it, easily assemble the students around it, and show my PowerPoints from there. Now I didn't have to rely on those old projectors and transparency sheets. (The older teachers know what I'm talkin' about!)

For this year, since we were in the basement, Tim and I would swap classes, with my students going to him for math and science and his students coming to me for language arts and social studies. Tim and I got along great. We were both laid-back teachers, with him being a little more on the obsessive cleaning side. After a day's work, he would come into my classroom, and we would talk about how the day went or if we were having any issues with students. While we debriefed, he would be unconsciously straightening out my desks and organizing my room.

Tim was also quite the prankster. Oftentimes he would send his students over to my classroom with something up their sleeves. One time, he had them collect Barbies, and they all gave the dolls to me when they walked into class. Another time, they came in with grocery bags over their heads, as if they were a shamed group of kids going to a sporting event. I got a kick out of it. Everything we did was in good nature and was never meant to be ill-intentioned.

Sometimes Tim and I would collaborate and pull something on our sixth-grade team. For example, there was a field trip where the sixth graders had to go on two different days because of limited space. So Tim and I would go on this field trip one day; and our other two teachers, Gary and Joy, would go on another day. When Gary and Joy went on their field trip, we had our students go up to their classrooms and switch their students' desks. These desks had the top that would flip open so you could put all of your supplies and school books in there. When Gary's and Joy's classes came back, there was mass confusion among their students as they opened their desks and realized that they had been switched. Unfortunately, there were some students who had extreme anxiety issues and didn't take this well, which caused Gary and Joy to do some damage control. They had one student who was EBD and wanted to murder Tim (thankfully, not me)—and boy, the rest of their students wanted to get back at us with all their hearts. Joy did think the prank was kind of funny. Gary, however, did not. He walked back to his room and slammed his door shut. Tim and I learned a lesson that day: don't pull pranks on Gary.

We did get Tim back with a prank that bordered on inappropriate—but it was magnificent! A teacher in our school had a son in our grade who was fun and game for anything. With his parent's emphatic permission, we had this student write a love letter in a sixth-grade girl's handwriting to Tim. I was kind of leery about this, but since it wasn't my idea, I was interested to see how it would turn out.

After school one day, we put the letter in a spot in the classroom where we were sure Tim would pick it up. Moments later, he found us with a panicked look on his face. He'd found the letter, and he didn't know what to do about it. He was absolutely fretting, and it was fun to see him squirm. "Wha . . . wha . . . what do I do about this?!" Tim said. "I'm definitely going to have to bring this to Mr. Boone! Oh my gosh! Oh my gosh!" The rest of us acted like this was a serious situation and pretended to not know what to do so that he could make the next step. He brought the letter straight to the principal's office, which was the icing on the cake. The next day, we let him off the hook; and he was a good sport about it, laughing in disbelief. But he vowed a retribution prank on the student who had written the letter. He did have to go to the principal to declare it a prank, too.

SORRY, I'M HERE FOR GOOD

As the new school year started and we got rolling along, I was finding my groove. My classroom management still wasn't the greatest, but I was developing the confidence of teaching like a veteran. Maybe that was in my mind, but I felt like I was getting along a little bit easier. Thankfully, that year, I once again didn't have the Synergy group—although I was yearning to get them again and try to get different results from my first year.

This year was the big year for my observations as well. If I did well enough for Mr. Boone and got tenured, which would create job security, then I could get my master's degree as well as the pay jump that would come after obtaining it.

The observations came and went again in the beginning part of the year. I pretty much did average, sticking to my strategy of just hitting singles and doing a prescribed lesson from the curriculum. Mr. Boone still wasn't giving me a ringing endorsement, but I didn't bomb like I had during my first year.

Toward the end of the school year, Mr. Boone finally let me know that I was going to be retained and, thus, tenured. I don't think he cared if I had gotten it, though, because the sixth grade was going to be heading to the middle school. So I wasn't going to be his responsibility anymore.

Getting tenured is a huge relief. It means that you don't always have to be looking over your shoulder to see if the principal is there with a pink slip. So it was a cause for celebration! I immediately told Carrie and my coworkers about getting tenured, and they congratulated me. I'm sure some of them thought, *Oh man, how did he get tenured?* I also went out with some friends to celebrate that weekend. Most teachers feel as if a giant weight has been lifted off their shoulders when they achieve tenure. It's also heartbreaking when you see teachers who are let go the year they were supposed to get it.

I know that tenure is also controversial with some people. What other job has a mechanism that guarantees your position for years to come and protects you from your boss firing you for any reason? Some people argue that teachers go into autopilot once they're tenured and that they don't care anymore. This couldn't be further from the truth. Yes, there are teachers who slack and may not be earning their keep. But what profession doesn't have those employees? The vast majority of tenured teachers work just as hard as they did on their first day. Most teachers know the great responsibility they have to their students, and they don't want to fail. Sure, we may know some shortcuts to make our professional lives easier and more efficient, but what person doesn't?

ELEMENTARY MEMORIES

At the end of the year, my team of sixth-grade teachers and I started packing and moving our items into a storage area so that we could move them to the middle school, which wasn't quite ready for us. I was sad to be leaving the elementary school, where I had started my career. I was especially sad to be leaving my oversized room with the built-in bathroom. However, there were parts of the elementary experience that I wasn't going to miss.

One piece I wasn't going to miss was recess. If the weather was bad, the students would have their recess time in our room, leaving us without that invaluable time alone to get things done. That's when school starts to feel like babysitting. Also, I was tired of having to hang recess over a student's head for behavior reasons. It was getting old. Sometimes I didn't mind going out and playing soccer or four square with the kids to develop relationships, but I was looking forward to removing that time from the schedule in middle school.

Another part I wasn't going to miss was our morning meetings. I felt like it took way too much time in the morning, but we were expected to do it. Morning meetings are important in gaining students' trust, developing empathy, encouraging respect, and using it for some academic features, but it was running its course by the time the students were in sixth grade. Besides, I was on our reading coordinator's bandwagon and thought the time could be spent on reading. Morning meetings would have been useful maybe twice a week for sixth grade. I would have liked to use them on Mondays and Fridays for personal sharing purposes. But now that we were moving to the middle school, the daily meetings were one less piece we had to plan for.

Finally, we didn't have to go to the elementary school lyceums anymore. This was another part of the day when our students had to go sit on the hard gym floor and watch a performance that was geared toward the third grade. I always hated playing cop and stepping around the sitting students to pull out anyone who was bored and misbehaving, then have them sit by me during the performances or speeches.

I was going to miss our coworkers, though. The elementary staff—at least where I'd been teaching at Five Hawks—seemed more connected than at the secondary level. Most teachers had worked with the same students you were working with, so you could talk with them about a particular student you were concerned about or how well another one was doing. As a sixth-grade teacher in middle school, I don't have as many opportunities to do that. Also, it seemed that school-wide decisions like celebrations, teaching placements, and staff get-togethers were more staff-driven than administrative. Everything was more inclusive as well. At the elementary school, there were more staff outings. We would go to sporting events, bowling, or other events together. I'm not saying that where I work is cold and isolated. It's just departmentalized, so it's hard to be as inclusive. For the record, I do love where I work, and my coworkers are great fun to be with.

Chapter 19

IN THE MIDDLE

When my team of teachers and I first started at the middle school, we had the chance to meet our new coworkers. This would be the first year our district would have two middle schools, as they had converted the old high school across the street into the other middle school. We also had a new principal, so this would be my second time starting in a new school with a new principal.

I was impressed with Sasha off the bat. He taught in Minnesota for a couple of years but came over from Russia before that. It takes guts to move to a different country with only your family and a couple of suitcases and then become a school principal in just a few years. Sasha spoke English fairly well, too, but he was aware of his deficiencies and had a great sense of self-deprecating humor about it—and still does to this day. I was wondering how he would get along in a community that wasn't very ethnically diverse at the time and how he was going to get along with the staff as a first-time principal.

At first glance, our staff seemed to have a good mix of veteran and young teachers. And over the first few meetings, it looked like the group of teachers was well-organized, intelligent, and engaging. It was a promising group that I thought would be fun to work with and learn from.

In our week of workshops before school started, we also received our new schedules. It would be a change for us ex-elementary teachers to be on a fixed schedule with bells. I was looking forward to it, along with the other differences from the elementary level.

I would be back to teaching two subjects again: language arts and social studies. Having had a few years of teaching these subjects back-to-back, I felt better about my knowledge of the content. The only part I would find difficult was fitting language arts into forty-seven minutes, since I was used to teaching almost double that in the elementary setting. I knew I'd have to make cuts to my language arts arsenal; I just didn't know if it would be cutting down on reading or writing. I was a big fan of independent reading, as I felt like students loved having the choice to read whatever they wanted. But I also liked to have the students get creative with freewriting. Plus, I still had to teach the curriculum and fit in our standards.

One language arts component we got rid of was spelling. There was much trepidation among the teachers about this. We were all wondering if this decision would lead to a massive decline in spelling skills.

As for my schedule, I felt like it was completely different. I would be teaching five periods: three in language arts, and two in social studies. I was also going to have two open periods. One period was going to be my prep period, and the other was going to be a team period where I would meet with my sixth-grade team. There were two sets of sixth-grade teams, and each one was pretty much in its own pod. I wasn't used to having two off periods, but that team time was invaluable. It allowed us to discuss students who were struggling, plan celebrations and activities for our students, and plan thematic teaching where we could combine our curriculum. And I have to admit, it was also nice just to have it as a second prep. Some days we would be overwhelmed with prepping our other classes, grading tests or compositions, or maybe from being out sick, so we could use the time for ourselves. That team time enabled us to get to know each other as well. We were all coming from different schools, except for Tim. So it was interesting to compare the different ways we went about our teaching.

Our back-to-school night was set up for students to get used to their schedules. The families would come in as if the first bell had rung, then get a ten-minute presentation from the teacher. Then they repeated this for each hour. At the end of the presentation, the bell would ring, and the students and their families would have a mock session of going to their lockers and trying out their locks before heading to their next class. I didn't mind this format, as I had my five different classes come in and the presentations went by quickly. I did feel like I didn't get a chance to meet the parents and students, though. The parents didn't have the time to linger around. It's nice to get to talk to parents, listen to their concerns, and have an opportunity to introduce yourself to the student more informally.

Finally, the new sixth graders arrived for their first day of middle school. It was amusing to watch them walk into the school. For years, we had been used to seeing them as the confident rulers of the elementary level, but now they looked younger and (for the most part) skittish and uneasy about their new surroundings. Anyone who has made that jump into a higher-level institution can relate to this. Some students, of course, came in with a bravado of knowing everything by showing their friends where their classes were, bragging about getting their lockers open first, or knowing what the teachers were like already. Perhaps this was because they had siblings who had taught them the ropes or because they were keen observers. But most of the students had a deer-in-the-headlights look. I stood there wondering if I'd had that look on my face on the first day of junior high—or even high school—back in the day.

It was fascinating how much longer the honeymoon period was for the students who were new to middle school, compared to the honeymoon period at the elementary level. For me, the honeymoon period in elementary school would last for maybe three weeks. But now that we were in the middle school, these students were the youngest, and they didn't see us as coddling elementary teachers anymore. So this honeymoon period went on for a little over a month. First of all, there were a lot of things the students had to worry about and get used to, like opening their lockers, getting to the right classroom on time, wondering where their old elementary friends had gone to, or evading the older students.

When the students finally sat down in our classes, they had a lot to digest. Some had a look of shell shock for quite a while. Also, they needed to get used to having seven new teachers for one day and to learn their classroom expectations.

I loved being up in this secondary level of teaching. For one thing, it seemed like the administration wasn't around as much, as there was a much larger staff compared to the elementary level, where the principal was more heavily involved with the staff and the day-to-day business of the students. That was fine with me! Also, I liked cycling the students as we had done when we had departmentalized during my second year of teaching. It gave us a chance to work with a wide variety of students; and if we had a stinker of a class, we would only have them for forty-seven minutes. The teaching team was also competent and professional. However, Janet, who was a veteran teacher in the next room over, was struggling after not being around during our workshop week.

Before the first day of school, Janet was almost at a loss as to how she was going to teach and how to decorate her room. I would go over to see how she was doing, and she would have this look of confusion on her face. Then she would go on a helpless rant: "Oh! I have all of this stuff that they just dumped at my door and didn't bother to put in the classroom! I haven't even begun to look at my curriculum! I don't even know how I'm going to get this organized in time!" I didn't feel that sorry for her, since she could have planned ahead if she had known she was going to be gone up until a day and a half before the school year started. She did refuse my help and told me she was going to come in during the weekend to get things set up. I was fine with that! It gave me a bit more time to set up for my class.

THE SHOE'S ON THE OTHER FOOT

As the school year started and progressed into the first few weeks, I wasn't the one having classroom management issues for once. It was Janet, who was still struggling to keep up with the new environment. It was probably the first time I'd watched somebody struggle with classroom management and content in the curriculum, and now I knew how others may have felt when they had been watching me teach during my first year.

That first class wasn't even particularly difficult. If I remember correctly, they were quite enjoyable to teach. One standard I go by is if I can't remember the students from a certain class. Then I know it was a good class. That might be a little crass to say, but I always remember the students who were making my hair go gray rather than the relatively quiet ones. I wish it was the other way around, but it isn't.

Anyway, this was Janet's first time going through the science and math curriculum, as I think it was her first year in sixth grade. And she wasn't prepared for it. It reminded me of when I'd been in my first year of teaching. The difference was that I had been a first-year teacher and spent countless hours trying to nail down the basics of the curriculum so that I knew what the heck I was doing, whereas Janet had been teaching for a long time and probably didn't have the patience or drive to put in the extra work anymore. It's harder to put in all that time the older you get. Plus, she had a family as well as a long drive home. She lived a half hour from the middle school.

Instead of consistently teaching that curriculum, Janet would have days where she would just give up and wing it. So I had students who would come to my class after hers and, on several days, tell me they had done origami (again) in math. Some of the students loved it and were getting quite good at it, while others were becoming extremely bored of it and were starting to wonder about the purpose of that class.

Some days after school, it looked like Janet had had enough. She seemed frazzled and distraught—feelings I was all too familiar with myself. "I just don't know what to do with these students," she would lament. "I just can't teach them this stuff!" It was hard to communicate and work with her. I would try to offer suggestions, but it seemed as if whatever I said went in one ear and out the other. I had only been in the district for a few years anyway, and maybe I just wasn't resonating with her. But Janet also seemed not to listen to the other team members who were helping her. She would often miss team meetings; and when she did show up, she wasn't helpful with planning or teamwork. It seemed like the rest of us had something to contribute to the group when it came to discussing students, parties, cross-curriculum ideas, and general school information. However, Janet didn't have anything to contribute and mostly tried to shoot down any idea we'd come up with for events or teaching. I wanted her to gel with us, but it just wasn't working.

It wasn't just the curriculum and the classroom management that were hampering Janet. Technology was starting to become a factor in our teaching. For the first time ever, we had electronic grading. The system we had back then was called Skyward, in which you could find your class, put in your assignments and total points, and plug in the students' grades from there. It was a godsend for me! I didn't have to rely on that red grading book anymore. The grades just added up, and you'd come up with an automatic letter grade and percentage for each student. This was heaven! Also, no more filling out report cards! For that first year, we just printed out the reports and mailed them. For the newer teachers like myself, we could switch over quite easily, since we had never relied on written grades so much. Janet's struggles were also because she had missed valuable training for our online grading system. She would ultimately keep records in both Skyward and in her red grading book, which was unnecessary unless the system crashed and we lost all records (which some teachers feared at the time). To me, I felt this took away time from planning, which was what I was still doing too much of.

We also received smart boards, where everything that was shown on the teacher's computer screen was also shown on a large screen in front of the classroom. That was, all the students could see the visuals much easier than using transparencies and outdated posters. If I was teaching about Mount Vesuvius, I could easily show images from the Internet for the first time rather than using a poster.

Janet's year of despair got worse when one of our students accused her of racism. This student happened to be in one of my classes. I was shocked when he came up to me and said, "Mr. Clinton, Mrs. Johnson [aka Janet] was being racist." I thought there was no way this could have happened, as I felt like Janet didn't have a racist bone in her body. She was a hippy progressive who often talked politics. I asked the student why, and he responded, "She's always punishing me and not the other students for doing the same things, and I'm not even causing the trouble!" This was especially surprising; the boy was an excellent student throughout the school, even if he was a typical middle schooler who sometimes got himself into minor playfulness. All I could say at that moment was for him to wait for Mrs. Johnson to have some time so that he could ask to talk to her about it. Instead, he went to Principal Sasha.

I didn't know who to believe. People have their unconscious bias—and I'll admit it's something I've been working on, so there could be some truth to that. Janet was a bleeding-heart liberal, but that doesn't absolve you from anything. Since I hadn't been in the room, I couldn't take sides. But it wasn't like this student went around accusing people of racism. I don't remember ever hearing him discuss anything on the topic. So I was concerned that this was happening, as was the administration.

The administration came down on Janet pretty hard. Principal Sasha brought her and the student's parents in, and they had a big meeting. After the meeting, I noticed Sasha had a series of observations of Janet and her teaching as he'd walk past her room to mine. Also, Janet let me know about this, as she felt she was being wrongfully targeted. She was on the verge of breaking and quitting right there. I felt like there was nothing I could do and that there were no words that would help her get through this. I think that when this all went down, she made up her mind that she was definitely not going to come back the following school year and was already looking for a teaching job that was closer to her home.

At the end of that ordeal, I still didn't know if I had done enough to support the student—and, oddly enough, to support Janet. The student and I got along great; as I said before, he was a good student and hardly any trouble. He had a good group of friends, and they seemed supportive in backing him up throughout the whole fracas. I just wanted my classroom to be a normal learning environment for him. On the other hand, I had to work through this with Janet, and I hated seeing her go through it. I truly believed she didn't have bad intentions, and I thought it could have been resolved between her and the student. Being a young teacher, it was an eye-opener for me on taking stock of how I was teaching students, especially students of color. Was I being fair? Or was I subconsciously favoring white students?

Chapter 20

WHERE'S MY HELMET?

Once our second year at the middle school dawned, my team of sixth-grade teachers and I were preparing for what was the worst group to pass through the Prior Lake-Savage school district in quite some time (or so it seemed). By the time we got to the workshop week, we immediately wanted to see the list of students we would have for each class. Just by looking at the students, nobody could quite tell if they would be naughty or not. Some might have had that look, but it was all a guessing game. Instead, we relied on behavior and the academic cards of each student that were sent to us by each fifth-grade teacher. On each card was a picture of the student and information about their academic performance and behavioral issues. We instantly jumped on these cards and compared the information with the students assigned to our classes.

I never did this at the beginning of the year because I always wanted my students to start with a clean slate. But after hearing about this class, I was cautiously interested—and when I looked through the cards, my stomach sank. These observations from the fifth-grade teachers were some of the harshest I had ever read. It was like reading profiles of serial murderers. We read and heard from teachers about students picking not only fights with their peers, but also physical altercations with teachers! Plus, there was your typical damage to property, stealing of school equipment, and other major disruptions. Since our sixth-grade team would share all of the students, we were already coming up with a game plan for how to work with them.

Unfortunately for me, I would also have a new schedule, teaching three preps instead of two. A new teacher was replacing Janet: a fantastic teacher named Angie, who would take up math. But we needed an extra science section, and I was picked to teach it since I'd had that one horrific year of teaching a science class. Plus, I was still the youngest teacher in the group. I started having unpleasant flashbacks to my FOSS goldfish days back at Christina Huddleston; and with this group coming in, I was wondering what disaster I was going to create. The problem with having three preps of language arts, social studies, and science was that I could potentially have some of the students that were on our radar for three whole hours out of the day—and that turned out to be the case.

By back-to-school night, I knew something wasn't right. Usually when we have this night, the parents and their children—especially the children—are on their best behavior. They are curious about the class and listen to what the new teacher has to say. At this one, however, some of the boys were overexuberant about having each other in class. "Yes, Brady is in my class!" one of them said. "Oh, man, Teach better not sit us together. Ha ha!" After the parents saw the students who were in the classroom, they had concerned looks on their faces, as if they couldn't believe these students would be in the same class together. Their faces and the heightened tension made me sweat before I even gave the quick presentation. All of my classes except for one—the last class of the day—were as unsettling as the first.

In one of my classes were twin boys and their mother. My team and I had been warned about these boys in particular, like "If you get the twins, make sure they're separated," and "If you get the twins, make sure you let the office know when they're coming after you dismiss them for behavior," and "If you get the twins, good luck!" Their mother looked extremely tired, and I could tell that it was probably from trying to chase them down for the last eleven years.

Once I started my presentation, the twins kept interrupting me with questions. "When's recess?" one of them asked.

"This is middle school," I answered. "There's no recess. Sorry!"

"That sucks!"

"Okay then. Now, about science, . . ."

The twins' questions were totally out of the ballpark; and they each had a blank stare, like they didn't comprehend my answers. They also had a shock of white hair each and several bruises and cuts to prove that they didn't care one iota about bodily harm. They reminded me of some of the troublemaking friends I'd had who had also been terrors in the classroom. (Needless to say, those old friends were still causing trouble in their early adult life.) It also felt like the twins were in sync with each other's thoughts, like how twins sometimes are. And I noticed some of the other boys snickering as the twins asked questions, as if their behavior was common and everyone knew what kind of havoc they were going to create this school year.

By the time the night was over, my team and I quickly convened in our pod with concerned looks on our faces. "Did you have the twins?" we asked one another. "Did they blurt out during your presentation? Did you also have this group of students? It's going to be a long year!" Everyone on my team got weird vibes from their classes, especially those of us who had had the twins. While there were other students of concern, the twins were definitely the standouts that night. We each took a breath and wished one another good luck for opening day.

I knew this would be a challenging class. But even a challenging group of students can have a honeymoon week, right?

Wrong. When the first bell rang on the first day of school, the students started piling into my class while I was out in the hallway, helping out students with their lockers and finding their classrooms. I arrived at the class a couple of minutes later and was relieved to see they were just sitting there quietly, waiting for me. I greeted them with a "good morning" and started taking attendance, playing a little game with the students so that I could get their names right. Then I noticed that one of the twins was absent. I was secretly hoping that he and his brother might have transferred to a new class or school and that I hadn't heard about it yet.

When I finished with attendance, I started to do a presentation about myself when the one twin, Barry, rolled into the classroom. It was already ten minutes after the bell had rung, but it was the first day of school. So I wasn't too concerned about why he was late. As I was about to welcome Barry, he strolled right up to a scrawny redheaded student's desk, took his pencil, and snapped it in two right in the boy's face. Then he saw the desk that was open right next to my desk (preferential seating, due to what I'd read on Barry's fifth-grade performance card), sat down, and just stared at me with a look that said, *What are you gonna do about it??*

Truth be told, I had no idea what to do. I had never imagined this situation happening within the first ten minutes of a student's middle school career. I looked around the classroom and saw the students' mouths agape in shock. Some of them were even covering their mouths, as if they were going to burst out laughing. The poor redhead was staring at his busted-up pencil with tears in his eyes.

Finally, I looked at Barry incredulously and asked him why he had done it. Barry just stared at me and said he'd felt like it. We stared at each other for a few more moments. I didn't want to start the year off by yelling at this student. That could potentially blow the vibe of the whole year. I also had a feeling that he wasn't going to apologize, as he had no hint of empathy or sorrow on his face whatsoever. So I just told Barry that we would talk after class.

Throughout the rest of the class, Barry kept on looking back at the students and making faces. I couldn't believe it. I was on the verge of kicking out a student in his first class of middle school. The students all stared at him, waiting for what he would possibly do next. So I lost my class after the first ten minutes of the new school year. I was in uncharted waters. I couldn't believe this was happening to me! If I was having issues now, what was the rest of the year going to look like?

When the bell rang, I took Barry aside and asked him if he was okay. There was no way a student in their right mind would be acting this way on the first day of school; and at this point, I'd had my share of troublemakers. He replied that everything was all right. I then asked him why he had broken that kid's pencil, and he just said that he'd felt like it. This was when I knew we had to get in contact with Student Services and the boy's parents—after just one period of being with him. But something was wrong. If the twins had been behaving like this for years, how come they hadn't had any type of intervention, at least for behavior services?

After that hour, I had his twin brother, Brody. It wasn't much different. He was just as disruptive as Barry had been. It was stressful because I didn't want to act like an unwelcoming dictator on the first day. It was also strange that the twins' peers were encouraging them. They would laugh at everything Brody did—even if it was malicious, like picking on a student, tipping over a desk, or climbing up the back wall cabinets and table. Everything that had been said about this group was coming true.

The worst class of the day was my only science class, which had both Barry and Brody, along with other students who were on my team's radar, including a boy named Joseph. (I'll get to him later.) The introduction for that class was an absolute joke. These boys knew they had power in numbers to run this class into the ground, and I felt like a prison warden without guards to back me up. I found myself yelling more and using punitive measures like holding the twins after class and sending students down to the office after the first sign of trouble as a kind of preemptive strike. I was starting to feel like there was a conspiracy against me to put all these boys in this one class. I was going to have my work cut out for me, especially given that science was my weakest subject to teach.

My last class was a small consolation, as I could tell they were going to be somewhat manageable. But as the final bell rang for the day, I walked out as if I knew I was about to witness a slow-motion murder for the whole year. The rest of my team came out with the same expressions. Our new teacher, Angie, who had taught for a few years in a tougher district before coming here, asked us what the heck had just happened. The rest of us reported that each of our classes had students who were going to need massive behavioral and academic help. We also knew we were going to have many happy hours throughout the rest of the year.

Unfortunately, the twins weren't the only students who were struggling. We had no good natural leadership in the grade—and when that happens, it's going to be a long year. Joseph, who I mentioned earlier, was having a hell of a time in our classes. We had received academic and behavioral warnings about him. The issue with Joseph, along with most students who are struggling, stemmed from trouble at home. His parents were divorced, his father was dating or married to somebody Joseph didn't like for one reason or another, and his mother was battling substance abuse. I wanted this school to be a bit of a safer place for him. Therefore, I was a little bit more lenient. It's hard, though, when the behaviors are affecting everyone in the class.

Joseph's problem was that he couldn't help himself from getting into trouble. It broke my heart every time I had to admonish him or have him removed from the classroom after he would go on a yelling and swearing spree for no reason. Then I would have a discussion with him about what had gone wrong, and he would be genuinely sorry. He couldn't explain his impulses, and I wasn't enough of a child psychologist to figure it out. Deep down, he was a good kid. He loved to play hockey and go fishing; and to get him focused or back on task, I would engage him in conversations about those topics.

My team and I had numerous discussions at our Student Action Team (SAT) meeting where I first learned of Joseph's home life to see if there was a way to get him tested for probable learning disabilities. The main roadblock to getting Joseph to see a psychologist and get tested, however, was his parents.

I had to give his dad credit. He came to every conference we had and had the utmost concern for Joseph, but he was at a loss. His first wife was pretty much AWOL, and now his new partner probably cared less about Joseph. The father was quite successful in the business sector and looked like he loved to spend his money. He just didn't know which direction to take Joseph. Unfortunately, he wasn't ready to get Joseph tested. My colleagues and I see this with quite a few parents when we suggest this. Some of them feel like there's nothing wrong with their child or like they just don't want to admit it. It's not like we want to test every student with whom we're having difficulties, but there are students with definite red flags who would benefit if we knew there was an underlying issue that needed to be accommodated.

As for the notorious twins, we were trying to fast-track them into our EBD classroom. We only made it about two weeks before we started to demand meetings with their parents—and boy, these meetings were something else.

First off, the twins' parents knew exactly what was going to be said at this meeting, as they must have been to more of these than any other parent in our district's history. When they came in, they looked tired and ragged, not because of their economic state—they were uber-wealthy and lived on the lake—but because their house was being run by the two boys, and the years of trying to control them had drained every ounce of the parents' energy.

Through the meetings, my team and I found out that the boys pretty much got anything they wanted from their parents. The parents seemed to just throw money at the twins to keep them at bay. While at the meeting, they were kind of laughing about a boat the boys had set on fire. I couldn't imagine being the parents of these boys, nor how it had gotten so out of control without someone getting killed. We even had parents who didn't want their kids in the same class as the twins.

At the meeting, the twins' parents were finally willing to give up and have their sons tested for EBD. We were elated that they were going to get more individualized attention, especially through our EBD teacher, Eve (who I think is probably the district's greatest teacher, given the environment she creates for students who need help emotionally). Also, in a self-interested way, this would be a game changer for my classroom, since I wouldn't have to feel like we were in a hostage situation every single day.

The testing and observation period for students going through IEP qualifications takes time and is laborious. There's much to be done to get the students the help they need. We can only accommodate so many students in the regular classroom. It would be a few months before there would be any real movement with the twins and some of the other students we were looking to get individualized learning environments.

In the meantime, we continued teaching. Science was a doozy. As I was saying, this classroom was berserk, and I had to do a song and dance to get their attention. This science curriculum—which, thankfully, wasn't FOSS, where I'd be killing animals—had some physics experiments that were doable in my classroom. A lot of the experiments dealt with physical changes and motions, so one thing I incorporated quite a bit was using candy for experiments and almost burning rulers to show physical changes to a point where I thought the sprinklers would have come on—which would have nicely encapsulated the year.

The students, knowing they were going to get some kind of food at the end of the experiments, largely did okay with the labs. But sometimes there were small outbreaks of candy flying across the room or a lab group eating all of their gummy worms before the lab started.

ANOTHER ONE IN THE BOOKS

The school year rolled on, and my team and I got some of our classes lined up with paraprofessionals by getting certain students into IEPs. Some students found a better learning environment in the EBD program, most notably the twins. So the year started to smooth out in terms of classroom behavior.

On the last day of school, we kept a close eye on that countdown. The last day is usually just fluff anyway, as the students go around outside and sign their yearbooks or notebooks. Once that final bell rang, the students all raced to their buses, and the teachers came outside to the front of the school to wave goodbye. There were teachers who were considering mooning the students as they drove off. I'm sure some of the kids shared that sentiment. As they drove away, I heard a collective cheer from my sixth-grade team. To cap it off, we had a nice house party to celebrate the end of the year.

Chapter 21

THE MASTERS

Now that I had a few years under my belt and was tenured, I started to finally finish what was left of the master's program by enrolling in the U of M reading licensure program. This would give me a K-12 reading license. I needed only three credits to complete my program, so all I had to do at the time was take one class and be done with it. But no—I decided to go into a whole program that was going to cost me thousands of dollars to take but would eventually end up saving me from becoming a second-grade teacher (which I'll explain in the next chapter).

As all teachers know, we're striving to climb up the mountain of the pay scale through our system of steps and lanes. We start in that upper left corner, where (I believe) my first paycheck was somewhere around $800 in 2002. Each additional year under our belt, we move down the ladder and earn a little more cash (as long as we're not on a pay freeze!). Then, if we earn more credits through professional development, we move to the right on the grid and earn ourselves even more cabbage. The faster we can do this, the better, as we don't want to waste years sitting on the low side of the pay scale when we can be earning way more if we do our professional learning early and often. That was why I took up the reading licensure program: I would get my license (aka the master's degree), allowing me to move closer to the next lane.

I was also saved by having most of my master's finished when I had gone through my student teaching. Coworkers who were around my age were also starting to go through their master's program, but they didn't go through the five-year program that included partial master's work like I had. They went through a four-year program with the student teaching but without starting the master's program. That meant they had to start the master's program from scratch. It's a lot harder to do that when you already have a full-time job; and a lot of the coworkers who were starting this already had young families, so their hands were going to be full. Another part (which I felt guilty about) was that they had to write a capstone paper to complete their master's. I had to proofread some of my coworkers' papers, and I was thinking I was lucky that I never had to write one.

I was hesitant about the reading license. I wasn't sure what it was going to get me in the end. I was teaching language arts, so I thought the reading license would help me become a better teacher. As I said, though, the price tag was steep, and I wondered if it would be economically sound to do it. However, the other classes that were being offered weren't appealing to me, as they weren't that relevant to what I was teaching. Had there been a class that was just three credits and applied to middle school English, I would have taken it in a heartbeat. But there wasn't anything that would fit. So the reading license it was!

All the courses I would be taking were night classes, obviously. I had to start investing in caffeine to stay awake during these classes. At that time, I prided myself on not having to drink any coffee or pop before, during, or after school. There are teachers at our school (and workers in any occupation) who consume great quantities of it. Tim, for example, pretty much goes through a pot of coffee every morning. Another coworker of mine would drink two Mountain Dews each morning. I didn't like the taste of coffee, and I felt like Mountain Dew would ruin my teeth. However, teaching a full day and then driving up to Minneapolis and sitting in a drab campus classroom started to put my attention to the test. Classes would go on for about two and a half hours, and often I would find myself nodding off—literal head-bobbing into sleep. I had to give in to the caffeine gods, so I found a soda vending machine with the energy drink AMP. It's like a Mountain Dew, just with more caffeine. If I took it on a day when I'd had a light lunch or skipped that meal completely, I would get the shakes after downing a sixteen-ounce bottle. But it did the job and kept me awake.

The classes I took were invaluable to my teaching. They opened my eyes to just how important reading is to ensuring our students are productive in society. I've come to believe that it's undervalued in our educational system.

The first class I had was Leadership in K-12 Reading. In this class, I was a bit outclassed by my peers, as most of them were administrators or reading coordinators for their districts. To top it all off, I ended up getting pink eye right away—and that made a fabulous impression with my peers, as they made sure to stay away from me like I had the plague. I wished that this class had been at the end of the program, because I didn't know how to be an effective reading teacher at this point. If you're not an effective reading teacher, how can you be an effective reading leader for the district? But I held on as best I could and got through the class. If anything, it taught me how to promote reading concerns within the school, work with reading coordinators, and possibly become a coordinator if I chose to during my career. Again, it was a little over my head and would have been a wonderful class to take later in my career.

After I finished that class, I had enough credits to get my master's, and that was exactly what I did. This also enabled me to get into the next lane of our pay scale. I felt like a millionaire! Well, okay, a thousandaire. Since I had my master's, I had lost some of the motivation to go through the rest of the classes. But they, too, could bump me through the next lanes of the pay scale. And that was what it was all about: the race to the max pay!

The next few classes were much more relevant in helping my teaching pedagogy. One of them was Reading in K-6, which was taught by Deborah Dillon, who I thought was a tremendous professor. She opened my eyes to how students approach reading in primary and early secondary grade levels. Even though this wasn't quite relevant to my grade level, it revealed how struggling readers could have been missing critical areas of reading from their early ages. Her class was also important for me in getting students to collaborate in, participate in, and discuss reading in my classes. Teachers today are finding that the more students can discuss reading—whether by sharing in their enjoyment or having critical discussions on reading topics—the better their comprehension. And this class brought that idea home. For example, it would help teach my reading extensions class a skill such as cause and effect. We would be reading an article about a boy who suffered a life-threatening concussion in football. Just by getting into a discussion about being seriously injured at one point or another with the students had them interested in the story. It does help that what the students read is also relevant to their lives so that they can make connections to the story.

The class that was really important to me was Reading in the Middle and Secondary Levels. The professor for this class was David O'Brien, who was married to Professor Dillon. O'Brien was a professor I could relate to. He didn't come off as overly stuffy or technical, but he added valuable insights on motivating older students to read. His classes helped me work with students who were struggling with reading and hated it with a passion. With him, it was all about appropriate reading level and choice—something students weren't given enough of in the era of classroom novels.

O'Brien's class helped me understand how to develop discussion techniques that triggered student engagement, as well as how to get students to collaborate and share what they had learned in their reading. This was similar to Professor Dillon's class. I used these techniques right away in my language arts class and noticed a huge difference. Students became more engaged with their reading. These techniques were nothing new; they were just best practices I hadn't been familiar with, such as jigsaw reading strategies and other effective small group discussion techniques.

With the jigsaw technique, I could break up the reading into smaller chunks and assign students to different chunks of the texts. When the students were finished, they would form small groups with classmates who had read different chunks and then lead a discussion on the part they had read. Slowly, my language arts class was morphing into a reading class. Students liked the discussions because they could move around and talk to classmates and not listen to me for a change. When the discussions were all done, we would have a whole-class discussion where we'd hit on the major ideas that were discussed. I even found that my more introverted students came out of their shells a little, as they were getting used to talking in front of a large group.

O'Brien's reading class also helped me in the area of writing. He showed us how to motivate the students who were most likely to shun writing. All that was needed was freedom of choice. I had already experimented with choice during my long-term sub job with compare and contrast compositions, but O'Brien's verification that struggling readers and writers do better with free choice started to influence most of my writing classes. Back in the day, students would have to follow a prompt that would try to guide them in their writing. But more often than not, students came to hate it because they didn't know what to write. As I learned from O'Brien's example, the prompt could still be used, but students could be given the option to write about anything. Not all students were suddenly writing like James Patterson or even jumping for joy while writing, but it was gratifying to see them be proud of completing a whole page of writing, even if it had taken them three or four freewriting sessions to do it.

After taking O'Brien's class, I felt like his strategies improved reading engagement and motivation in my class. We were using small group strategies more, and the students didn't have to listen to me drone on about what I thought the reading was about. The students could now have a say in their learning. Granted that it was slightly louder in the classroom, and it might have seemed even more chaotic than usual. But the students didn't have this beaten-down zombie look when they left my classroom. (Well, most of them anyway.) Instead, they left the class a little more invigorated than usual.

One thing I wished there had been some information on in O'Brien's class was how to diagnose students who were struggling at reading—or, rather, on what they were struggling with and why. Yes, students who were struggling with reading were now more eager to get into discussions in my class, but they were still lagging behind and couldn't close the gap with their counterparts who were passing our standardized tests. I had several students who seemed to be reading more and had better participation in the class but were still testing at 10 percent of their reading grade level or lower. I didn't have a firm grip on how to figure out why these students were struggling. I couldn't put two and two together to at least figure out if it was phonics work or something much more complicated (like a form of dyslexia) that was getting in the way. It wouldn't be until later in my career that I would grasp diagnostic testing among my struggling readers.

After O'Brien's class, I had to take a class on using professional development throughout the whole school system. Again, this class was devoted mainly to reading coordinators throughout their districts. I would have loved to have taken this course ten years later, as I wasn't ready to be a reading coordinator for the district quite yet. However, this class helped me become more vocal about reading issues that might arise within my school, which was becoming more common.

More and more, schools were being held to a higher standard on their state standardized tests, as the state of Minnesota was to the Minnesota Comprehensive Assessments (MCAs). Principal Sasha was entirely fanatical about these test scores. In a way, it was good that he was concerned about how our school was doing on standardized tests. On the other hand, it brought immense pressure to language arts and English teachers to make sure our test scores were improving. I used some of the strategies I was learning at the U of M whenever Sasha asked for advice or ran a professional development session. It was perfect timing, as our school was constantly setting reading goals as part of our school improvement plan.

POWER UP!

My last course of the program was in the one area where I was lacking: how to prevent reading difficulties. Our instruction included diagnosing students with reading difficulties. The course was taught by Deb Peterson, who I felt was more knowledgeable in diagnosing reading difficulties in primary students. Still, I learned some strategies I could finally employ at the secondary level to find out where students were and what I could do to help with reading difficulties. It was basic, but at least it was something.

Reading teachers are often met with indifference or resistance when we present to other teachers who are experts in their curriculum but not in reading strategies. "Oh, great," they would say. "Another reading strategy. When the hell am I going to find the time to fit this in?!" Sure, some teachers are willing to learn and implement these strategies. But most of the time, we'll get glazed-over looks from our audience. It's hard to convey why reading is important for all areas of study and to try to have a whole district commit to them. A lot of my coworkers were quick to scrutinize how they could even use the strategies in their own class.

After taking Deb's class and receiving a grade for it, I could finally take the test for my reading license. Throughout the program, I had heard stories about teachers who had failed the test to get this license. Our professors at the U of M were confident that we would do well, as they boasted a 95 percent passing rate from students who had taken the test while other smaller universities only had a 50 percent passing rate. I'm not sure if that was the case, but I was also hearing of teachers suing these institutions for not preparing them enough for the exam.

The night before the exam, I wanted to make sure I didn't have a repeat of what I had done when I'd taken the Praxis exam five years earlier. There was going to be absolutely no late-night binge drinking; this was going to be taken hangover-free. What a world of difference it made. I arrived at the testing site with plenty of time. When I took my seat in the classroom, it was nice to have people show up after me. I didn't even break out into a cold sweat like I had last time. I pretty much knew everything the test was asking of me. Much of the exam had something to do with planning and organizing reading instruction, the use of assessment tools, and professional development within the school. The test was almost too easy, to a point where I thought there must have been something wrong and I was sure that I'd failed it. But as it turned out, I ended up passing it, and now I could add a reading license to my arsenal.

When I got it, I didn't even realize how rare it was to have a reading license in our district. But it turned out that I was one of only three or four teachers who had one—and having this license saved my hide.

Chapter 22

CAN YOU READ?

A s it turned out, I would be changing positions because of two reasons. One was because of my newly acquired reading license, and the second was because we were experiencing budget cuts and starting to cut staff. This was hard on the non-tenured teachers, as they were most likely going to be let go. Meanwhile, young tenured staff members like myself were facing the probability of moving to a different school within the district to teach something else. Luckily, because of my reading license, I stayed in the middle school while my friend Jamie was slated to head to the second grade. He went to teach in South America instead.

My new teaching position was to be the reading teacher of our middle school. I would be taking over for another fantastic teacher, Pam, who would be heading back to the English department in our school. During my time in the reading licensure program, I talked to Pam quite a bit about how she taught the class. She was talented in working with struggling readers and would be tremendously helpful as I started teaching this class. I relied on her more than I probably should have! "What curriculum did you use? How did you do independent reading? How did you deal with students who were misbehaving?" My questions for her were endless.

For that first year I was going to be teaching the reading program, we were going to have an every-other-day approach with seventh and eighth graders. I was still going to be teaching two sixth-grade language arts classes, too. I would be taking on students who weren't passing the state standardized test (the MCA) and who didn't have an IEP. These students were going to be a handful, as for the most part they were the ones who hated reading. I had to figure out a way to motivate these students into thinking that reading wasn't bad. I hoped this would lead to higher test scores on the MCA, our state's reading and math standardized test.

I also had a problem with the curriculum. I looked over the materials Pam had taught the previous years, but I found them to be dry. It was not content that these students would be engaged with. Some of these materials were in curriculum kits with small booklets that weren't relevant to or engaging for today's students. I pretty much went through any curriculum we had and cobbled together specific readings that I thought would be somewhat interesting to the students. I also aligned my curriculum with the state's standards to make sure students were getting more practice in the areas they needed to improve. Testing was starting to reach its zenith in high-stakes importance. Suddenly there was a lot of pressure on me to make sure these students not only improved their scores on the MCAs but also passed them. I always dreaded when the results of the MCAs were available, as I had nightmares of all of my students sliding backward in their scores.

The other part I wanted to focus on was reading for enjoyment. Because of the classes I had taken for the licensure program, I had to start building up my library so that the students could have choices and find books that would be at their level. Thankfully, I had coworkers who were switching from English or language arts to another subject, so I got some books from them. I also got some books from Carrie. However, my classroom library was still weak, and some of my books were pretty old and not palatable to the incoming seventh and eighth graders. Books like *Maniac Magee*, *Anne of Green Gables*, and *The Westing Game*—which are classics, don't get me wrong—were just not going to resonate with my new students.

As the new school year approached and the students started to come to my reading class, I started to understand that the students were quite aware of their reading abilities and felt like they were being singled out because of it. They were not happy to be in this class. "We're in the dummy class!" they would say out loud when entering my room. These were also students who were used to getting in trouble; and at this stage of their educational career, they weren't too interested in learning. Naturally, my classroom management—which I'd thought I had been getting better at—was collapsing. Each time I would introduce a reading skill with an article, there would be some serious groans. I had students ask to go to the bathroom and come back a half hour later. Also, the side talking was unstoppable, even when I had students separated with empty desks between them. I didn't know how to handle a class full of students who all felt that school wasn't for them. They felt like they were the sludge of the school because they believed the rest of the school saw them as "stupid." So why listen to Mr. Clinton anyway?

I approached this class the wrong way. I went along for the first few weeks thinking that we would be a happy family and set up our expectations through the students' suggestions and I could dive right into the teaching. It didn't happen that way. They could have cared less about coming up with shared expectations, because they didn't want any. So going straight into the curriculum and making this into a reading-only class wasn't going to work.

I found that the students needed the expectations right away. So I scrapped whatever lessons I had for the day coming up and went old-school with my expectations and consequences—in other words, the simple "No talking when the speaker is talking, and be respectful to your classmates and yourself." I had to show them this through modeling. I also had to have separate expectations for when we were independently reading. The students had to sit in their seats at first to gain my trust that they could move around the room. They also couldn't sit by their friends. In these cases, I would move a student to a spot where they couldn't make eye contact with the other. I had to model the heck out of this and give them the reasons why as well.

I also figured out that the students needed to learn why it was important to read. What were the real-world consequences if they didn't read? I had to do some heavy-duty research on why reading is important for the brain and to show how much more you have a chance to graduate if you read more—which, ultimately, would earn you more money. When I tied money around those reasons, the students seemed to listen more. They also needed to have a say in the whole discussion around reading. Some would say, "I need a book that is not thick," or "I want a book with more illustrations in it." These were reasonable, and I found that at least we could build on those. To say these changes totally straightened out my classes would be ludicrous, but at least it made the management a little better.

My first eighth-grade class was a challenge, to say the least. Looking back, the students in this class had several issues going on at home, and school was just not that important to them. They were starting to overtake the classroom; and for the first time, I needed Principal Sasha to come in and stop the flood. He was a bit hard with them in telling them to shape up, but that is what I really needed to do. Give them some tough love as well, rather than having them walk all over me. However, I needed to have this classroom not be quite so punitive, but also a place where they could feel like they were making progress.

I had to start by making the students aware that there were books out there that were interesting. I realized that they would get into discussions in our class if they had skin in the game, so I knew that historical or science fiction wasn't necessarily going to be their cup of tea—for most of them anyway. (There were a couple of students who liked those genres, especially if they were a bit on the rated-R side.) These students, including my seventh graders, were coming from backgrounds where they had already dealt with issues most of the student body wouldn't experience during their adolescent years. So they needed something they could identify with. It brought me back to my YMCA volunteering days, when we had realized we'd brought white-dominated magazines for our Black students to use for collages. I realized then that I had little to nothing here that resonated with these students.

Now, almost all of these students hated reading and never did it outside the classroom. There were a couple who did like to read and did read outside of school, although that could have been purely to try to impress me. (I did implore them to be honest and told them they weren't going to be judged on this.) The majority of the students also knew where they were in terms of their reading abilities. Most of them knew they struggled in this area, with a few exceptions.

As for what books the students liked to read, *Diary of a Wimpy Kid* was almost unanimously the number one choice. If you're unfamiliar with that book, it was written and simply illustrated by Jeff Kinney. It's about a boy who struggles hilariously in school and family life, written in a diary format at about a fourth-grade reading level. Kinney probably made bazillions off his book. Some students had *None* written down.

For the books the students didn't like, I noticed that these books were generally assigned as whole-class novels, like *The Giver* or *Where the Red Fern Grows*. I was heartbroken about *The Giver*. I usually did that as a read-aloud, and I loved it! But I could understand *Where the Red Fern Grows*. The students didn't have the background knowledge, and they found it hard to identify with. Some of the students had, of course, written *All of them* when it came to what books they hated.

With preferred genres, my students were all over the map. For the most part, though, there was a clear gender divide. Most of my boys liked sports, military, humor, and horror. This was about it. My girls were more open about what they wanted to read.

Getting to know the students' hobbies outside of school was important for a couple of reasons. First of all, it was a way for me to get to know them more and get into conversations with them. For example, if a boy liked to play video games, I could talk to him about what games he was playing. If a girl liked to play soccer, I could talk to her about games she might have coming up. Developing an interest in the students helped me gain some trust from them and convey that I wasn't some stiff teacher who didn't care about them. And the final reason to know their hobbies? I could hook them up with books that would align with their interests, which could also introduce them to new genres.

Now that I had the students' information from the survey cards, I had to get wise to which books were out there that would be of interest to them. The students didn't know how to pick out books for themselves for a variety of reasons. Some didn't know any authors who were good. Others were terrified of books that didn't have illustrations or were over 200 pages long. And for some students, the sheer number of books in the library was overwhelming, so they didn't want to ask for help.

My first major help in getting books into the students' hands was our media specialist at the time, Judy Haugh. She was tremendous at letting me know what books would be satisfying for my students, who preferred young adult books that had coarser content.

Even though Judy gave excellent recommendations, the problem was finding the right book for each student. It's hard to determine which book is going to be good and at that student's reading level. I had to do an enormous amount of research on the books I was looking into. That included reading the jacket copy and even going on Amazon to read reviews and summaries. I also had to read the first few pages just to see if the vocabulary was going to be an issue—and most of the time, it was. If the first page consisted of many multisyllabic words that I felt were above a ninth-grade level and with concepts I felt the student had no background knowledge in, it wasn't going to work. I was just hoping that the students would get the gist of it, sort of like with the Harry Potter effect, where children were absorbed in those books even though they were way above their reading level. I found that if I had a short stack of books based on the interest survey, the students were more apt to pick out a book. And if they liked that book, they would have a better understanding of what they would like to read next.

The other source I had to use (and still use today) is the Scholastic Book Club. Now, when I taught regular language arts class, I would always hand out the Scholastic flyer that contained new books. The students would fill them out at home, then bring them to class with a check from the parents so I could put in the order for them. Since I was ordering the books, I would get points toward free books the more our class ordered from them. It was great, especially if you had a class full of readers.

Unfortunately, with my reading classes, these students could have cared less about spending money on books. So it came out of my pocket. I struggled with this decision and still do today, as I know I've spent thousands to build up the class library. I'm not adept at finding school funding for books, basically because it takes a while to get approved for orders on materials that cost a lot of money, and I typically want my orders done ASAP. But in the end, it's worth it to me just to see one struggling student glom on to a book—and I get an even deeper satisfaction when that struggling student brags that they finished the book, and it was the first book they have completed since third grade. That's my financial contribution to the school.

Once I had the new books from the library and Scholastic, I had to find a way to bring awareness to the students. That was to hold book talks. I can't remember where I had seen them first, but I started using this practice toward the end of my first year with the reading classes. And for the most part, the students appreciated those talks. With my worst-behaved class, I had to make the books and the book talks like I was promoting a rated-R movie to get them interested. But in general with the book talks, I would take a book I had found and try my best to promote it by first asking a discussion question that would prompt the basis of the book. For example, for *This Is Where It Ends*, which is about a school shooting, I would ask my students if they knew of any school shootings or what they would do in the event of one. This would bring up a good discussion, and I would eventually introduce the book. Then I would read the back cover and first pages to give them a little taste of it.

I was wondering if I may have been crossing the line, though, because some of these books were sexually graphic and violent young adult books. But then I thought, who cares? As long as the students could read something, I wasn't going to care. I found that there were actual video book trailers online that helped promote the books as well. I enjoyed it when, after finishing a book talk, the least likely of readers would raise their hand and meekly request to read the book. Hell, sometimes students would get into flat-out shouting matches over a book.

"I want that book!" one student would say.

"No!" another would yell. "Back off! I asked Mr. Clinton about it before class! That's mine!"

By now, I was starting to get a little better at getting books into the hands of my students and was still stressing the importance of independent reading. I would automatically have twenty minutes of independent reading during this stretch, but even this was almost too much time for my readers. Stamina was the issue here. These students always faked it or just never read for longer than ten minutes. Telltale signs of this included me finding students on the same page after five minutes or simply staring into space. I found out that I had to start with ten minutes, then gradually build up to twenty. Most students built up this stamina, but there were a few who had reading deficiencies I wasn't catching and were having issues with this.

TAKE YOUR READING MEDICINE

Now that the "reading for enjoyment" part was improving, I had to get the class going on the "reading to learn" part. I found that my improvised collections of readings weren't working too well. They were out of date, and students weren't connecting with them. I had to find something that would catch their attention and let me teach the reading strategies at the same time.

Another teacher recommended Reader's Theater plays from Scholastic's magazines. I started using these magazines to help with fluency, then discovered that they contained interesting articles. Oftentimes students would prefer to read the magazines instead of their books because they found the content to be more interesting. So I went to our school secretary to see if we could order these magazines as class sets— and I was able to do it!

Scholastic's magazines weren't the only source I could rely on as time went on. Websites like Newsela, which had a great selection of nonfiction stories that you could adjust to a student's reading level, started to pop up. There are also a wide variety of short story websites I uncovered to help with fiction.

The magazines and the online resources fit perfectly into what I was teaching. Back then, I was using a Laura Robb book called *Teaching Reading: A Differentiated Approach*, which had lessons that lined up perfectly with the standards I was teaching and could be used for any type of literature. That manual saved my hide that year.

The magazine articles created more conversation within the classroom. I found that it was more important to keep those discussions going rather than trying to jam the lesson down the students' throats in record time. It seemed that they could get a better sense of what we were reading, and this included the students who typically never shared in the conversations. Often, we wouldn't even get to finish the lesson that day because the discussions would go on and on, but the students' engagement seemed to carry over into reading time. There were students who liked to play the game of how long they could keep the discussions going so that they didn't have to do any reading that day. Sometimes there was a problem with prolonged discussions and not getting to the actual lesson. And since our classes were every other day, the content we talked about two days earlier would largely have been forgotten by the next meeting. Thankfully, we turned into an everyday class after our first year.

Even though the students were becoming somewhat engaged, I was still having difficulty figuring out why students were struggling. I couldn't find a way to efficiently diagnose students. One student who led me to believe in the importance of diagnosis was a boy named Henry. I finally had a chance to teach him when he arrived in eighth grade. He hadn't been in my sixth- or seventh-grade classes because he hadn't wanted to be; and his parents didn't believe he had a reading deficiency, even though he had been scoring well below state norms for the past few years. It was also well-known that Henry was a tremendous troublemaker. I hadn't had him in sixth grade for my language arts classes, but I'd heard his name mentioned by teachers all the time—and from the office calling him down to Student Services through the PA system. (Going down to Student Services meant you had probably done something wrong and were about to meet somebody in the administration.)

Henry was, again, one of those students who was extremely approachable and likable when you were in an informal conversation with him, even though he was a troublemaker. He was, in a way, socially beyond his years when he talked to adults. He could carry on conversations and ask high-level questions. However, he couldn't read worth a lick.

Whenever our class was about to get into a reading activity, Henry would complain like I had never seen a student complain before. "Man, we have to do this again?!" he'd say. "We just read yesterday! Why do we have to read again? I'm *sick* of this!" He would act like he was going to the dentist's and principal's offices at the same time. And during these class reading sessions, Henry would never raise his hand to read aloud, which was strange because he was by far the most talkative student in our class. It wasn't until I started working with small groups that I discovered the problem.

In small group reading, where I would have the students read to me one-on-one, Henry would stumble over every word, even in a fourth-grade level reading text. If we had to read the sentence, *Samantha ran to the shore with great urgency to save Bryan,* Henry might have read it out loud as, "Sam . . . ah . . . run to the store . . . ah . . . in rapid . . . urn . . . to . . . ah . . . sail with Ryan." Right then and there, I suspected there were probably some underlying dyslexic issues.

By eighth grade, most students should be reading at 160 words per minute (wpm). Most of my struggling students were in the 100 to 140 wpm range. Some were at or above their grade level but were having comprehension issues. With Henry, he was reading at only 40 wpm. Here was a student who had no problems talking and getting into deep conversations but could hardly read at a second-grade pace. I knew this was dyslexia, but I didn't know how to address this reading problem. I didn't know exactly how it worked. It wasn't just mixing up your *d*'s and *b*'s; it was much more complicated than that.

I had a conversation with Henry about this and asked if anybody thought he had dyslexia, and he said no. I was blown away by his answer, because he had been through years of schooling reading like this. I then asked him what it was like to read words on the page. He told me that when he was reading, the words tended to jump in front of each other and the letters would rotate. I wasn't an expert in this, so I then asked Henry about independent reading. He would often complain about reading, but I would observe him doing it during independent reading time. He told me that most of the time he just faked it, but he did mostly read *Diary of a Wimpy Kid* because there were illustrations and the words were more spaced out.

The only part of the reading class that Henry liked was when we did Reader's Theater. I did note that Henry loved reading the plays. He loved being the exhibitionist, and I wished he would have been in the school plays. Reader's Theater gave him the chance to reread his lines before we would put on the play so that he wouldn't sound like he was stumbling all over the place.

At our SAT meeting, where a handful of teachers get together with administrators to discuss students who need possible special education (SPED) testing, I brought up Henry. He was usually discussed for behavior issues, but not this time. During this meeting, we had his parents in to set up testing for SPED and ADHD and recommend outside testing for dyslexia. Unbelievably, they wouldn't go for any of this, insisting that nothing was wrong with their child. Henry's parents were both educated and extremely well-to-do, so I was taken aback by why they didn't want any resources to help their son. The meeting ended, and there was nothing else we could do for Henry.

Knowing I was going to have him for the rest of the year, I dove into research about how to work with middle school students with dyslexia. This even cleaned up some of the previous misconceptions I'd had about dyslexia not being a sight issue, but rather a brain issue that deals with sounds of speech and how they deal with letters and words on paper. I tried everything with Henry, from using enlarged text and different colored paper to help settle the letters and words, to using colored transparency paper to cover the white paper with text, to having him work with a paraprofessional one-on-one. These strategies seemed to help a bit, and I thought Henry was at least noticing that I was going the extra mile to help him. So he wasn't being as much of a pain in the ass in the classroom and was willing to give anything a try. But in the end, I felt like he would move on to the high school and have to start all over again. That was a shame.

SO MANY READING PROBLEMS, SO LITTLE TIME (AND EXPERIENCE)

Aside from working with students with possible dyslexia, there were students in my reading classes who were struggling with basic phonics skills. It took me a long time to figure out how to work with students who have these problems.

Part of the reason why I failed to focus on phonemic work with students when I began teaching reading was that I just didn't have the time or resources. I had roughly fourteen to twenty students in my reading extension classes. That may not seem like a lot, but when they're all struggling with reading fluency, vocabulary, and comprehension, it sometimes feels like I have a class of forty students. I did have a paraprofessional in my classes at one point. But to be honest, she was used to making sure the students were on task during instruction. Also, I was more concerned about teaching reading strategies and trying to get the students hooked on reading rather than finding out what they really struggled with. I felt like if they could just learn how to use the reading strategies and get the gist of what they were reading, they would be fine. I can't say I was totally wrong in this assumption, though. We did have some success in improving scores on standardized reading tests, but it could have been better.

Another reason why I didn't focus on the root of the problem was that I felt like it was too overwhelming to pinpoint each student's problem in reading. On top of lesson planning, grading, and going through standardized assessments, I felt like it was impossible to have adequate time with over 100 students to observe their reading and come to a conclusion about what areas of fluency they needed help in, what areas of comprehension each student needed, and whether there was an underlying issue such as processing or dyslexia. And even if I could identify that issue, what strategies would I use to help a student with their specific reading deficiency?

I did have one resource that I could quickly use at the beginning of the year: the Qualitative Reading Inventory, in which a student reads a passage out loud and you time it and mark any mistakes during the read-aloud. After the reading, the student has to recall what happened during the reading and answer a series of questions for comprehension. Here, I could at least see what words the students were struggling with, but it wasn't specific enough. Also, grading the comprehension and recall could be subjective. Each assessment also took around fifteen minutes, which was way too long to do for a whole class. So I just continued to rely on the Aimsweb progress monitoring of the students' one-minute reads and look at their fluency. If they were struggling with the latter, I would come up with fluency exercises. However, this still didn't attack the root of students' specific reading deficiencies. It wouldn't be until much later, when we added two more teachers to our middle school reading program who were incredible at diagnosing, that I could get to the root of my students' problems.

As we started the reading program, we noticed how important it was to close the testing gap between students who were proficient in the state testing scores and students who were not. It was my job to do this. If the district was going to invest in me doing this, then I had better show results. The other middle school across the street from us also started a reading extension program and moved two teachers in to teach it. One of the teachers who would be teaching those classes at the other school was Kristen. The only way I had worked with Kristen before was through sixth-grade language arts, when I had taught it before becoming a reading interventionist. And I have to admit: I was pretty intimidated by Kristen when I first met her before the reading classes even began. She was one of the most headstrong teachers I had ever met, and she could be quite challenging with fellow teachers. However, I eventually found her to be one of the most thorough, well-researched teachers I've ever worked with.

Kristen was the one who got me to understand data and diagnostics whether I liked it or not. She would show up with binders of data and assessments of students she had. I felt quite inadequate during those meetings. However, she inspired me to be more diligent in keeping reading records and data on progress through assessments. Sometimes I would walk away from a meeting and wonder, *Where does she get all the hours in the day to come up with all the data on student reading and diagnostic tests?* She was even married—and busy with kids! I was starting to feel like my turf as the reading guru was being trodden on like I wasn't quite the expert I'd thought I was. But in reality, Kristen was extremely talented in getting to the root of a reading deficiency in a student—and, ultimately, I was grateful for observing how she went about taking careful data through assessments.

Not only did Kristen help change the way I was teaching, but Olivia (the other reading teacher at the second middle school) has also had a tremendous impact. She's much younger than me and Kristen, but she's wise beyond her years and well versed in reading research. She can connect with the hardest students to reach and does a great job bringing the community to her reading classes.

THE ONE AND ONLY KATHY

As the years went by, I worked with a paraprofessional who changed my life: a seventy-year-old woman whom the middle school's vice principal recommended. I was wary of this choice because I didn't know how the paraprofessional would handle the students in my classroom, since they could be on the mischievous side and didn't seem to respect their elders as one would hope. My vice principal, though, vouched for her vehemently and said that she was the perfect person for these students. I was still dubious.

When I first met my new paraprofessional, Kathy, I felt even more doubtful. To me, she seemed to be way too eager about the school year and was going about 100 miles per hour. She talked and walked so fast for her age, and I could hardly keep up! She kept asking if I had anything for her to do, which was helpful. But at times, I needed to get things done on my own.

I was getting worried that if I didn't find something for Kathy to do, she was going to implode. I was also concerned about her positivity and her belief that everything was great. I was getting the sense that she thought I was this awesome teacher who changed the lives of every student I taught. She would think that everything I'd told her that we would teach that school year was some profound, life-changing teaching method. I was worried she would be massively disappointed with the realities of my teaching capabilities. I felt like she would start to sour on the students when she realized that they wouldn't respect her because of her age and lack of connection. I thought she was going to be in way over her head; these students needed an extra body to help teach small groups, and she wasn't going to be able to effectively do that. But as it turned out, I couldn't have been more wrong.

First of all, I hadn't known Kathy's background at all. One day, when I was explaining to Kathy that some of my students may be coming from difficult situations at home, she said, "I can definitely relate to what they're going through. Oh, yes." Yet I was thinking, *There's no way this Bible-thumpin' lady knows anything about what they're going through—and she'll probably be appalled when she finds out!* So I asked her, "How can you relate?" She answered by telling me that she had been a wild kid, smoking cigarettes and anything else she could light when she was barely a teenager. She then dropped out of school and started experimenting with drugs. Around that time, she developed a relationship with a man and became pregnant. However, she and her boyfriend were busted for some type of crime, which I believe was drug distribution. While she was sitting in jail, pregnant with twins, her boyfriend (the father of her unborn children) died of an overdose. It was then that Kathy devoted her life to Jesus and cleaned up.

However, hard times would still follow. Kathy struggled with raising her twins because she lacked a degree, and her oldest boy was developing the same tendencies she'd had while growing up. Eventually, he got into the drug scene—and trouble. One night, he was arrested for a drive-by shooting and murder. He was later sentenced to prison for forty years.

Kathy said that this just about crushed her, but her faith and her daughter pulled her through. She remained active in the communities of mothers who had lost their children to gun violence, either from being murdered or committing the crime of murder. She became an advocate for parents who were struggling with the loss she was going through, even though her son was still in prison. Kathy would often tell me stories about the women she volunteered with, especially one whose teenage son had been murdered by another boy who was just fifteen at the time. When her son's murderer got out of prison twenty years later, the woman forgave him, and he moved into the apartment next to her. This woman essentially became a surrogate mother to the boy who had murdered her son. After hearing these incredible stories and finding out about Kathy's background, I knew she was the perfect paraprofessional for my class. I now knew she could relate to the students and what they were going through even more than I could.

Now, back to Kathy and our students. When the class came in, they didn't know what to make of Kathy. When they first saw her, they probably thought exactly what I had thought. Here was a woman who was so out of touch that the students assumed they could have some fun at her expense.

First of all, they saw the energy Kathy brought every day to the classroom. It was boundless. She would go from desk to desk, encouraging students even in the midst of their eye-rolling and sighing. But she went on, undeterred. Whenever the students tried to take advantage of her by covertly doing something that would humiliate her, she wouldn't get upset or lose her cool. She had been through hell in life, and this was child's play. Instead, she would forgive and talk to the student in a way that would make them feel bad for what they had done. The students were flummoxed by Kathy. They would have these looks of confusion on their faces. There were perplexed stares, as if the students were trying to solve a puzzle. They were used to no forgiveness and only harsh punishments. Yet they were getting the exact opposite. In turn, the students developed respect for her.

Kathy also created a fun dynamic between the two of us. In a way, she was a student in my classroom. She would sit in the back of the room whenever we were doing a whole-class teaching lesson and would participate as if she were a student. And whenever we were in a discussion about a topic, she would raise her hand in an almost impatient wave to get my attention, like an elementary school student. Our students would be eager to hear what she had to say, as they would all turn to listen to her and get into another discussion if they agreed or disagreed with her. Sometimes I felt it was a little distracting, as time was passing on what I really had to teach. But the level of engagement she brought to the students far outweighed my agenda.

Kathy and I couldn't have been more different in our tastes for literature. I loved reading books with tragic endings, whereas she loved inspiring books. Whenever I had a class discussion about books like the Escape from Furnace series, Kathy would playfully boo and hiss and act like the book was the devil itself. This would inspire my students to want to read it more! She would also give her own book talks about inspiring books she had read and left some of my students wanting to read those books themselves.

Kathy also loved our read-aloud sessions where I would read from a novel, and she would help create an engaged environment because of her "audience participation." As I said earlier, I loved tragic books, and most of my students did as well. Whenever the protagonist would suffer a massive breakdown, Kathy would let it be known that she was mortified through a series of sighs or reactions of disbelief or incredulity. For instance, I would get to the point of the book and read something like, "'Just then, Jeremiah turned the corner only to see the soldier strangling Sophia, and her limbs going limp——'"

"OH, NO!" Kathy would cry out. "MR. CLINTON, DON'T TELL US SHE'S GOING TO DIE, TOO!!'"

The students just loved watching Kathy do this. Sometimes I would invent portions of the story to have the protagonist prematurely killed just to get a reaction from her and them.

Kathy was also great at working with the students one-on-one. They were extremely comfortable working with her because she got them. She understood where they were coming from and had enormous empathy for them. The students started to trust her. Kathy might not have been the greatest at teaching the concepts I wanted to teach in small groups—which could have been due to my not explaining things well enough—but her relationship with the students was far more important than her teaching capability.

By the end of each school year, the students were sad to leave—not because they were leaving me, but because they were leaving Kathy!

Chapter 23

TEACHING SAVIOR

A s I reached my late twenties and early thirties, I was perfectly content with where I was in my life. I was extremely lucky and had everything going for me. But I was still ignorant of outside distractions from my personal life that were becoming louder and louder and would eventually turn my world upside down. The only thing that would save me was my job.

In my early thirties, I was hitting a consistent stride in my teaching career. At work, everything was fine. My private life was also going along . . . well, okay. I had a great group of friends and family, but my love life was heading into turmoil. I just hadn't realized it yet.

At that time, I had been dating a woman, Denise, for roughly five years; and there were some plans for us to get married—although I was completely oblivious to this. You see, I'm pretty dyslexic when it comes to reading relationships and what my partner is looking for. They may write down what they need from me explicitly on how to move the relationship along on a cue card and show it to me, and I'll read that cue as if it's in Mandarin.

Denise and I had a complicated relationship, to say the least. First of all, she was beautiful, smart, and probably way out of my league. However, I didn't take heed of this. She was a bit blunt, which may have rubbed my friends the wrong way from time to time. But I wasn't too concerned about that. When I'd met her, she had been going through dental school while I'd been teaching. We'd had a typical midtwenties relationship, aside from me being completely ignorant of her wants and needs; and things were going well, at least for me. We had enough common interests in politics, sports, recreational life, and making appearances at social gatherings. However, looking back, whatever we did was based more on what I was interested in doing.

When Denise graduated from dental school, things started to become more complicated. She was determined to move to the East Coast to start her own dental practice, and I was completely against this. I had no bargaining power, aside from my friends and family being in Minnesota and how it would be incredibly difficult to quit a teaching job and find a new one in an area where I had no connections. I was also in my late twenties, and I thought I was going to be too old to be offered a new job. That was my worry anyway. This shouldn't have been a hard decision, since Denise was going to be the breadwinner times five compared to my salary. Still, the roots run deep in Minnesota for me.

We had a year and a half of intense arguments about our future. I did not want to move out to the East Coast; and while Denise half-heartedly applied for positions in Minnesota, her heart was set on the east—and she wanted me to come with her. There was nothing I could do to change her mind, so I relented. She was great at arguing her case of getting ahead faster in opening her own clinic, and I just couldn't put any dents in the armor. Who was I to stop her anyhow? I was just some mediocre teacher.

The plan I had in my head was for her to be a dentist for two years and eventually take over the practice or start her own. The problem was that she would be working for someone else for two years, then possibly move somewhere else to start the practice. It would have been fine if I was in a different career, like business or some other profession, where I could just quit and find another job. But teaching is a different animal.

One of the states Denise was looking at was Massachusetts. I would have to apply for a license in that state, and then I would only have a small window of time to be hired in the area where she would open her practice. That was if they were even hiring—and it wasn't looking good in the areas Denise was considering practicing. I couldn't find a lot of teaching positions that were open when looking through the state's education website. Plus, even if I was lucky, I couldn't just get a teaching job and teach for a year or two, then move to a completely different district or state. Looking back on it now, I probably could have made it work. But at that time, it just seemed too daunting to me, and I was perturbed that this had to happen.

After a few months, Denise finally landed a job out in Northampton, Massachusetts. I remember when we packed up the U-Haul and hitched her car to the back of it, with our cat inside the car. When we were driving out of Saint Paul, Denise started hyperventilating over the life change that was about to happen. "You deserve this," I said as she was literally hyperventilating in a bag and then sobbing as she realized she was moving away from the only home she had known. For the first five hours on the road, I was in a pissed-off, selective mute mode; and she was leaning against the window, staring out at the landscape, probably thinking, *How am I going to get rid of this guy?* Yes, I was an ass that day, and I was starting to pour lighter fluid on the sticks to light our relationship ablaze.

We made our way to Massachusetts, where Denise would be working for a small dentist's office in hopes of starting her own in a couple of years. She and I made a deal: I would pack up and head over to the East Coast during the summer. I would also come over whenever I had a break during the school year. She would then come over on some of the weekends when I didn't have any additional days off.

It worked out quite well. We didn't go through long stretches without seeing each other; and we traveled around quite a bit, exploring the northeastern coast while I was there for two summers. However, I was still nagged by this whole process and was ignoring the fact that Denise wanted to get engaged and married. "We should just elope," she would say from time to time, followed by a nervous laugh from me. But I just didn't want to wait until she had her own practice so that I wouldn't have to worry about finding work right after I accepted a new teaching position.

Not only that, but I was still making myself out to be a martyr over the whole long-distance thing where I'd have to drop everything and move to be with Denise. I remember driving in that U-Haul on the way to Massachusetts and telling her, "I'm giving up my friends and family to be with you." She would just sit and stare out the window, though. I don't know why this made me feel good. Maybe it was just to make her feel the misery I was feeling about the prospect of ending my career for the sake of hers, but it didn't have to be that way. I would remind her often about what I was about to give up just to spend the rest of my life with her. Now, looking back, I suspect that this was wearing on Denise, and she was getting sick of waiting on me and dealing with my attitude. Plus, she was smart and attractive, and she could have anybody she wanted out there. She'd had enough of me; I just didn't know it.

I knew we were going through some troubles when, during the third summer, Denise became more curt during our conversations and less interested. It was unfortunately during that time that I had finally resolved to move to Massachusetts for good. I was actually enjoying my time out there and liked the area. Unfortunately, Denise was getting sick of me wasting all of that time and making her feel bad. Whenever I had breaks during the school year, we used to be excited about getting together and planning all sorts of things to do. But toward the end of our time together, our conversations about getting together were losing enthusiasm. "You don't have to come out here if you don't want to," she would say. I knew this wasn't good, but I ignored it, thinking that things would get better.

Out of the blue—or, really, it shouldn't have been—I received an email from Denise one day. It was just a two-sentence statement, as dry and cold as a Minneapolis night in January. Of all ways to communicate the end of a five-year relationship, this was how she told me she'd had enough of me, and we were through. I couldn't believe it. I felt as if my world had been ripped apart. I tried to fight my way back to her; and for a while, it looked like I would get back to her in a last-ditch effort. But in the end, Denise found somebody else. I was shattered. I thought that I'd had her wrapped around my finger and that she was never going to break up with me, but I had ignored all the signs of how I was destroying the relationship by making her feel horrible.

I had to teach the day after I found out that our relationship was truly over. I was a wreck. I remember telling my brother that night that it was over and just heading straight to bed. Then I woke up the next day, wondering what was the point of living. I just lay in bed for the longest time, contemplating if I should even go to work. *How am I going to make it through the day?* I thought. *How am I going to tell my coworkers?*

My sister? What are they going to think? Shit! I got dressed and could have been wearing two different shoes for all I cared, then headed to school.

On my drive to school, it was around six in the morning. So it was dark outside, and I was driving on the freeway when a dump truck was merging onto the freeway at an unusually high speed. I noticed it was going to be merging a little behind me, so I didn't change my speed to let it merge ahead of me. Then I heard a large crash and a screeching sound, and I noticed that the dump truck's headlights were now vertical rather than in a normal horizontal position, and sparks were coming from behind it. The truck had merged too fast and tipped over, missing me by two seconds. I wished then that I'd been under that truck. I was too far ahead now to stop.

When I got to the school, I went to Carrie's room and told her what happened. It was better to rip the Band-Aid off and let everyone know via my sister that I had been dumped for another guy. When Carrie finally arrived fifteen minutes before the students came in, I walked in to tell her. Unbelievably, I couldn't control my emotions. I started crying like a little schoolboy. It was the first time in my adult life that I couldn't keep it together. "Oh my God, Blair, what's going on?" was the reasonable question she asked. Once I blabbered to Carrie about what had happened, she said, "Blair, you have to go home. I'll get someone to cover for you. You're in no condition to teach today!" I told her that there was no way in hell I would leave. I honestly didn't know what I was going to do with myself if I had to go back home and be all alone.

Once the bell rang, I looked at Carrie and saw the genuine look of fear and concern on her face. I had to straighten up and get into my classroom. She told me that she would be in to check on me during the lunch hour. I had only five minutes to stop the water faucet behind my eyes and get the redness out.

When I walked back to my class, I was still in somewhat of a dream state. I didn't feel, see, or hear anything. I was a zombie. When I entered the class, though, all of that changed.

I was trying and failing miserably to get the day's lessons in order when the students started to file into the classroom. Immediately, something happened. My demeanor and attitude changed. I knew I was going to be all right, and the kids were the reason for it. That morning, I had been a man drowning in the sea in the middle of a Category 4 hurricane. But when the students came in, I saw the looks of wonder, excitement, innocence, and resiliency on their faces. It was like a buzz that was created by them just by being there. It was as if the sunshine was fighting to push away the thunderclouds—and it was succeeding

Just then, I realized I had a girl in my class who had lost her father to suicide the year before, and she was one of my most positive and bubbly students of the year. I also had twins whose parents were going through a divorce that year and were now talking about the Minnesota Wild hockey game and how they were elated that the Wild had won. Another student who came from an extremely broken home was talking to a new friend she had just made. And yet another student who had been having trouble making friends all year was staring at me with curiosity about what I was going to teach them today.

I stood a changed man . . . somewhat. My problem was life-changing, but some of these students were going through an awful lot more than I was and would face more tragedies, as we all do. I had their learning and their future in my hands at that moment. Suddenly, what I was going through shrank to insignificance. I had an important job to do—a job to help make sure these kids were safe, respected, engaged, happy, and enlightened. I'd just had a major failure in my personal life, but I didn't want to fail these students.

That day, I taught like I had never taught before. My voice was more assuring and confident, even after what I had just gone through. I also made sure I had no downtime to myself at my desk while the students worked independently. I went from desk to desk, calling up small groups and conferencing with as many students as I could during independent reading. I wanted them to be happy, and I was teaching with an emotion I never had before. They were more important to me than I had ever imagined. I didn't want them to go home that day. I would have taught them 24/7 if I had to. They were the only ones keeping me sane and happy without even knowing it.

When the students left for the day, my sadness started to seep back in. I just stood there in the classroom, watching them exit. Thoughts of losing someone I had loved were creeping back into my consciousness. I didn't want to sit at my desk to think. I didn't want to go back home to dwell on how my life had just tipped upside down. So I stayed late at work just to keep my mind off my current situation. During that time, I realized just how important teaching was to me. For those seven hours when those students were in my classroom, they made me feel important and wanted just when I had been cast off by my longtime girlfriend. I realized I needed them more than ever. My situation was a bump in the road compared to some of the things the students had been through (and would go through). I remembered one student who had witnessed his mother's death in an accident on a camping trip, the boy I taught who had lost his twin sister (whom I had also taught) in a senseless car accident, and all of the other students I had who didn't have a consistent place to call home and had to move because of the trouble that was following them.

My coworkers and I were constants for the students, and the students were constants for us. It might have been a rough year for me, but every day I drove into school, I knew I could count on the students to take my mind off the things that were going on around me.

I'm totally thankful that I was teaching during that time. I also wondered how people in other professions dealt with trauma while trying to work. I imagined having an office job and sitting there by myself, stewing and lamenting over what had just happened to me with no outlet or distraction. Maybe I would have just stared at the computer screen and tried to make sense of what I was doing. Or maybe I would have been sitting in conference meetings all day, unable to pay attention and not caring about work for weeks and months. But with teaching, I couldn't not care. I couldn't let the students down.

Chapter 24

TESTING, TESTING

A s the years of my being a reading teacher rolled on, so did changes from above that would alter the way I taught reading, whether I liked it or not.

Let's face it: school has become a performance-driven enterprise. It's not like the days when I was in school, when the attitude seemed to echo John F. Kennedy's mentality: *Ask not what your school can do for you. Ask what you can do for your school.* (Well, pretty close anyway.) We had to obey the law and the authorities in that system. Now, it's almost reversed: *Ask what your school will do for you (in achieving higher test scores).* Education is now an outcome-oriented business. School administrations— and even us teachers—compare ourselves relentlessly to other schools in how we're performing, especially in math, reading, and science. If our standardized test scores are good, that's great—but how can we score higher? And if those scores are sinking, then we need to make significant changes in how we teach. The stress can be unbearable at times.

State testing wasn't considered all that important when I started teaching. We took the MCAs, but nothing was done after that. We didn't look at the data on how we had done as a grade level, track our scores from year to year, or even look at how we compared to other school districts. We just took the tests, and that was it. We didn't do anything with the data on how well or poorly our students were doing. (Well, at least I didn't!)

Then the Bush administration arrived and introduced No Child Left Behind. It was game on from there as far as the arrival of data and analytics. For the first couple of years, I felt like there was no urgency to find out if we were successful as a school and making progress in improving student achievement on the MCAs. But then money and status got involved: money in the threat of losing funding if we didn't perform and the arrival of the Quality Compensation Program (Q Comp), and status in that we must do as well as—if not better than—our neighboring districts. As a young teacher, it took a while for me to grasp this concept of data collecting. And looking back on it, the data wasn't that specific. The MCAs were taken, and we'd see how well we had done as a district. There wasn't anything that showed how your specific class did and if you, as an educator, were creating growth in test scores with your students. I felt like I had some cover if we were falling short of growth goals because there was no way they could trace my class. But that would change later on, unfortunately.

The reward of money due to performance was most stressful to me, and it unjustly made the core classes of math and reading the targets of scrutiny throughout the school. I had trouble understanding how No Child Left Behind determined funding based on performance-based testing in each district. I was kind of oblivious to this because, in part, I knew we were pretty good as a district when it came to reading scores, since—let's face it—we were in a secure socioeconomic area and always tested well on the MCAs, whereas schools in the inner cities were constantly being threatened to be defunded because they weren't reaching their arbitrary numbers in reading and math. So No Child Left Behind was a fundamentally flawed system.

My friends in these struggling schools would comment, "Man, we are on the verge of losing all of this money, and students will be leaving this school in droves if we don't get our scores up!" I felt bad about this. I knew my friends were good teachers, and this was an unfair system. Those teachers had to put away any type of creative teaching they had and teach the students to the test. They were starting to become disillusioned because of the pressure for their students to meet state standards.

Thankfully, No Child Left Behind was abandoned, and the Every Student Succeeds Act (ESSA) was passed under the Obama administration. This was promising because the states set their own achievement levels, and it did away with the punitive measurements of No Child Left Behind. With this new law, schools could also evaluate themselves in other areas rather than just math, reading, and science scores. They could rate themselves in school safety, for example. However, our district (along with most districts across the nation) still has a huge emphasis on reading and math improvement; and depending on the school administration, the stress is still there for improvement.

This was the case for our school. Around the time ESSA was implemented, we adopted Q Comp, which had us setting up academic goals for each school. If the goal was met, the whole school was rewarded with a bonus of extra money in our paychecks. At the beginning of each year, a committee made up of teachers and administrators would come in and decide what that goal would be. It could have been in reading, math, science, or student safety. Well, it was impossible for every class to teach science or math in their curriculum to raise the school's overall test scores in those subjects, school safety was almost impossible to keep accurate data about, and the public didn't care about school safety data in our neck of the woods. They wanted the meat and potatoes of the core class data. That left reading as the only area to hinge our goals on every year. It was much easier to implement reading across the curriculum, and it was what parents were looking at when it came to how well their school district was doing. This wasn't fair for our English teachers or our, ahem, reading instructors.

I was on the committee that set this school improvement goal, and everybody else feigned interest in coming up with a different goal other than reading. They would say things like "Maybe we should have a math goal this year!" and "You know, we've had a reading goal for the past two years. Maybe we should do a behavior goal." But these goals never happened because, as I said, not everyone could implement science or math into their teaching. So reading it was, every year.

Every year, we set our reading improvement goals for the school to increase by 3 percent from the previous year's MCA test scores. For the first couple of years, we were successful, and we got our bonus of a couple of hundred bucks—which is the jackpot for us teachers! Knowing that all of the teachers got the bonus made me feel pretty good. Jokingly, I wanted to go around to everybody and ask them if they were going to buy me a round because my expertise in teaching reading had gotten them their bonus. But I knew some teachers wouldn't have taken that joke so well, especially the English teachers who were more responsible for the improvement of test scores.

But then something happened: we stopped meeting our goals. Nothing is worse than when the principal announces to the staff that we didn't reach our reading goals from the MCAs and that nobody would be getting their bonus. I felt like a disease whenever I was in those staff meetings. I wanted to slip away to the exit and escape. It was honestly hard to look at the staff and wonder if they were thinking, *What's going on in reading, Blair?! How come we didn't get our bonus?!* This was when I started to become a bit disenchanted with how the system works in a data- and performance-hungry environment. I was feeling pretty shitty about the whole deal. I wondered if I should just go back and teach social studies so that I wouldn't have to be on the hook when it came to our school reading goals.

I had a couple of theories about why scores were falling or stagnant. First, our district was already one of the top reading districts in the state, and it was kind of like the Icarus complex. We were trying to fly higher and higher to the sun, where we just kind of burned out and didn't get to where we wanted to go. Second, our testing format had changed. The MCAs went from a pencil and paper format to an all-online format. This had a dramatic effect not only on our district but also statewide. Reading on a screen for hours on end isn't conducive to reading comprehension. It's hard for students (and adults) to focus on the text and reread information that's pertinent to the questions. Finally, students (and, again, adults) are just not reading as much anymore. With social media dominating our lives, we're leaving behind sustained reading.

Even though testing and data have firmly entrenched themselves into our school system and have created a somewhat stressful work environment, I'm still committed to developing a love of reading in our students. I may not be the greatest reading teacher, but I'm lucky to have found my calling, even in today's challenging world of screen media.

Chapter 2 5

GETTING SOCIAL

W henever I meet with my friends and coworkers, we often get into the topic of social media. We lament how much time their children or our students spend on social media, all the while checking our own Instagram posts, Twitter accounts, and whatnot. Look at any time you go to a bar or restaurant. Sometimes I notice couples or families glued to their devices. It doesn't happen all the time, but it seems to be an increasing trend. One thing my coworkers and I do agree on, especially since most of us are over the age of thirty now, is that we were lucky that we didn't have social media when we were growing up.

Our version of using social media in the classroom back then was passing notes. Sometimes I'll tell my students about the days when my friends and I would pass notes, and they'll look at me like I'm some caveman who just stepped through a time portal. They're probably thinking, *You mean, you would actually have to use paper and pencil to write a secret down to pass to somebody?* Now, I'm not sure exactly how I would have gotten in trouble with social media back then. I probably would have taken a compromising picture of a friend and spread it around on Instagram or some other platform. If I wasn't going to get in trouble with the school, I was surely going to get in trouble with my mom. So thank heavens we didn't have it!

When my friends and I hit high school, especially in our senior year, we were introduced to email. Some of us scoffed at the idea of sending a message online when you could just call someone to talk. But once we were in college, we discovered email's benefits, especially the capability of emailing more than one recipient at a time. Mind-blowing!

By the time my friends and I were at the end of our college careers, the first signs of social media other than email (if you consider that social media) started to pop up. Obviously, widespread cell phone usage wasn't happening at that time, so everything revolved around the clunky desktop computer. I vaguely remember one social media site that was called Hot or Not, where people would post pictures of themselves and you'd rate them as "hot" or "not." My roommates and I had a fun time trolling that site. In fact, a photo of one of my roommates became almost a cult classic while we were discovering the term viral. He racked up 9s and 10s with this ridiculous picture of his—and he was ugly as sin!

HERE TO STAY

By the time I got into teaching, social media was starting to grow up. The first real site was Myspace. We look back and kind of laugh at it now, but it was a revolution, especially for the younger generation. I didn't have Myspace, which was a social networking site where people could post their favorite music or photos. But many of my friends did, and my new students were starting to get into it as well. I remember the students asking to follow one another on their Myspace accounts. I even saw the first signs of social media fighting when a student wouldn't let another student follow their account (or however it went back then). Those incidents were few and far between, though, because no students had access to a cell phone at that time. And as Myspace was picking up steam, so was another site that would come to dominate our social landscape: Facebook.

I remember Facebook starting to make its way to our students (and everyone else) in the middle of the first decade of the twenty-first century. By this time, probably 20 percent of students had cell phones, which were by and large flip phones. I had my own at the time, and BlackBerry phones were fancy back then. You couldn't have any screen time on these phones yet, but they were becoming more advanced. Students and adults alike still had to rely on desktop computers for their social media. But students were now more engaged with Facebook; and I think the reason for this was that they had more immediate access through the use of their computers, whereas there was only one phone per household. This was the students' first crack at forming an online community with their friends. They desperately wanted to become friends with one another on this social site, sort of in the same way Myspace was used.

Full disclosure: I have, to this day, never subscribed to Facebook—except for one time because of a subscription to something for my reading courses, and it took me forever to delete my account. I have all the friends I need here, although other friends get annoyed if I miss out on information from other friends that was only posted on Facebook. I don't want to know everything about everyone!

YouTube also came out during this time, but it took a little bit longer to grab hold of the students' attention. Nobody had sufficient knowledge at that time to be creative enough to post videos on that website. There wasn't any real talk about it. But that was about to change with the iPhone.

When the iPhone came, it changed the game completely. By the end of the decade, students were still reliant on their Nokias or used flip phones. (For adults, I remember the Motorola Razr phone being the popular choice.) But then a friend of mine got the first iPhone, and we were blown away with all the phone's apps and Internet capabilities. At that time, we had no idea what a game changer this would be for society—and even for education.

We didn't see students with iPhones until after 2010. Once the first students brought them in, it was game over. A student would come marching in, saying, "I got the new iPhone!" and all the other students would gather around to look at it. Since we're in a well-to-do district, whenever a student brings in a flashy new piece of technology, invariably there will be other students who will request the novel object from their parents—and then more and more will invade the school. This was the case with the iPhone, as well as the Samsungs and the Motorolas. But the crème de la crème was the iPhone. Students who didn't have one were subject to phone shaming, especially if they had an outdated version. Even I was shamed for my iPhone 3 when my students were coming in with the iPhone 5. When smartphones infiltrated our schools, the social media boom really hit.

At first, Facebook was still the rage early in the 2010s because of its gaming options. Students (and adults) were preoccupied with games like

FarmVille and *World of Warcraft*. We started having issues with students bringing in their phones and trying to sneak in playing while school was going on. For some kids, this became a time when it was more important for a sneak attack on a village through their phones than actually passing their science class. We didn't have policies in place (and even today, we still struggle) to deal with students and their overreliance on smartphones. At that time, we thought gaming was bad.

Then came a social media platform that really blew it up. Snapchat came completely out of nowhere for us teachers. I don't even know how it got started, other than some college student made it up for a class—and became an instant millionaire. Before Snapchat, students didn't spend time on Facebook because of its complexity, and Twitter wasn't quite their thing because of its mass following and how it required reading and typing. With Snapchat, though, you could take photos or videos and send them off easily with a quick caption to a more focused group of friends. Best of all, these photos would disappear after ten seconds. Now we had a problem.

A few students were using Snapchat with devious intentions, and there would be reports from parents about harassment and the like. In the classroom, I was having difficulty getting my students to put those damn phones away! As a school, we didn't have a clear policy because some teachers would have their students use their phones for their lessons. This would create confusion and haughtiness from the students who were forced to put their phones away, because they would say, "Well, Mr. So-and-So lets us use them!" I had to have a strict policy on phones especially during my reading classes, where we relied heavily on print paper. This was an ongoing problem for me. Sometimes I would collect up to three phones per class period because students would be trying to secretly use them.

Boy, those students would try any means possible to hide their screen activity during class. The classic move was to rest their phone on their lap, where it would be visually blocked by their desktop. The greatest tell would be them staring down at their lap for minutes on end, with their hands underneath the desk. Usually, I would just stare at the student until they noticed I wasn't talking anymore, and then they would find me (along with the whole class) staring at them. The jig would be up then.

Another classic maneuver would be during independent reading time. I liked my students to get up and move to wherever they wanted to be comfortable during independent reading. The only places they couldn't go were out in the pod outside the classroom (unless a couple of students were reading the same book and wanted to read aloud to each other) or under my desk. Some of the sly students would try to get to a corner of the room where they would have their book and would hold it up like they were reading, only to have the phone hiding inside the book. During this time, I would try to conference with my students, but I would also get up to observe readers between conferences. As soon as I approached these corner-dwellers, they would become uneasy in their body language—and lo and behold, their phone would be uncovered. Another score for the teacher!

Sometimes things would get so bad that our class would have a frank conversation about cell phone usage. I would admit that if I was their age, I also would have a problem with this. I would also tell the students about phone addiction and how adults can be the same way, but how we had to recognize situations where we could and could not use them. I would then try to apply real-world situations for norms on using cell phones. Most of the time, it would work. But then the lesson would wear off, and we would have to revisit it another day.

By the end of the 2010s, a new social media platform had come to life: TikTok. I first found out what this was from a student in my reading interventions class who was obsessed with it. This student, Rashad, had major reading deficiencies (more specifically, a second-grade reading level). He was one student we were trying to get identified for special education pronto. He was failing all of his classes and was struggling on the social interaction front. Rashad was incredibly emotional and would switch from being extremely happy to confrontational with another student in the blink of an eye. He also tried to be the jester, entertainer, and center of attention in all of his classes. So TikTok was the social media outlet he was craving. Rashad loved to dance, and he would come into the classroom to show me all of his dancing videos on TikTok. I had no idea what TikTok was, though. I thought it was just this fringe social media site. (It even reminded me of the old Vine GIFs that were around a few years back.) But I was wrong.

Within the next two years, TikTok exploded. Gone was Snapchat. All of the students were watching other people's dance routines and music videos, among other things. It's amusing to watch a trio of students doing some sort of dance routine. Sometimes they even try to get us teachers into the mix, but I'm an old wet rag and won't embarrass myself over it.

There are teachers who are innovative and know how to incorporate social media platforms like TikTok into the classroom and use it for their curriculum. Some use this medium to produce videos to explain concepts they're teaching in the classroom. During the COVID-19 pandemic, a friend of mine used TikTok to connect with students and lighten up their day, since they had been stuck in the house for so long. I do believe that social media can be used in positive ways for students. However, I have trouble convincing myself of its necessity. I'm an old-fashioned Twitter guy; I just want my headlines for news and quips from my comedians.

Social media is obviously here to stay, especially with our students. I can't blame them for reaching out to it. In fact, social media can help students who are having trouble socially to find an outlet to relate to and not feel alone. But it also has its obvious downsides of bullying and shaming other students. I'm always pining for the world before social media, but we have to deal with it. It's important to take interest in what students are using for social media, just to know what's going on and how it's affecting them socially and academically. It's also up to us teachers to use social media for teachable moments on how students can appropriately use it, as they may not be getting that at home.

Chapter 26

TECH SUPPORT!

A s social media has advanced and seeped its way into our education system, the technology it relies on has also been changing at warp speed. I'm always trying my hardest to keep up with the changes so that I don't look like a complete caveman in front of my peers. But at times, it can be a little overwhelming. It's amazing to see how far we've come with using technology in comparison to when I was in school.

WHO NEEDS MARKERS ANYMORE?

By the time I started teaching full-time, I still used the projector quite a bit, as the curriculum we were using for language arts and social studies had premade transparencies to be used along with the instruction. However, as I stated earlier, I was starting to find out that PowerPoint was much more visually appealing to the students. I could get more detailed pictures from the Internet and copy-paste them onto slides! Also, the power of the "Transition" effect on PowerPoint slides was (and still is) my jam. I know this sounds prehistoric, but this was revolutionary for us teachers at the beginning of this century. This also meant not having to clean those damn transparency sheets at the end of every class.

The next evolutionary technological piece that eventually buried the old projector and transparency sheets was the smart board. If you don't know what a smart board is, it's a six-by-four-foot board that is connected to and displays what's on your desktop computer screen. You can also control what's on your computer by touching the board, and you can draw on the board with different colored smart board pens. I think we started to get them in 2006, when we moved from the elementary school to the middle school. At the time, the boards had everything I needed. I also had (and still have) two projectors: one for the smart board, and one for the regular whiteboard. They were great for projecting my texts. I didn't have to rely on the hope that students could see where I was on the reading. They could follow along easily with the smart board, as I could go from page to page and underline important text. Also, students liked to draw on the text to show what they were talking about during our discussions.

Some of the teachers became wizards with the smart board. Within the program setup with the smart board were many games and ways to manipulate the board that would fit your curriculum. I didn't have the patience to work with all the bells and whistles; I just wanted to show what I had on my computer (which was mainly graphic organizers) so that I or another student could write on the board. Basically, it was my big transparency sheet. I've finally started to use some of the smart board's updated programs for my reading students, though, as they do have pretty good items for phonics work, multisyllabic practice, and Greek and Latin root work. The smart board has programmed games where you can slide the correct prefix to the base word and make it into a game-type setting. The students are much more inclined to be manipulating the smart board rather than practicing or copying down notes. That's not to say that I've completely abandoned having the students take notes, though.

Here Comes the Tech Devil

As the smart boards firmly entrenched themselves into the school culture, the speed of technology started to pick up. Students could now have their own devices at their fingertips. And now there are enough desktop computers for all classes if you schedule things wisely and don't wait until the last minute. If you can't sign up for them, then not to worry, since the school also has laptops that can cover roughly a third of the student population—and that number is increasing. Students are also being supplied with their very own iPads now. So there's no excuse for students not having enough technology at their disposal, at least in our district. I do know there are districts out there that lack the technology for students to keep up, but that's just it. Are we relying on tech too much? In my humble opinion, I think we are.

Around 2011, we started to hand out iPads to each of our eighth-grade students for a one-to-one initiative. At first, as a reading teacher, I thought this was going to be great. I felt like students were becoming so reliant on their devices that they might start reading more on their iPad rather than complaining about reading a good, old-fashioned book. Hell, even I was reading *A Game of Thrones* on my iPad at the time.

Our school gave reading with the iPad a good effort. The librarian, Gina, and I found a virtual library where students could check out books to read on their devices. There was a problem with this online library, however. First of all, there weren't nearly as many choices as the students had in their own library. I would say the virtual library had about a tenth of the books compared to what the school library had— and that's a generous estimation. Not only that, but most of the books weren't even that current. It was difficult for students to find something that they could relate to on that system, which was the leading virtual library at the time. Plus, whenever there was a book checked out by a student on the virtual library system, another student couldn't check out the same book. I thought that the point was to have unlimited access if we could digitize a library! The students were quickly getting fed up with it, and so was I.

Another problem was the lack of free books on the web that students could download to their iPads. I ignorantly assumed that there would be a treasure trove of books available to them. Well, it turns out that this thing called property rights needs to expire for a book to become eligible for free reading online. Those books are generally classics that are over 100 years old. You can imagine my students' unbridled excitement at finding out that *Civil Disobedience* by Henry David Thoreau was free to read!

Since books that interested my students had to be bought online, the students would take the time during independent reading to shop for books (if they even had the means to buy them). This would be immensely frustrating, as they would pretty much take up the whole time looking for a particular book. Let's face it: it was a good excuse to look for books and not do any of the reading.

Also, students were learning to manipulate the system with their iPads. They would pretend to have a book to read, go off into a corner of the room, and proceed to watch whatever YouTube video or video game they could discreetly play.

I felt defeated by the iPads. What I thought would be progress in students' education, especially in reading, was actually the opposite. The students were showing less motivation to read than in all my time as a teacher, and I felt like there was no way I could change course. I even tried several methods to get the students to independently read. First, I stopped letting the students move around the room and had them put their iPads on the desk so I could see them. I also had the students write the page numbers they started and stopped on. (This was too easy to manipulate.)

This type of reading in the class wasn't conducive to learning. I still needed to conference students during independent reading, so this method was easily manipulated by the students. I would then confiscate iPads from students if they were using the devices inappropriately. But this just made me feel like a cop. Also, I didn't want to have massive complaints from students who were caught using their iPads inappropriately. This wasn't what I was paid to do. It was to a point where I didn't want to do independent reading anymore. The students were also getting annoyed with the restrictions. They felt like they were getting unfairly punished when others were breaking the rules.

The only solution I had was to educate students about why I felt like the iPads were constraining their learning. So I decided to do some research on the effects of reading on a screen compared to an actual print book—and I found ammunition. There were published reports on how students fared better in reading on paper rather than on a screen. For example, students can recall information they read on paper better than what they read on a screen. This made sense to me, since when we are reading a book and need to recall information we may have forgotten, we can page back to where we generally know the forgotten information can be found. But on a tablet, most of us don't have the spatial memory to swipe back to the page where we lost certain information.

Students (and adults) are also more distracted when reading from a tablet. They tend to start reading, then remember they can quickly check out something online with just a click of the button. There are also notifications that pop up on their screens that seem to scream, Click on me! The user may have good intentions to go back to their reading, but that may never happen. With a print book, they don't have that option.

Another benefit of reading on paper, I found, was motivation. When we start reading a book, we get to visually see how far we've read and how close we are to finishing it. So we generally know how long it will take to finish a book. My students would be more excited about coming to the end of the book after seeing how little they had left to read. They always liked to show their book with how far they had read. But when it comes to tablet reading, you can see the number of pages that you've read. But for the students, it was hard to physically know just how much that was. It didn't motivate them enough to finish the reading.

I also read information about eye tracking for digital reading compared to reading on paper and found out about the F-pattern. If we're on a digital device, our eyes typically scan the top of the page of the text, then scan largely the left side of the screen (sort of in an F-shape), leaving out important information we could read. This hampers linear reading, which is the capability to read all the way across a text, line by line. This pattern happens less often in paper reading.

After doing this research, I was ready to present to the students why we had to go back to paper reading. I put this information in a Power-Point presentation—because what better way to teach this concept than on a screen!

After I taught the lesson, I felt an unexpected relief. Most of the students agreed that the iPads were getting in the way of their learning. "I don't like the iPad because we don't really have that many choices, and the notifications start to bug me," one student said. They all agreed that reading on paper or print books was easier than reading on the screen. They also noted that they liked to know where they were in their book and see they were making progress or close to done with reading it, as opposed to not knowing exactly where they were when reading on an iPad. However, they didn't agree with my F-pattern theory. I don't blame them; I didn't, either, when I'd first read about it. But now I'm constantly aware of it when I'm reading digitally.

We soon ditched the iPad reading for books, unless a student needed it for visual purposes. I noticed then that my students were much more engaged with their books and more settled in their reading than when they had been reading on their iPads. That's not to say that this process went swimmingly. Students, just like adults, are preoccupied with their screens; and it was hard for some of them to give the iPad up just for independent reading. I did have some students who were legit reading on a screen, like a Kindle, where the screen mimicked the softness of a paper page to the eyes, and there wouldn't be any notifications. Sometimes I would allow this, but I would still try to guide those students to regular books.

Now, I'm not saying that the iPad is a thing of evil and that all screens should be thrown into the abyss. (Well, maybe cell phones. . . .) But I do rely on iPads in my class. I'm not totally from the 1930s. iPad usage has been beneficial in cutting down on magazine copies and provides an efficient way for students to write notes, work on graphic organizers, and type up discussion points for other students to read and comment on, among other things. There's no stopping tech!

THE CURMUDGEON OF TECH

That deluge of technology can lead us astray today. We have hundreds, if not thousands, of different ways to teach, assign, grade, and meet through technology. It can all be a little overwhelming for teachers, including myself.

When I was going through my first few years of teaching, technology was advancing at a rapid pace. Some teachers (or maybe most) thought that the students were different than we had been when we were growing up, which is true because of our obvious lack of technology during that time. We also started to think that students were wired differently because they grew up reading and manipulating screens (rather than sticking fingers into electrical outlets like we had) and that we needed to get the students prepared for the technological age when they graduated. In my opinion, it was to a point that if we didn't introduce a lesson using the latest form of teaching technology, we feared that we were holding our students back and they would be left behind by the more technologically advanced students after graduation.

I was feeling the pressure of this as a teacher. It got to a point where I thought I was punishing the students by asking them to read from an actual book and not incorporating any type of technology into my classes. I was afraid of being typecast as the teacher who would never incorporate the latest teaching methods and would only teach the same method for the next twenty-five years. There was this pressure, I felt, that if we didn't load up our students on the latest technology, they would be coming out of high school like prehistoric people and couldn't compete in the new tech world.

It took a professor of technology to help me realize that it's okay not to shove all sorts of tech down our students' throats. This professor made us teachers realize that students are not wired all that differently from us. They don't have a technological advantage over us because it's all about training. We, as adults, are perfectly capable of learning new technological skills just as easily as students who have prior experience with the skill we're learning. For example, in getting myself up to speed with video recordings and streaming for distant learning during the COVID-19 pandemic, I learned more about technology than I cared to know. I became proficient in just a few hours (or days) at the most. Translate that to our students. Of course, they need to learn the rudimentary tech that's important for everyday life at our schools. But do they have to have virtual reality, social media, or the latest interactive apps in every lesson we teach? Technology will most likely have changed by the time they hit the real world anyway, and students will have to learn a whole new system that may not resemble anything they were exposed to in our teachings.

This is where I'm proud to be a curmudgeon of a teacher. Why are we so concerned with showing off how we're teaching the latest technological learning gadgets when there's no real research that shows they're advancing students' reading, writing, or mathematical skills? I'm proud to have my students read regular papers and print documents and books. I consider it an honor to watch students fight their way through concentration lapses to understand the strategies they're using for reading. I feel like this is the real work that helps us identify where students are in their learning process. If I just used fun reading apps or relied on an online curriculum, I would never really know how a student processes their thoughts or exactly how much reading help they need due to an unnoticed reading disability. And no, I'm not shutting out new technology. I just feel like we need to pump the brakes and go back to basics. But unfortunately, as I stated, the COVID-19 pandemic forced our hand with alternative teaching strategies.

Chapter 27

THE PANDEMIC

I have to admit, I didn't know a whole lot about pandemics before 2020 hit us like a loaded freight train of dynamite. I was aware of books like *Fever 1793* and the endless dystopian novels like *The Eleventh Plague*. I also remember when the US had the H1N1 influenza pandemic in 2009, but it never registered as anything too dangerous. If someone got the flu during that time, we joked that they had H1N1, but we never felt like it would kill anybody we knew or even make its way to our community. It came and went as just a bad flu season, it seemed.

Then came the Ebola epidemic in 2014. For some reason, I felt like the public was terrified of this because of the horrific symptoms patients exhibited when they contracted it. We were watching the horror stories unfold in Africa and thought about what would happen if this reached our shores—and then it did! The news cycle seemed to be on full coverage of the virus as if it were spreading like wildfire (even though in the end, only a couple of people died of it in the United States). Still, it was enough for me to grab reading material and use it for my reading classes. My students were generally interested in how it could spread and were curious about whether it would make its way here.

Neither of these outbreaks were what I imagined an epidemic or a pandemic would be like. They came and went without significant damage to human life or the economy. I felt like our science community was up to the task of squashing any type of viral pandemic, so I never thought our lives would be altered by anything. Sure, we would probably get more of those H1N1 types or another Ebola scare. But it wasn't like we were living in the medieval era, where we were going to get a raging plague and people would just spit up black bile and convulse right there on the sidewalk. I mean, our government leaders and

Health and Human Services work hand in hand to make sure we swiftly contain these viruses, right?

Well, I guess I was wrong in assuming that, and so were many of my colleagues during the winter of 2020.

ARE WE IN A BAD MOVIE?

I remember hearing about a viral outbreak happening in China some-time during January of that year. At the time, I didn't think much of it. My awful stereotypical thinking—which was along the lines of, *Well, there always seems to be this weird viral breakout in China, but they'll get it under control and it won't amount to much here, anyway*—was off the mark on this occasion. It wasn't until later that month that the country started to notice it was coming to our shores. My colleagues and I still didn't think too much of this, as we were hearing it was nothing more than just a really bad flu, and we thought that this was going to be contained right away.

But when the entire city of Wuhan had to be quarantined and the pandemic started to ravage Europe, most of us started to watch more intently from the sidelines. Then the virus started to spread throughout the West Coast and seemed to slip through the back door and hit the East Coast. This was now something I wasn't familiar with. We started hearing about massive death counts coming from places like Italy and the surrounding European countries, and air travel was shut down for the first time since 9/11. My coworkers and I, along with our students, were starting to wonder if this was seriously going to impact us.

The virus continued its spread, it seemed, at an uncontrolled wildfire pace. The country watched as New York City turned into what seemed like one of those dystopian pandemic novels, with hospitals being over-run by the sick and dying. By early February, the US was in a declared state of health emergency.

Still, my coworkers and I kept on teaching as if we were going to complete the school year. I didn't have any notion that we would be closing schools, but then I started to hear terms like "community spread" and "pandemic status." The virus had reached our state, and we were starting to accumulate cases. Now my colleagues and I were seriously wondering if we were going to finish the school year, as many schools around the country had started closing. At first, we thought we might only close for a week or two—not the whole year—in hopes that the virus would subside. But, of course, it didn't.

By early March, my coworkers and I knew it would only be a matter of time before our school district would be shutting down. We were speculating on what was going to happen, as we were noticing schools across America starting to shutter and attempt to go into a long-distance learning format. Students were even starting to ask us if we were going to shut down. It felt imminent. The question was, how long would we be shut down?

Teaching during this confusion was surreal. My coworkers and I had never taught during an impending pandemic, and it was difficult to tell the students what was going to happen because we didn't know. I went along with my normal plans of reading interventions. Everything was going along fine, but I couldn't shake my worry about what would happen to my students if we were to shut down the school.

The strange thing about this pandemic, especially during March, was that we never felt threatened from where we were. It was ravaging the East and West Coasts, and it seemed to only attack the elderly. But again, we were starting to see the virus make its way into middle America, and we knew it was only a matter of time before it would hit us.

"Are we going to shut down?" was the question I would receive from my students as we were going over our reading lessons. I didn't want to be an alarmist, so I told my students that I didn't think so. However, my feelings were the opposite of what I was telling them.

By late March, the virus was here, and Minnesota started shutting down its schools. I remember when my coworkers and I got the call to close down. In a way, it kind of felt like a snow day. I honestly thought we would figure something out and be back in the building shortly. However, schools were closing up for weeks at a time, and we announced that we would be out for two weeks. Eventually, like the rest of the schools across the country, we closed for in-person learning for the rest of the year. My coworkers and I suspected that this would have happened eventually. Nonetheless, we were shocked. Now we had to figure out a way to reach our students remotely, and nobody had any experience with how to do it.

A Real-Life Milton Waddams

Right away, our district gave me and my coworkers a week with no contact with our students to get remote learning up and running. This was a cram session for us and our teams to get together and figure out what tech tools they were going to use to reach out to their students. In the meantime, the district administration was trying to figure out how to make sure all students had access to their teachers and what the expectations would be for teachers to reach out to their students.

As for me, I was lost in the shuffle. Since I was now a full-time reading specialist without a class and I met with my students only three times a week, I was not a priority. I was just a teacher who saw students for twenty minutes at a time during what wasn't a graded class. I knew I was stuck between a rock and a hard place. Students were now expected to learn a whole new way from teachers who had to learn a whole new way of teaching. These kids were going to be overwhelmed, along with the teachers; and I felt like if I demanded that my intervention students get served, it would be throwing another monkey wrench in the process of trying to make this work.

I wasn't the only one who was in the sea of despair. Worse off were our SPED students. They had IEPs that were bound by law to get the specialized education they deserved, and that was now out the window. Our SPED teachers didn't know how they would serve their students, and the district was also trying to figure this out. This put me even lower on the totem pole, as it was necessary to find a way to service our SPED students.

Regular classroom teachers were busy meeting with their departments to figure out new ways to reach out to their students, who were now going to complete the rest of the year learning remotely. Our line of work, along with every other job that had never dealt with working from home, was caught with its pants down. We didn't have the resources or the infrastructure to sufficiently reach all of our students adequately, but it wasn't due to a lack of trying. This was happening all across the nation.

My coworkers and I had to become tech gurus in communications overnight. We had to find every resource available to teach our lessons and make sure students were responding to the teaching and the lessons. Quickly, we (along with everyone else around the world) would get familiar with videoconferencing through Zoom. For myself, I found it fairly simple to use the videoconferencing platform, as did most teachers. Eventually, we would use Google Meet, as there were some technical loopholes involved with Zoom at the time.

Once videoconferencing was nailed down, my coworkers then had to figure out how to get their lessons available for all students online. They would by and large use our learning management system (LMS) Schoology, where they would have to reorganize their online pages to make them remote-learning friendly. Homework and videos of their lessons would have to be uploaded in a way that would be easily accessible for all students. I observed as other teachers found several mediums to record themselves to get their lessons out.

As for me, I was still languishing in educational purgatory. The priority was to get the students in contact with their primary teachers and make sure they just got the minimum amount done to be successful in this new normal. I was initially told to help the English teachers with anything that needed to be done regarding reading. I felt like this suggestion was just something to make me feel like I had something to do. Frankly, the administration didn't know what to do with me at that point—and I didn't blame them! I didn't even know what to do with myself. The last thing that other classroom teachers wanted to do was deal with me. They were just concerned about getting their classes up and running. In my futile attempts to work with teachers, I would say, "Hey, if anyone needs any help with reading online, let me know! I'm totally available!"

"Okay!" they would reply. "Thanks, Blair! We'll let you know." And I would nod back, knowing I was most likely not going to have any takers.

So there I was, sitting on the sidelines, waiting and trying to find something to do that would be helpful. Being the only full-time reading interventionist in middle school was awfully frustrating and lonely. I had nobody to work with, which made it difficult to bounce ideas off anybody. There was no prior situation like this to fall back on and use. My other interventionist colleagues were only part-time and were more concerned about working with their English departments, which was understandable. I would sit in on department meetings, but there was no way that my ideas of meeting with my intervention students would be considered, since most of the students were having a hard enough time doing well in school in the first place, let alone spending more time in online learning.

After a week of workshops, the time came when it was no longer safe for us teachers to even be congregating in the schools. So we would be working from home from then on, along with the rest of the nation. Thankfully, after that week of getting everything set up for our students, the other teachers were somewhat ready to teach remotely from home. However, now that we were relegated to our homes, I was really cast off into the abyss.

And so all of my coworkers and I were stuck within the walls of our homes. As for me, I had no students to reach out to. Since I'm a reading interventionist, my students are not graded in my classes. We only worry about the progress they're making on state tests and other assessments we take. Well, the state's department of education can-celed our state assessments, and there was no way we could perform our own assessments in reading. So I was thinking to myself, *What's the purpose of my position for the rest of the school year?*

I felt embarrassed and useless by this, like I was going to be ridi-culed for not having anything to do. I was convinced that my coworkers would think, *Wait! We're working our asses off, setting up online learning, while you're just sitting there with nothing to do!* And that was where my sense of uselessness would come in. I felt like a boxer with no arms. I was racking my brain to figure out how I could participate in any type of teaching.

As for my coworkers, they were told to only teach about 50 percent of what they would normally teach for the school year, because we didn't know if the students were even going to keep up. Parents now had to be the helpers, and this was a significant challenge for students who were coming from a single-parent home. I was tentative about asking if there was a way to get my students to meet with me during the week. If teachers were going to seriously cut out that much of their curriculum so that students wouldn't be overloaded, it wouldn't make any sense if I was going to add work back in by having students meet with me for extra reading. I even asked the school administration, "What would you like me to do with my reading students?" I was told not to worry about that for the moment, though, so I was essentially shot down. The administration didn't want to put any more work on the students; and in a way, they were right in that decision.

So I had to sit at home and try to figure out a way so that at least I could still be seen and somewhat earn my paycheck. I went about creating folders for my intervention students' Schoology accounts and tried to get them to practice on our reading learning site, IXL. In this system, students were given practice reading questions that would ultimately chart their growth, and then they'd be prescribed more questions based on their growth. (Whoopee!) During the rest of the pandemic, only three out of my forty or so students attempted to get more practice in using IXL, and they probably averaged thirty minutes total for the four months we were away from school. It wasn't working at all. Again, I was feeling defeated. Every time I logged in to the site to see if there was, by chance, any significant reading going on, there was no progress.

I made another attempt to reach my students by recording read-alouds and posting questions to get a discussion on a topic. I would read short nonfiction and fiction stories that would be of high interest to my students. First of all, I had to become an expert at using iMovie, which wasn't as easy as I thought it would be. I first wanted my read-alouds to be a news report type of broadcast. I wanted to read the article and have visual clips that went along with the article inserted in the video. This took forever for me to cut and edit those visuals. Then, once I was finished, I would watch what I had put in—and found that the visuals would only be up for a second. So I had to do it all over again! Finally, when I was finished, I had to export the video to my files—and that would also take forever! A fifteen-minute read-aloud was taking me two hours to produce. I was spittin' mad!

After posting two read-aloud videos during the first two weeks, I was kind of excited to see if they would gain any traction. But they didn't. All that time I had spent messing with iMovie, and I only got one comment from the prompt! I still had to make myself feel like I was contributing, so I continued doing the online read-alouds—but now in costumes. I figured I had to find a creative way to get the students into some form of reading comprehension. So I first dressed up as a pirate, with an eyepatch, a wig of long hair, and the closest thing I could find to a pirate shirt. I also dressed up as a rocker (I even played my lousy guitar, dammit!), a beachcomber with a sun hat and a Hawaiian shirt, and a billionaire in a suit and tie and with my hair slicked back. (That one was pathetic.) I had fun doing it, but I was still getting absolutely nothing in terms of discussion posts from the students. I didn't know if I was even getting any views on the videos. Again, I was rather dispirited.

But it turned out that I wasn't the only teacher who was having trouble getting students to engage in their learning and complete their assignments. Every once in a while, I would have a chance to Google Meet with some of my coworkers, and they also expressed concerns about having major issues getting a hold of students during that time. We had a massive number of students who had just fallen off the map completely—and these weren't just our struggling students, but also straight-A students. It was so bad that our administration pretty much told us to pass them if they completed only 10 percent of their assignments. It was something we teachers never would have thought we would have had to do in our careers. Not only that, but other teachers were reporting rampant cheating. I don't blame the students entirely for this. If I had been their age, I would have totally tried to gain advantage over the system as well. I would have either been at the house of a friend who was smarter than me and ridden his coattails or asked for payment to help other students cheat. (Probably the former, since no friend would have trusted me to do their homework for cash.)

THE REAL EMOTIONAL COSTS

There was also the issue of parents who had to be at work because they were essential workers, so they couldn't monitor what was going on with their child's online learning. These students in particular struggled, especially if they came from a single-parent home and had to be with grandparents or other members of the extended family who might not have known the ins and outs of the child's curriculum. At one point, I heard a heartbreaking story from Carrie after she had done a Google Meet with a student. The boy broke down crying, because he was at his grandma's and she couldn't help him that much, and also because he missed his friends. As I talked to Carrie about this on the phone one day after school, she was pretty emotional about it. So was I, since I knew this student and he was such a great kid.

The emotional toll of being separated from peer contact was real for most of these students. Our district and many others across the country were trying their best to provide child care services for students who didn't have parents at home during the day. But it was impossible to meet the needs of all of our students during a pandemic.

TROUBLE AT HOME

Opinions were also coming in fast and hard from parents about the new normal of remote learning. As I talked to my coworkers, they said that some parents had expressed that they now understood what teachers had to go through with their children. Some parents realized that their kids were not as intelligent as they had assumed and found that they had to spend a significant amount of time trying to teach their children at home. Some parents even discovered that maybe the teacher was right about their child not being motivated in class and missing assignments, or that the teacher wasn't losing their homework all the time as their child had claimed before. There was a new appreciation from parents for what teachers endured daily, and now they couldn't wait for their child to go back to school. I even started to see hilarious memes of parents drinking wine to soothe their nerves while working with their children.

There were also parents who were extremely frustrated with the whole process. One of my best friends was part of this group. He couldn't stand the way teachers were posting their assignments in their LMSs. He would complain about having to go on to Seesaw to look at the assignment, then go to YouTube to find a video of the lesson, then go onto another LMS to complete the assignment, only to find an email on yet another LMS that the assignment wasn't due.

WASTED YEAR

By the end of the school year, it seemed that we'd had a complete educational system failure. Again, the entire planet had had its way of life upended, but we teachers were especially frustrated about how we couldn't properly teach our students.

By the time June hit, I honestly felt like I had already been on three months of summer break. I know that may be horrible to say, but I felt as if I hadn't done anything worthwhile to advance any student's reading skills. Sure, I had made some more read-alouds and monitored IXL, but those were hardly picked up by any of my students, no matter my pleas and reminders on our Schoology email system. I know there will be armchair quarterback teachers out there who would have found a way to reach those students, but I just felt like I was lost in the middle of a pandemic hurricane in which I had no other tools available to me. Maybe I hadn't been creative enough. I just felt hopeless.

I was constantly getting friendly jibes from my coworkers about how nice it must have been to sleep in. They would ask me what was on TV, if I had taken a nap that day, or if I had gone golfing or to the beach. I know it was all fun and games, but deep down inside I felt like I wasn't part of the staff anymore. I was kind of like that guy Milton in the movie *Office Space*; I just kind of sat there, and people wondered what exactly I was doing. I was half expecting to have a boss drop me an email and demote me to the boiler room the following school year when we started teaching in person again.

I would sit there, listening to my teacher friends as we talked during our Google Meet happy hours, saying how they were staring at their computer screens for ten straight hours, answering hundreds of emails a day, creating Google Meets every hour, and making video lessons on the spot to help students who were having trouble understanding lessons. I often heard about how they were busier with teaching remotely than they had been at the brick-and-mortar school. They often found themselves up late at night, helping a student either academically or emotionally. I was frustrated that I couldn't share their misery in this environment—and that's the truth. I didn't feel like a teacher at all.

Finally, the real summer break hit, and I didn't have to worry about pretending to work for the time being. Usually, whenever the summer started, both students and teachers would celebrate with a sense of accomplishment now that their students could move on, and we teachers would have a chance to take a breath. We would often have several staff celebrations at teachers' residences or at restaurants, too. But since restaurants were closed then, we just had a small get-together at a coworker's house. It didn't even seem like an end-of-the-year party, because we didn't have any good memories to look back on.

My coworkers and I were still in a state of uncertainty as well, because we didn't know what to expect for the upcoming school year. Were we going to teach in person? Were we going to have this so-called hybrid learning system that we had been hearing about? Or were we going to go back to remote learning again? We just didn't know as the summer started. We had nothing to look forward to. We weren't talking about upcoming classes we were expecting, what challenges they may represent, or how fun they would be to teach. We didn't have any idea about what we were going to do to change our teaching for the upcoming year. We were just kind of sitting there in a distance circle, drinking our beverages, lamenting distance learning, and asking what-if questions the whole time.

After we went our separate ways for the rest of the summer, there was nothing to look forward to. It was as if I was staring into the never-ending expanse of the desert for my summer break. I also had a summer job with the Minnesota Twins—and they obviously weren't going to be playing with any fans in the stadium, so there was no work for us. This didn't hit me as hard as others who had lost their main job and source of income. In fact, this made me feel lucky that I had my teaching career.

As the summer plodded along, there was no word on what was going to come. Debates were raging on TV over what the government should do about school openings for the upcoming year. On one side was President Donald Trump, who was all "Damn the torpedoes!" and wanted everything to open back up regardless of the immense health risks of COVID-19 spreading like wildfire. On the other side were the doctors and epidemiologists who were warning against a full opening of schools.

The problem with President Trump and his push to reopen schools was not only that it wasn't rooted in science and the medical advice from top doctors, but also that it was influencing a loud minority of the public. The argument we heard was, "Well, children rarely get sick from COVID-19. So what's the big deal about opening the schools?" It was as if people didn't understand that teachers may have someone living at home who has a health condition that makes them susceptible to going to the hospital and even dying from the virus.

One of my coworkers, who lives down the street from me, was going on leave, since she had a compromised mother-in-law living at home. Hell, even if we didn't have somebody like that who lived at home, we had to be careful about going to visit our elderly relatives. Not only that, but if one teacher tested positive for COVID-19, then we had to contact trace everybody who had come in contact with that teacher, regardless of whether they were symptomatic. Then, when teachers who had come in contact with the first teacher also tested positive, we would have an emergency where we wouldn't have enough substitute teachers to cover those classrooms for two weeks.

I realized that my friends who were giving me a hard time about not going back to school (again) were the ones who were working from home but also had their kids with them, so they were itching for them to go back to school. Some friends who did work away from home could socially distance themselves from their coworkers using their office space. I often told them to imagine having fifteen students crammed into their office for at least six hours, then asked them to tell me how to stop the virus. They usually didn't have anything to say after that.

On the other hand, I could see why it was vital to go back to school, and that was for mental health reasons. I was losing it myself, being cooped up in my house. I couldn't imagine what it was like for students who need peer interaction.

By midsummer, three options were emerging on how the school year was going to start. The first option was to continue distance learning from the state. The second option was the hybrid learning model we had been hearing of throughout the summer. This was where school districts would find a way to hold only half of the students in school each day, switching with the other half every other day. The last option—and the least likely one, at the rate that things were going in terms of trying to defeat the virus—was to go back to having full classrooms like we'd had before the pandemic hit. Most of us had a pretty good feeling that this third option wasn't going to happen, since our district couldn't get the COVID-19 infection rate down low enough to meet the threshold of having all of the students back in the classroom.

One thing I knew for sure was that if we had to go to hybrid learning, it was going to be a logistic nightmare. I didn't envy those who were in charge of figuring out the scheduling of students going to an every-other-day format, what communication systems we would have with students who were at home on their off days, and how we would deal with staffing if there was an outbreak at our school.

As the summer came to an end, my coworkers and I started to see school districts make their decisions based on guidelines from our governor, Tim Walz, as well as state health officials. Basically, depending on which infection rate category your district fell into, your school would either reopen with distance learning, hybrid, or full opening. The announcement was going to be made by the governor, and we teachers were fully tuned in to what he would say about reopening our schools. When Governor Walz laid out the infection rate thresholds, we immediately went to our city websites to find out exactly where we stood. I was on text threads with coworkers from my school and friends from school districts in and around the cities, and we were all trying to find out where we stood with the infection rates.

With my friends in our district, we had some trouble finding this information at first. I found what I thought was our county infection rate, and I had to do the math to figure out the infection rate for the last two weeks. (That was what the governor was implying districts should do.) Of course, I calculated it wrong and texted out a number that would have us doing distance learning again. But somebody smarter than me got the correct calculations and showed that we fell into the hybrid model category.

Now, this was just a suggestion from the state. Districts had the authority to do what they wanted, so my coworkers and I didn't know exactly what our district was going to do. What we found out was that most school districts fell in the hybrid category. However, shortly after the announcement, my friends who taught in Minneapolis and Saint Paul found out they would be teaching distance learning, even though they didn't fall into that category. This was surprising, and we started to wonder if our district would do the same. Ultimately, our school made the decision to go with the hybrid model, since we clearly fell into the category of infection rate that recommended it.

I now knew there would be trouble ahead for me in figuring out how I was going to do interventions with my reading students. If they were only going to be coming to our school for two days a week, how was I going to pull them out of electives like art, phys ed, music, foreign languages, and choir? I usually worked with my students at least three days a week, and that meant the elective teacher would only get their students once a week for in-class instruction. I knew this wasn't going to go well, especially with the classroom teacher, the student, and potentially the student's parents. So I knew I was about to get railroaded again.

Once the school year began, my fears came true. My job wasn't necessarily a priority. Again, I got it. Core classes and electives had to figure out how to even teach in a hybrid model, which had never been done in our district or most districts across the nation. Our administration was feverishly trying to figure out the logistics of scheduling two groups of the student body, working with students who opted for full distance learning rather than being in the hybrid group, and working with teachers who were going to be teaching from home full-time.

Not only that, but the district administration was incredibly difficult to get a hold of for help. Our testing coordinator was busy implementing a new assessment to identify students who needed interventions—and she was also getting that ready for the elementary level. Our student support staff had myriad complications and obstacles to work out with the general district staff.

So I was left to my own devices again. My two part-time interventionists were understandably busy, working with their English department to get their classes ready for hybrid learning. Interventions were the last thing on their mind. It was incredibly frustrating.

During this time, I started to review the students I'd had during the last school year, sorting through old standardized test scores to see which students would requalify for interventions again this year. When I approached the district administration to get the go-ahead to contact parents about interventions, I was told that we couldn't use their old assessments, since they were now invalid. Also, we were going to use the new assessment that the elementary level was using to identify students. Now I had to wait for an extra two weeks because the English department had to assign the assessments to students who would take this reading assessment at home with their iPads. (Like nothing could go wrong there.)

So there I was again, sitting at my desk for the next two weeks, just doing reading intervention research and filling in for teachers who were gone and couldn't be covered by regular subs. Strangely, I didn't mind this from time to time, as I had a chance to interact with students and not lose my sense of what it was like to be a classroom teacher. However, I felt a little bit like a building sub, just waiting to be called on to fill a classroom.

I did help my sister, though. Carrie taught one hour of a class called SAIL, which helped students who were targeted for academic assistance. I also had a twenty-minute study period class right before lunch, as always. It was weird, because when you're a teacher (even an average one) and you haven't taught for a long time, you find yourself teaching anything to students who are just in your class for study hall. That was how much I was trying to feel useful. I looked forward with enthusiasm to Carrie's SAIL class, as it was a time when I could support students in any subject area they needed help in—including math!

I also, once again, had a hard time sharing the emotion my coworkers were going through in the beginning weeks of the hybrid model. It was awful for them. Not only did they have their regular students in front of them, but they also had to check in with their distance learning academy (DLA) students for at least ten minutes in every hour of their classes with Google Meet. This was quite the tap dance; teachers would have to leave their students who were in class for independent work during this time and go to their laptops to teach the students in DLA for ten minutes. If you know anything about teaching, the schedule doesn't always jive the way you want it to during the day's lesson. In-person students may have questions while you need to get to your Google Meet, or the lesson may take longer than expected. And what if there was an interruption during class, like a sick kid, a technical difficulty, or a fire alarm? I witnessed this firsthand while helping out with Carrie's SAIL class. At least there I could help the students who were in the classroom while my sister went to help the online students from her desk. Other times, I would walk by classrooms where teachers would be outside in the hallway, giving additional help to online students so that they wouldn't be disruptive to their in-person students.

Teachers also had to figure out a way to plan for students who were at home for their off days. So my coworkers were now planning for two separate student groups each day. This also became a problem, because no matter how easy teachers tried to make their lesson for students who were home each day, they would end up with a massive number of emails from students who couldn't access the video for their lessons, didn't understand the PowerPoint, didn't know how to upload and transfer a PDF file, or were just generally confused. Some parents were mystified at how slow teachers were at getting back to their students. When I had conversations with other teachers, they would tell me how they were frustrated by these impatient parents.

What the parents had failed to realize was that, while they may have an office job where they can answer loads of emails at their desks, teachers are in front of students most of the day. They also have a prep hour to get their tech ready for the next class or meet with students they missed, and they're lucky to even fit in a lunch without other working duties. That just leaves them with the end of the day to respond to emails—and that's if there isn't another staff or committee meeting. So by the time a teacher gets back to their desk, there may be a stack of emails that can take hours to get through. This was a trying time for everyone. There were added responsibilities for parents and their children, along with teachers who had to teach three different groups at a time. Nothing good was coming from this.

As the first few weeks progressed, I observed and listened to teachers discuss the obstacles they faced day in, day out. I felt horrible about this, as I was on the complete opposite end of the spectrum. After work on a Friday, we would meet up for an outdoor happy hour, and I would feel left out of the conversation on how our staff was struggling to keep up with the new demands of the job. "I feel like I'm emailing parents until I go to bed!" was a common sentiment. "I just feel like I'm glued to my laptop at all times of the day!" was another.

I saw great collaboration among teachers to solve these issues. As for me, I felt like I was the backup punter of a football team, standing there and cheering the team on with no real solutions. If I did offer a suggestion to help make their working life a little easier, I felt as if I was looked at that way: like the backup punter, offering suggestions to the defensive coordinator about stopping the run. It's not fun to go from being part of a team to being looked at like, *Oh, it's just Blair. He doesn't have students anyway, so what the hell does he know? Lucky bastard.* I was starting to realize what it must be like to be an administrator pontificating to teachers about pedagogy in a teacher's areas of expertise—especially if the administrators haven't taught in a classroom for more than ten years.

Slowly, the ball started to roll for interventionists like myself as the school-wide reading assessments were finished. (Well, at least 80 percent of the students were completed. We still had DLA students as well as students who were assigned to take the assessments at home and were most likely never going to take it regardless of all the emails and phone calls to home.) We finally had a meeting to figure out what to do with the students who qualified—and what we found out was exactly what I'd feared was coming. We had to figure out a way to do interventions remotely.

I wasn't concerned about figuring out how to do lessons with a small group of students through Google Meet or using new technology for recording read-alouds for students. What I was concerned about was how we reading interventionists were going to schedule these students. It was hard enough to negotiate with elective teachers to pull students out of their classes into our interventions, but now we were going to have to try to get permission from parents and schedule interventions when students were free. This was going to be a logistic problem in many ways.

The first issue was contacting parents to schedule their kids. It was already hard enough to get the permission slip back from parents to enroll their children in interventions. Now I had to have them actively participate in scheduling these interventions. For the most part, students who are struggling in reading also come from homes where it's more difficult to communicate with parents. Not all cases are like this, but many are.

Another problem that the school administration expected was that parents might be reluctant to add another course to their child's schedule. In prepandemic times, we couldn't add more instruction time to the students' schedules; there were only seven hours to the school day, and we would pull the students out of an elective class. But now we would be adding roughly an hour a week for instruction, and we felt like parents would think this would be academic and time overload for their kid.

As reading assessments came in, reading interventionists like myself reached out to parents for permission for interventions and to start scheduling sessions. After a short while, we had the schedule set up and the students ready for sessions through Google Meet during their distance learning days.

What transpired was disheartening at first. I had a horrible time getting students to show up for their Google Meets with me. I would be waiting in the classroom, staring at my screen as the minutes ticked by. I didn't want to be off-screen; I felt that if my students didn't see me right away, they would just log off. So as the minutes ticked by and they didn't show up, I would just check emails. After about ten minutes, which was half of the session, I would note the student's absence. The other interventionists and I used a shared Google spreadsheet to keep track of attendance, and it wasn't looking good. For the first week of interventions, I was getting about 50 percent participation from my students. Each time a student missed a session, I would email them through their Schoology account. This would improve attendance a little bit, but I had to find a way to increase participation—or else this was going to be an absolute disaster.

One way to solve this problem was to deploy Operation Candy. I told students that each time they showed up for their session, I would put candy (primarily Jolly Ranchers, Starbursts, or other assorted bite-size candy bars) into their "candy bank." Once each quarter was over, I would find each student to deposit their candy bank (which was just a sandwich bag) right into their backpack. Some laughed at the notion of the candy bank; others wondered if I could just send it to their house after a while. Regardless, this helped get my attendance up to around 80 percent. There were students who just didn't show up, no matter how many emails or calls I sent. I didn't feel too bad about this, as this was par for the course for the rest of the staff and their classes.

While my attendance was getting better, I was getting increasingly annoyed with cameras being turned off for my Google Meet sessions. I mean, it was just a small group; and in most cases, it was one-on-one. So it wasn't like there were other students to judge. Facial expressions, to me, were important in reading so that I could see if my students were confused, bored, or engaged. About 25 percent of students did have their cameras on during our lessons, but the rest of the students didn't. So I would just be staring at a dot with the student's initials on it when reading to them.

Hybrid Education

As my coworkers and I progressed through our first quarter of hybrid teaching, I was surprised by how well-behaved our students were. I don't know if it was like this in other districts, but the students didn't have too much of an issue with face masks. Of course, we had to remind a few students to keep their masks above their noses. But for the most part, it wasn't a huge issue. Along with the masks, the teachers had to get creative with their classrooms to make sure students were six feet apart. Disruptive behavior was down, as students were socially distanced; and the masks kind of worked as a muzzle against any type of blurting out. It also helped that less than 50 percent of the student body was there. What was kind of sad was that we teachers couldn't have any Halloween celebrations or fun events because we'd have to do that twice—once for each group—and that would lead to even more missed curriculum. I don't think the students minded, since they were only in school for two days out of the week anyway.

As November was coming up, my coworkers and I were paying close attention to our county's infection rate. Along with the rest of the United States, as we headed into the winter months, it wasn't looking good. We were already past the state's recommended infection rate threshold, so we should have been total remote teaching. But I felt like we were just trying to make it to the second quarter, which we did. By the last week of the quarter, it was announced that we would all be back to remote learning. This didn't affect me, as I was already teaching students on their distance learning days.

For this go-round of remote teaching, my coworkers and I could teach from home or go to the school. I chose to head in, as I hated being stuck in my house all the time. I don't have any kids to keep me on my toes, nor anyone else to pass the time with when I have nothing going on. (I really could have used a dog at that time. It seemed like everyone in my neighborhood was getting a new puppy because of being home all the time.) Going into school retained some bit of normalcy for me, but most of the teachers chose to teach from home. This was understandable, as most of our staff had children at home who also needed to learn remotely.

It was odd, to say the least, when it came to teaching remotely from the school. There were six of us who showed up every day. One or two others would sometimes make it in every other day. The school was eerily quiet, and it kind of had an office feel to it. Our classrooms were like our own cubicles (albeit very large cubicles), where we were facilitating online meetings. During our prep time or lunch break, we would often see who wasn't busy teaching and go have a chat. At the end of the day, we would leave right away as long as there wasn't a staff or committee meeting we had to attend. I was still feeling pretty empty when I left the building, though. It felt as if I only put in a half day of work due to how much interaction from a typical school day was missing.

Is This Ever Going to End?

The winter was brutal. My coworkers and I didn't know if we would ever go back to school because infection rates and deaths were at an all-time high throughout the country. I would stop by one coworker's classroom, and he would give me constant updates like, "Welp, our county just went up in our infection rate again. I don't know how this is ever going to end." But after a few weeks, the lockdowns seemed to be working. Infection rates went down, and vaccines were starting to wrap up their clinical trials.

As we were ending our second quarter, some of my coworkers and I were trying to predict when we would be going back to school. I felt like the rates were still too high, and nobody had been vaccinated yet. So we probably weren't going to come back until the start of the fourth quarter, and it would be under the hybrid model. I was wrong yet again.

Word came pretty fast that we were going to start hybrid teaching by the start of the third quarter. This kind of took me and my coworkers by surprise. Some teachers were not for this; we hadn't been vaccinated yet, and the infection rates were still too high for hybrid learning according to our state's recommendation on when schools should reopen. However, I could also see that parents were getting fed up with how long their children had to stay at home. School districts across the nation were losing students to private and charter schools and, in turn, were starting to lose revenue. Just from the few students I had, two of them transferred to the Catholic school in town. I also talked to teacher friends who were losing up to 300 students within their district. The heat was on for superintendents to get students back in the classroom before they bled any more revenue for the upcoming school year. This was how I felt the decision was made. In a way, I don't blame the administration for doing this. Heck, I was all for students coming back. They needed to be back, especially those who were struggling socially. I also wasn't having fun staring at that laptop all the time!

As our students came back to the middle school (elementary schools started having full classrooms a few months before us), it felt like the third start of the school year. This time, we only had half a year left of school. For the most part, nothing was out of the ordinary for a second go-round of hybrid learning. My coworkers and I did have a little more protection, with face shields and transparent partitions for our desks. But it was still a pain in the ass for teachers to have to juggle teaching a live class and teaching or answering questions from students who were on their distance learning days. This still didn't apply to me, as I continued to teach students who were on their distance learning days.

As we approached the end of the third quarter, the vaccines were starting to make their way through the nation's elderly and first responders. Teachers were up next on the list to get the vaccinations. Most of us started getting them by the end of February, receiving our second shot at the end of March. Getting that final shot at the Minneapolis Convention Center was the most liberated I had felt in a long time. I was sitting there, waiting to be released and hoping this would be the beginning of getting back to normalcy. Infection rates were now on a serious decline, to the point that it was announced that we were finally coming fully back to school by the start of the fourth quarter.

When students were fully back, it was like a shock back to reality. The noise was back in the school. We had students laughing and congregating in the hallways again. Even though they were supposed to stay distanced from each other, it was impossible (and laughable) to try to enforce this. Students still weren't using their lockers as well, in hopes of keeping their peers from gathering there. So with all the time between classes, students walked and talked in groups around the hallway. If they stopped, we would urge them to get moving, as the hallways were busier than ever with nobody in the locker bays anymore.

Our classrooms now only needed to have students separated by three feet, which allowed us to have our full classes. There were a few classes that had more students than what was allowed per size and distancing requirements, but we managed.

As for me, it was the first time I had students in my classroom again, period. It was strange—and a relief—to not be staring at the screen for hours on end and to finally see a face instead of a dot. I built a much better rapport with students in class rather than on-screen; and most, if not all, teachers will agree with this. It felt like conversations were more fluent. I didn't have this awkward moment of waiting for a student to say something.

I also felt like having students in the classroom had a huge impact on their learning, especially for my interventions. I could demonstrate reading strategies much more clearly than on a shared screen on a laptop. I could also hear each student's reading better, whether they skipped a word or pronounced it correctly.

The students seemed to appreciate being back in class, as most of them hadn't seen some of their friends in over a year. Of course, the teachers' usual complaints about classroom behavior returned to prepandemic levels, so I knew we were close to being back to normal. And yes, I would have been one of those teachers complaining if I had been back teaching English or reading extensions.

The end of our full-pandemic school year was finally approaching. Most of the staff couldn't wait to end this year of abnormality. We were looking forward to the next school year, when we wouldn't have to split time between live students and those who were hiding behind their avatars in Google Meet. We were also looking forward to teaching without face masks! Just to be able to show emotion on our faces and let students know we're smiling (or even upset) without having to tell them is huge. Although I did joke about how I didn't have to pluck nose hairs regularly while wearing a mask.

The last days of school kind of went unceremoniously. There were no big send-offs or end-of-the-year staff parties. We just wanted to be done. It was as if we got used to ending the school year with all the interruptions of the past year. It was extremely anticlimactic. With this ending, it was just one big shoulder shrug. We had done what we could. What was it going to look like next year?

And this is where we are as I finish this memoir. What permanent alterations did the COVID-19 pandemic reap on our education system? Most teachers already know that many school districts are going through budget shortfalls as students are leaving their districts, and we suspect that a whole generation of students fell behind because of the lack of structure they were used to and the quality of teaching that can't be captured in distance learning. One can hope that the resiliency of our teachers—and especially our youth—can lead us to a better place in the end, however that may look.

EPILOGUE

....

So this is what you get out of a midforties average teacher. Some of you may be wondering why I didn't do more in my teachings, and some of you may feel like I've done okay.

There are other topics I wish I could have covered, like building relationships with coworkers, the political side of teaching, and the usefulness (or, maybe for some teachers, the lack thereof) of a union. But this is getting pretty long as it is.

But this is it . . . so far. I feel like I'm not that special when it comes to being an educator. No, this wasn't a book about how I went into the inner city or a rural area and turned around disenfranchised students. I didn't make up a curriculum that magically cured dyslexia or reading problems. Nor did I change a culture of learning for an entire district. This was meant to show the life of a teacher who's trying to do a good job, and it's up to the reader to decide whether I did or didn't.

Trying to grow into this job is a constant endeavor. It never stops. From my youthful years of trying to grasp what it meant to be a respectable teacher, to my later years of trying to keep up with the latest research and best practices of being a reading teacher, it's a constant transformation each year—and even each day.

Overall, I do think I chose wisely in picking this profession. No, I won't be buying that house on Lake Minnetonka anytime soon. But this profession has brought me a wealth of happiness, thanks to my coworkers and especially—whether they know it or not—my students.